The Forging of an African Nation

The Forging of an African Nation

The Political and Constitutional Evolution of Uganda from Colonial Rule to Independence, 1894–1962

G. S. K. IBINGIRA

The Viking Press · New York
Uganda Publishing House · Kampala

Copyright © 1973 by G. S. K. Ibingira

All rights reserved

First published in Canada by
The Macmillan Company of Canada Limited

Published in 1973 by The Viking Press, Inc.
625 Madison Avenue, New York, N.Y. 10022

SBN 670–32369–1

Library of Congress catalog card number: 72–91025

Printed in U.S.A.

This book is also published in East Africa
by Uganda Publishing House Ltd.

*To all those, irrespective of race,
tribe, or religion, who staked all
they had in order that Uganda
should remain free*

A Biographical Sketch of the Author

Grace Stuart K. Ibingira, the son of Mr. and Mrs. Alfred Katebarirwe, was born 23 May 1932 in Ibanda County, Ankole District, Uganda, where his father was then serving as a Gombolola Chief.

He began his formal education at Mbarara High School (1942–1950), and entered Kings College, Budo, in 1951; he passed out of Kings College, Budo, with a Cambridge School Certificate, Grade One, in 1953. He then read law at the University College of Wales, Aberystwyth, graduating in 1958 with honours, *magna cum laude*. He completed his postgraduate research work at the University of London in 1959.

Mr. Ibingira was called to the bar of the Middle Temple, London, in 1959 and enrolled as barrister of the Supreme Court of England. In the same year he began the practice of law in Kampala, Uganda, as an advocate of the Uganda High Court. One year later he entered the Legislative Council of Uganda, having been elected by the Eishengyero [district council] of Ankole.

In 1960, Mr. Ibingira actively participated in promoting the merger between the Uganda People's Union (U.P.U.) and the Uganda National Congress (U.N.C.) to form the Uganda People's Congress (U.P.C.). He was a founder-member of the U.P.C. and served as a member of its Central Executive in addition to being the party's legal adviser from its inception. He also served as U.P.C. Chairman, Ankole District, for the three years preceding his election as Secretary-General of the U.P.C. in 1964; he held this party post until 1966.

Mr. Ibingira participated extensively in both of Uganda's two pre-independence constitutional conferences with the British Government in London. In 1961, while in the Opposition, he accompanied Milton Obote, then leader of the Opposition, to London and served in drawing up the East African Common Services Organisation Treaty which replaced the East African High Commission upon the independence of Tanganyika in that year. In the same year he actively participated, as a member of the U.P.C. delegation, in the conference that drew up the Internal Self-Government Constitution of Uganda. In 1962 as Minister of Justice he was the principal spokesman for the Government on the Constitutional Committee which, as part of the Uganda Independence Conference, drew up the bulk of the Uganda Independence Constitution. In addition, he participated in numerous international conferences of both a political and a legal character, including the first conference on the Rule of Law ever held in Africa (Lagos, 1961).

Mr. Ibingira was largely instrumental in forging the alliance between the U.P.C. and the K.Y. (Kabaka Yekka) political parties, which enabled Milton Obote to become Prime Minister and to lead Uganda to independence. In 1962, after the U.P.C. won the pre-independence elections, Mr. Ibingira was appointed to the senior Cabinet rank of Minister of Justice. In charge of the nation's legal system, he pioneered the reformation of what was called the African Law Courts by initiating the machinery to integrate them with the superior courts of the country. By so doing he made separation of the judiciary from the executive a reality for three-quarters of the people of the country, who settled most of their disputes in the lower customary courts. In 1964 Mr. Ibingira was made Minister of State in the Prime Minister's Office in charge of Public Service. But most of his time was now absorbed by his work as the Secretary-General of the U.P.C.

Mr. Ibingira has long been committed to East African unity of Kenya, Uganda, and Tanzania. When Obote forbade his ministers to attend a meeting in 1963 at the University of Nairobi,

Kenya, to discuss federation with representatives of the other two states, Mr. Ibingira defied the ban and made a passionate appeal for an East African Federation.*

He is a keen believer in African unity but insists that if such unity is to be meaningful and a source of real power, serious attention must be given to African regional integration as a stable base for a continental approach at the level of the Organisation of African Unity. Otherwise, he feels, the O.A.U. will be little more than a debating club, passing resolutions it has neither the unity nor the ability to implement.

Mr. Ibingira has been honoured by two independent African states: the Republic of the Sudan awarded him the Grand Order of the Two Niles in 1963, and the Emperor of Ethiopia awarded him the Grand Order of the Queen of Sheba in 1964. He is the designer of the national flag of Uganda, which has flown since independence.

Because of his conviction that Obote was betraying the principles on which he was elected, Mr. Ibingira organised a movement within the U.P.C. and outside it to put restraint on Obote's wild ambitions. The rift in the U.P.C. led to Mr. Ibingira's arrest in 1966, along with four other senior Cabinet members, when Obote abrogated the Uganda Constitution. He and his four colleagues were imprisoned at the Maximum Security Prison of Uganda for almost five years. He was finally released by the Uganda Army on 28 January 1971, when President Obote was toppled from power by a military coup d'etat.

After prison Mr. Ibingira was determined to settle in private life as a legal practitioner in Uganda but was prevailed upon by his Government to represent Uganda as Ambassador and Permanent Representative at the United Nations, a post he has held since August 1971.

* Included in Colin Leys and P. Robson, eds., *Federation in East Africa: Opportunities and Problems* (Oxford University Press, 1965).

Preface

The writing of this book was completed before my arrest and incarceration on 22 February 1966; I have had no reason—after five years in prison—to recast any portion of it other than to make a few revisions and additions in order to bring the material up to date.

I have always held, and still hold, the view that the future is inseparable from the present and, in turn, the present is indissolubly rooted in the past. No political leadership or constitution can afford to disregard this basic fact. Bearing this essential reality in mind, I have attempted to highlight the political and cultural forces that have—all along—shaped the Uganda Constitution during every stage of its evolution.

This is not a political analysis by a political scientist, nor is it a complete historical or constitutional study, but if to some reasonable extent this work develops and conveys the effect of the various political and cultural pressures associated with Uganda's constitution-making processes, my labour will not have been in vain. President Obote's "revolution" might be topical, but in order to assess its causes, execution, and ultimate collapse we must go back to the period covered in this work. We must first know what and who we were yesterday; we can then more intelligently plan what to become tomorrow.

The periods covered in this book fall into two distinct parts: the first part, in which I was not personally involved, begins with the foundation of colonial rule in Uganda; the second part deals with the period after I joined the Legislative Council in 1960 as a

Member from the then Kingdom of Ankole. I have made a determined effort to avoid using the personal pronoun when covering events I was personally involved with; however, this has not always been possible when discussing specific events and circumstances in which I was one of the dramatis personae. In these instances I have freely expressed personal opinion.

As a Founder-Member of the U.P.C. and official on all the major party organs from 1960 until 1966, as well as Minister of Justice from 1962 to 1964 and Minister of State from 1964 to 1966, I was rather well placed as both observer and participant in the events covering the momentous years just previous to our independence on 9 October 1962. At certain specific places in this book I have briefly dealt with events beyond independence in order to conclude a point begun earlier, such as the "Lost Counties" issue. I have made few such alterations in the original text. The Afterword, of course, was added after my release from prison, but my Summary and Conclusion remains unaltered.

Writing on political events that have sometimes been pregnant with emotion during our history, I am perfectly aware that some prominent people may hold different views from those expressed in this book. It is healthy that it should be so, "lest one good custom should corrupt the world".

I cannot conclude this Preface without expressing my thanks to those partly responsible for the publication of this book. First, to Mr. Mathew Rukikaire and Mr. Perez Kamunanwire, who— in the midst of very hectic political activity—gave me unfailing support and encouragement to persevere and complete it. Secondly, to Mr. John Sambwa, who so efficiently typed the manuscript, in spite of his numerous other duties. Finally, to the staff of my publishers, the Uganda Publishing House and The Viking Press, whose skill and patience made it possible to publish this book.

It is necessary to conclude by stating that, while the foregoing have shared my burden in one way or another, they have no responsibility for the various opinions expressed in this book or for any shortcomings it may bear; I alone am responsible.

GRACE S. K. IBINGIRA

United Nations, New York
14 April 1972

Contents

A map of Uganda at the time of independence appears on page 237.

The Forging of an
African Nation

1. Introductory Comment

Physical Features and Climate

The Republic of Uganda, which is popularly known in the world of tourism as the "Pearl of Africa", is situated astride the equator between latitudes 4° N. and 1° S. and longitudes 30° E. and 35° E. It is an entirely inland state with its capital, Kampala, 874 miles by rail from the east coast of Africa on the Indian Ocean. With an area of 93,981 square miles, it is comparable in size to the United Kingdom or Ghana.

The preponderant relief element is a plateau, approximately 4,000 feet above sea level, with an elevational movement that reaches an exceptional expression in the fabled snow-capped "Mountains of the Moon" (the Ruwenzori Mountains) rising to heights of almost 17,000 feet.

From Lake Victoria (through which runs Uganda's border with Tanzania) flows the River Nile, bisecting the country on its eventful flow northwards to the Mediterranean Sea. On the eastern side, Mt. Elgon (14,178 feet), an extinct volcano, forms the border with Kenya. One of Uganda's most picturesque scenes is formed by the western side of the Great Rift Valley, stretching from the north southwards with a number of lakes and land abounding with wildlife, which has been developed as an attraction for an increasing number of tourists.

Although astride the equator, Uganda is, nevertheless, blessed with an equable climate owing to its high altitude. Temperatures in most parts range from 60° F. to 80° F. all year round, and rainfall averaging about 50 inches a year is fairly well distributed, although there is a dry zone stretching across the country from south-west to north-east.

The People

As the subsequent account will show, Uganda before British rule was not a single state comprised of one tribe or race. On the contrary, there were many tribes, and in most cases each was independent of the others, possessing its own social organisation, language, and territory. The concept of Uganda as a nation state, therefore, is a direct result of Uganda's colonial experience after the British arbitrarily carved out the boundaries of today's Uganda, including within its borders a diversity of tribes who must evolve a common destiny in an indivisible sovereign state.*

Since the fortunes and patterns of Uganda's political and constitutional evolution under British rule were inseparably linked with and influenced by the characteristics of its diverse peoples, it is essential to mention the broad groupings of these peoples—now numbering nine and a half million.

The country can be divided in a variety of ways: it can be divided politically, in terms of regions—Eastern, Western, Northern, and Buganda; it can be analysed linguistically or ethnically into Nilotics and Nilo-Hamites of the northern districts and the Bantus of the southern, eastern, and western parts. But it has been more familiar to speak of Uganda's subdivisions in terms of regions. We take the Northern Region first.

(1) The *Lango,* a Nilotic tribe, traditionally pastoral, have also become agriculturalists. The tribe had several powerful clans but lacked any really strong central authority. It was from this

---

* About the people and their country, the Constitutional Committee of 1959 observed: "Uganda is an artificial unit containing within its borders a very wide range of types of country from arid plains to lush lakeside areas, and a variety of different tribes with different languages and customs." (The Wild Report, p. 34, para. 147.)

tribe that the first Prime Minister, A. Milton Obote, came.*
(2) The *Acholi* based their political and social organisation before British rule on a system of clans under the leadership of a hereditary chief, Rwot. They are noted for their bravery and martial spirit.
(3) The *Karamojong* by reasons of history and colonial design are the least developed of Uganda's tribes. They are typical, elegant Nilo-Hamites in physique, and they have long been intimately tied to their cattle and were traditionally a warrior people. They have no paramount chiefs, and authority has been traditionally vested in the elders of extended families; social life is on an age-grade system.
(4) The north-western districts of West Nile and Madi are inhabited by the *Jonam, Alur, Kakwa,* and *Madi,* whom arbitrary national borders have divided among Uganda, Sudan, and Zaire. The largest West Nile tribe, however, are the *Lugbara,* who are an agricultural people and, like the Madi, have been separated from their kinsmen in Zaire. Of all these tribes it was only the Alur who had a strong tradition of hereditary chieftainship.
(5) The *Iteso* are a half-Hamitic tribe and the second largest in Uganda. They migrated from Karamoja about two centuries ago and eventually settled in the area they now occupy, having found it an ideal pastureland. Constitutionally they had no hereditary ruler, and while the clan system exists in Teso, it has few of the usual characteristics of that found among the Bantu or Nilotic tribes. The most important social unit was the extended family, which comprises all the relatives of a household who have sprung from a common ancestor three or four generations back.

The Southern Bantu linguistic group covers roughly the remainder of the Eastern Region, the Western Region, and Buganda. These may be conveniently divided into the former kingdom and non-kingdom areas.

* Mr. Obote and his Government were overthrown by a military coup d'etat on 25 January 1971. He now lives as an exile in Tanzania. Obote always used the title "Doctor" and was usually referred to as "Dr. Obote". This was not an academically earned title; he was awarded an Honorary Doctorate of Law by Long Island University (U.S.A.) in 1963.

(1) The *Baganda* are the most numerous of all Uganda tribes, numbering nearly one and a half million. Although their kingdom was abolished, it was never by their popular consent but rather by force; they are an intensely "kingly" society. They evolved a powerful, highly centralised feudal kingdom whose monarchy went back to about the fifteenth century. Because of its historical connection with the expansion of British rule in Uganda, Buganda became the centre of Uganda. The traditional king, called the Kabaka, still very much exists in the minds of a good many Baganda, although the office of Kabaka has been abolished since 1966.*

(2) The *Banyankole* inhabit the former Kingdom of Ankole, which was substantially enlarged by British intervention. The former ruling aristocracy of Ankole, the Bahima, were not strictly Bantu but Hamitic, and are part of an aristocracy of pastoral feudal lords who spread to Karagwe, Rwanda, and Burundi. The majority of Banyankole, however, are the traditional agriculturalists, the Bairu. With the advent of democratic processes the Bairu inevitably reached the ascendency in political power. The traditional king, called Omugabe, cannot be said to have enjoyed the same support as the Kabaka did in his kingdom; this was because of the rivalry between the Bairu and the Bahima, in which the Omugabe, being of the Bahima, was resisted by a section of Bairu who favoured republicanism.

(3) If the advent of British rule helped to build the Kingdom of Buganda, it had the corresponding effect of diminishing Bunyoro, the kingdom of the *Banyoro*. Bunyoro, the most ancient and once the most powerful of all the kingdoms in Uganda, lost much of her territory to Buganda as a result of conquest by the British. The Banyoro and Baganda engaged in intertribal warfare.

(4) The *Batoro* occupy the former Kingdom of Toro, which was

---

* The terms "feudalism" and "feudal" gained such widespread currency in Uganda political life that they soon became accepted as terms connoting the traditional and largely reactionary "kingly-tribal" systems of local government in Uganda. Strictly speaking, "feudalism" in Uganda—as a specific form of government—deviated considerably from the norms associated with European feudalism.

the youngest of the kingdoms. In addition to the Batoro there are two other tribes, the *Bamba* and the *Bakonjo*. These two tribes never fully accepted the rule of the king of Toro, called the Omukama, who was of the Batoro. Indeed, there were times of armed insurrection by these people in their attempts to secede from the kingdom and form separate administrations. They cannot have regretted the demise of the Kingdom of Toro.

(5) Among the non-kingdom Bantus, the *Basoga*, east of the Nile and south of Lake Kyoga, live as farmers in circumstances akin to those of the Baganda. Although they had no central authority at the advent of British rule, they nevertheless developed small principalities, each with its own hereditary ruler. Later they consolidated their central authority, acquired a kinglike ruler, the Kyabazinga, and imitated the kingdoms in matters of government. The post of Kyabazinga, like those of all other constitutional heads and hereditary rulers, was abolished in 1966 by the Obote Government.

(6) The *Bagisu* are essentially a people of the mountains. Cut off by the invasion of the Nilotic and Nilo-Hamitic peoples from the north, they took refuge on the well-wooded slopes of Mt. Elgon, which they call Masaba.

(7) The District of Bukedi in the Eastern Region was specially created to embrace a mixture of Nilo-Hamites and Bantus, such as *Jopadhola* and *Iteso* on the one hand, and the *Bagwere, Banyoli, Basamia* and *Bagwe* on the other.

(8) Finally, living in Kigezi, Uganda's beautiful south-western section, are the *Bakiga*. Traditionally they appear to have had no centralized form of government above the extended household unit, despite the fact that they are bordered on the north by the western kingdoms of Uganda. In the same district there are substantial minorities of *Banyarwanda* and *Banyarujumbura* (Bahororo) who, at some stage in their history, were monarchical in political structure.

Uganda is, therefore, historically a country of diverse tribes and varied traditional institutions—with "republican" and monarchical institutions, with wandering pastoral people and comparatively more settled cultivators—and, today, with an increasing number of merchants and professional people.

The purpose of this work is to trace the impact of the British colonial rule on such diverse peoples and their ultimate attainment of sovereign power as a single independent state in the world community of nations.

2. The Foundations of British Colonial Rule

The Establishment of British Rule in Uganda

The Berlin Conference of 1884, which was convened for the express purpose of drawing up acceptable methods to be followed by "imperial powers" in acquiring territory in tropical Africa, was the official climax to the colonial expansionism that had gripped industrial Europe by this time. Indeed, the methods of acquiring territory became almost standardized. In the words of one of Britain's greatest proconsuls on the African continent:

> One can see what it means: it is moral annexation. The evolution of colonial empires of this kind follows a well known process of which the stages are in a measure inevitable: first travellers, missionaries, and traders; then treaties of commerce and friendship; then a kind of Protectorate half-concealed under the form of an unequal alliance; afterwards the delimitation of spheres of influence and the declaration of a kind of right of priority; then Protectorates properly so called, the establishment of tutelage, the appointment of Residents, and all that follows in their train; and finally, annexation pure and simple.[1] *

Following the travels of the English explorers Speke and Grant, the first positive attempt by British people to extend their

* Numbered reference notes begin on p. 293.

influence over what is now Uganda, it can reasonably be said, was through the Imperial British East Africa Company, the company trading under a royal charter which had been formed partly to thwart German imperial ambitions in the East African hinterland.[2] Missionaries also played a vital role, but more will be mentioned of them later. The Company's existence was brief and crowded with momentous events, but was unquestionably instrumental in making it possible, through the activities of its servants such as F. J. Jackson and Captain (later Lord) Lugard, for the British Government to formally accept responsibility for Uganda on 1 April 1893, although responsibility was accepted with considerable reluctance. Sir Gerald Portal raised the British flag that day to mark the beginning of imperial rule by proclaiming Uganda a British Protectorate.[3]

British rule was established in the territories now comprising Uganda through two principal methods which went hand in hand: through "treaties" or "agreements" with native rulers and by military or quasi-military conquest. Portal had negotiated a treaty in 1893 with Mwanga, the Kabaka of Buganda, which, like the one it superseded, promised British "protection" for Buganda. In return he extracted a promise from Mwanga not to enter into treaties with other powers and not to go to war without British sanction. The formal announcement of a Protectorate over Buganda was made in the *London Gazette* on 19 June 1894, and in August of the same year Colonel Colvile, who had succeeded Sir Gerald Portal, signed yet another treaty with Mwanga similar to the provisional one Mwanga had made with Portal. When E. J. L. Berkeley succeeded Colvile in 1894 as the first substantive Commissioner in Uganda, the Protectorate was still limited to the Kingdom of Buganda, although the British sphere of influence extended far to the north and west.

Meanwhile, before his departure, Colvile launched decisive military campaigns against the unyielding ruler of Bunyoro, Kabarega.[4] After a series of campaigns westwards, Kabarega was defeated; and, as Professor K. Ingham writes, one result of the war was that Bunyoro suffered terrible devastation. Famine and disease attacked the population and defeat destroyed the spirit of the survivors. A military occupation of Bunyoro was undertaken, not for the purpose of annexing Bunyoro, but solely for the need to prevent any resurgence of Kabarega's power.

In the west, Major Cunningham made a treaty with the Enganzi, the Prime Minister, of the Omugabe's Kingdom of Ankole in 1894,[5] and another treaty was made by Major Owen with the Omukama, ruler of Toro, in the same year. Both these treaties promised peace between the subjects of Queen Victoria and those of the rulers. The rulers undertook to make no other agreements with any other power, nor to cede territory to such foreign powers. The provisional character of these treaties ceased when in 1896 Berkeley was granted authority from England to add Toro, Ankole, Bunyoro, and Busoga to the Protectorate.[6] When Trevor Ternan became Acting Commissioner in 1899 he adopted a stern policy against Kabarega, and so Bunyoro continued to suffer the vicissitudes of a lost war until the Banyoro felt so oppressed that they broke into rebellion and stormed the British Fort at Hoima, driving away the British-placed Baganda chiefs from the kingdom.

Shortly after the treaties of 1894 with Ankole and Toro, a number of other unofficial treaties were made with some of the chiefs along the Nile Basin north of Lake Albert with a view to establishing information posts. Within one year from 1898 Major Macdonald, intending to expand British influence northwards, made more than thirty treaties with the chiefs north-east of the Nile.[7] When they were approved by the British Government in 1899, Berkeley despatched Lieutenant Colonel Cyril Marty to the chiefs for renewal of contact. He established four posts: among the Acholi, the Madi, the Alur, and the Bari. But even then the Protectorate administration was not properly established. It was not until 1910 that it established itself in Acholi, after some application of force to crush the Lamogi Rebellion.[8] It was in 1914, after adjustment of the boundary with the Sudan, that the northern part of Uganda effectively came under British rule.

The Protectorate administration opened up the territory lying north and east of the Nile—today the Eastern Region of Uganda—with the aid of a distinguished warrior and administrator of Buganda, Semei Kakungulu.[9] In 1896 he started building a series of military posts in Lango. He extended this scheme all the way to Teso, linking all the strategic positions behind him with military posts. He was attacked in Lango but resisted and won. In Teso between 1899 and 1904 he established a well-ordered administration with a hierarchy of chiefs. Indeed, the same administration was applied in Lango[10] and later to what came to be the Northern and Eastern Regions. Kakungulu imported his method from Buganda, but so acceptable had it become in most places that some areas, such as Teso—after a period of time—claimed it to be their indigenous sytem of government. In 1911 a new boundary was drawn up on Uganda's southernmost tip to include what is now Kigezi District; and by 1914, as Professor Ingham notes: "In general . . . Uganda had assumed its future geographical outline, and the pattern of its administrative future had already been firmly imprinted upon the diverse tribes of the Protectorate." [11]

It was not until 1900, however, that a more comprehensive and lasting agreement with Buganda was signed, called the "Uganda Agreement".[12] It was this Agreement that, for the first time, formally propounded the principle of "indirect rule"—a principle we shall examine elsewhere. Further Agreements were also made with Toro[13] and Ankole[14] in 1900 and 1901 respectively and, although they were not as exhaustive and did not confer as much power to the rulers as the Uganda Agreement did to the Kabaka, they were similar in spirit and in various fundamental aspects. They were all solemn documents; they all accepted British "protection" and promised loyalty to the British Crown, and they confirmed and regularised the constitutional set-up for administering their respective territories through a hierarchy of chiefs.* Since the making of treaties or Agreements with native rulers had so much bearing on the foundation of British imperial rule in Uganda,

---

* Article 6 of The Uganda Agreement read, "So long as the Kabaka, chiefs, and the people of Uganda shall conform to the laws and regulations instituted for their governance with Her Majesty's Government, and shall co-operate loyally with Her Majesty's Government in the organisation and administration of the said Kingdom of Uganda, Her Majesty's Government agrees to recognise the Kabaka of Uganda as the Native Ruler of the Province of Uganda under Her Majesty's protection and over-rule."

it is not out of place to examine the legal propriety and sanctity of these documents.

The Legality of Agreements with Native Rulers

After a period of uncertainty it was finally and firmly established in 1926 by a judgement of the Privy Council that such Agreements with "Native Rulers" can never bind the British Crown even if it had by virtue of such Agreements acquired the jurisdiction in the territory from which its right to govern is challenged. Thus, in the case of *Sobhuza II v Miller and Others,* Lord Haldane said in their Lordships' judgement:

> What is the meaning of a Protectorate? In the general case of a British Protectorate, although the Protected Country is not a British Dominion, its foreign relations are under the exclusive control of the Crown, so that its Government cannot hold direct communication with any other foreign power, nor a foreign power with a Government. . . . the Protected State becomes only semi-sovereign, for the protector may have to interfere, at least to a limited extent, with the administration in order to fulfill the obligations which international law imposes on him to protect within it the subjects of foreign powers. . . . But it may happen that the protecting power thinks itself called on to interfere to an extent which may render it difficult to draw the line between a Protectorate and a Possession.[15]

As we note elsewhere, Lord Lugard himself declared that, in practice, the distinction between a Colony and a Protectorate had no practical significance; in fact it did not exist, except in legal theory—and even then thinly.

This was a judgement in justification of an Order-in-Council which had contravened the authority by which Britain acquired a foothold in Swaziland. After this judgement, the principle enunciated was followed with unmistakable consistency. Twenty-five years later, in 1957, Lord Justice Denning gave judgement for the Privy Council in *Nyali, Ltd. v A.G. of Kenya* in no less certain terms:

Although the jurisdiction of the Crown in the Protectorate is in Law a limited jurisdiction, nevertheless the limits may in fact be extended indefinitely so as to embrace almost the whole field of government. They may be extended so far that the Crown has jurisdiction in everything connected with the peace, order and good government of the area, leaving only the title and ceremonies of sovereignty remaining in the Sultan. The Courts themselves will not mark out the limits. They will not examine the treaty or grant under which the Crown acquired jurisdiction: nor will they enquire into the usage or sufferance or other lawful means by which the Crown may have extended its jurisdiction. . . . Once jurisdiction is exercised by the Crown the Courts will not permit it to be challenged. . . . It follows, therefore, that in the present case we must look, not at the agreement with the Sultan, but at the Orders-in-Council and other Acts of the Crown so as to see what jurisdiction the Crown has in fact exercised; because they are the best guide; indeed they are conclusive, as to the extent of the Crown's jurisdiction.[16]

These two cases have been cited in justification and with approval in all the constitutional cases brought in Uganda to test the legal propriety of the Protectorate Government's conduct when it has been *ultra vires* the various Agreements with native rulers. In 1954, in a case designed to test the legality of the British action to withdraw recognition from the Kabaka of Buganda and deport him, which the Baganda submitted to court as being contrary to the Uganda Agreement of 1900, the Attorney-General of Uganda argued that, "whether just or unjust, politic or impolitic, beneficial or injurious," the deportation and withdrawal of recognition "was no matter on which a court of law could give an opinion." [17] Sir John Griffin, the Chief Justice, accepted this on the basis of its being an Act of State; the question of deportation was not a justiciable issue, for the Crown was by law the judge of its own case in such a matter.

When, as late as 1960, a contravention of the Ankole Agreement by the Protectorate Government was alleged, it was justified by the High Court of Uganda and the East African Court of Appeal on the same grounds.[18] It is beyond dispute, therefore, that within Uganda and in British municipal law, these Agreements lacked the force of law and bound the British Crown only during its pleasure. The question, however, which the indigenous people in these Agreement States asked often until independence—ruler and ruled alike—is whether the British protecting power did not commit a fraud, and, if the law was such that the treaties had no legal force, why this should not have been disclosed to the rulers and chiefs when they were making these Agreements. The plea of *ignorantia juris non excusat* (ignorance of the law is no excuse) could not have applied, for what was the law and who made that law, and by what authority other than the ultimate sanction of force? It is a well-established postulate of jurisprudence that what is legal or permitted by law is not what is necessarily equitable or just.* While it is a principle of English law that treaties can have no force of law unless enforced by an Act of Parliament, it had never happened before that so many treaties were concluded with literally hundreds of rulers from the dependencies when there was no intention of giving them the legal force of other treaties.

Yet in the early 1900s the policy of the British Government and British Courts seems to have been quite hesitant regarding the nature of these agreements or treaties. Thus, in *Katozi v Kahizi* it was ruled by the High Court of Uganda that its jurisdiction in Ankole was limited by the Ankole 1901 Agreement and that an Order-in-Council could not alter existing Agreements.[19] Later, in 1908, it was also held (in *Nasanairi Kibuka v A. E. Bartie Smith*[20]) that the Crown could not acquire powers in Buganda which had not been granted by the Agreement.

Indeed, in support of *Katozi v Kahizi,* the Secretary of State issued instructions to the effect that "the validity of the Uganda Order-in-Council of 1902, in so far as it nullifies this reservation

---

* Otherwise, a series of legislation by some states should never be criticised as unjust and offensive to notions of civilized conduct generally acceptable by international law, since they are almost always properly enacted by their respective legislatures. For example,

(1) Regulation No. 2 passed by Hitler under the Reich Citizenship Law (Germany, 1941) depriving Jews of German citizenship in his campaign for their depersonification; and

(2) Various enactments of the Republic of South Africa against the Bantus: e.g., The Preventive Detention Act, the Group Areas Act, The Suppression of Communism Act, and the extraordinary "Sabotage Act".

(contained in the Agreements) is open to question. In these circumstances, I am advised that the Uganda Order-in-Council 1902 should be construed in such a manner as not to impair the right thus reserved." [21]

If, then, it is true—as in fact it is—that the question of concluding, terminating, or honouring treaties with foreign states is an Act of State,[22] being a prerogative of the Crown and therefore unquestionable in a British court, it is equally true by the law of nations that once treaties are concluded, they import to the contracting parties rights and duties whose binding force is not merely moral, but legal.[23] From all this several interesting questions arise which we cannot leave unanswered. Were native states competent to make treaties in international law? If they were competent, were these treaties valid? If they were not valid, or if the states were not competent, what was the purpose of making them?

Generally, only states can be parties to treaties.[24] But even as Oppenheim says, "non-full sovereign states, however, can become parties only to such treaties as they are competent to conclude. It is impossible to lay down a hard and fast rule defining the competence of all not-full sovereign states."

Indeed, it is not essential to a state that there should be complete sovereignty. It was decided in *Duff Development Co. v Kelanten Government*,[25] "It is obvious that for sovereignty there must be a certain amount of independence, but it is not in the least necessary that for sovereignty there should be complete independence. It is quite consistent with sovereignty that the sovereign may in certain respects be dependent upon another power." Furthermore, Article 1 of the Montevideo Convention of 1933 on the rights and duties of states defines the essential prerequisites of statehood to include: (a) a permanent population; (b) a defined territory; (c) a government to which people render habitual obedience; and (d) capacity to enter into relations with other states.*

* Starke, *An Introduction to International Law*, p. 83. It is interesting to note that these conditions have not been strictly followed: in 1948, when Israel was proclaimed a state, its territory was not properly defined; nor did the governments in exile which received recognition during the Second World War command "habitual obedience" in their occupied territories.

While it is of course true that by the end of the nineteenth century all the African kingdoms were technologically backward and unversed in European culture, it is almost indefensible to contend that some of them, in the light of the general principles of law stated above, did not fulfil the essentials of statehood and therefore did not possess the capacity to conclude treaties with legal force. Indeed, the thorough constitutional set-up of Buganda's administration in the Agreement of 1900 reduced into writing what had for long been practised, for, as Mary Stuart wrote of the early British explorers to Buganda, they were struck to find "a people whose dignified sense of order seemed so like their own." [26] There is no doubt that the Baganda did understand the general importance of concluding a treaty. Lugard had to admit:

> In Uganda the case is different [from most of tropical Africa]. There the people most fully understand the nature of a written contract and consider nothing as absolutely final and binding unless put on paper. They are very clever and far seeing, and every clause of the treaty made was discussed for several days amongst themselves before it was presented to baraza for the signature of the King and Chiefs.[27]

It is inescapable to suppose that if a people of this prudent calibre had been informed of the extent to which the British would claim exemption from legal liability under the cover of Acts of State, they would have preferred not to make such empty agreements, and it would have been more understandable for them to be subdued by conquest. The anger that gripped the native signatories of these Agreements when the British rulers suddenly said they were not legally bound was certainly and obviously from just cause.

In fact, if the African kingdoms had the capacity by international law—which they should have had—the Agreements into which they were induced by the British would have been vitiated by the material fact that, while they all along believed that the Agreements bound both parties equally and legally, the British all along knew without so disclosing that they could never be bound by such Agreements. It is a fairly settled principle of international law, to quote Oppenheim again, that:

Although a treaty was concluded with real consent of the parties it is nevertheless not binding if the consent was given in error, or under a delusion produced by a fraud of the other contracting party. . . . Although there is freedom of action in such cases, consent has been given in circumstances which prevent the treaty from being binding.*

Even the great British proconsuls in Africa questioned the propriety of concluding Agreements with African rulers. Lugard termed it "the farce of acquiring jurisdiction by Treaties".[28]

it was surely more justifiable for the European powers frankly to found their title to intervention upon force . . . instead of assuming they themselves derived the right of intervention through cession of sovereignty, under the guise of "treaties" which were either not understood, or which the ruler had no power to make, and which rarely provided an adequate legal sanction for the powers assumed.[29]

It was well established by the law of nations that a colonial Protectorate, which Uganda (or Buganda as such) was before independence, had no international legal personality, nor did it have any *locus standi* in international judicial tribunals. The reasons why are not too difficult to answer.

It was the nations of Europe alone which were the judges in this matter of when a state had become a State; of what standards of development it must have reached and whether or not it had capacity to contract international obligations. It seems logical, though unjust, that norms of international relations at that time should have denied recognition to dependent territories, for were it not so, it would probably have meant endless embarrassment and anxiety to imperial powers as delegations, petitions, and claims endlessly flooded international tribunals from native potentates in protest against European imperial rule. In effect, international law, and all the standards it applied, was not in fact international; it was regional, being wholly European in origin and content.

In conclusion, it is fair to say that, although the British were

* Oppenheim, p. 804, also "Harvard Research" (1935, Pt. III). It is also well established in the English law of contract that misrepresentation of a fundamental nature can vitiate an otherwise valid agreement.

never legally bound by the Agreements with African rulers, for political reasons they adhered strictly to them and departed from them only in rare cases when it seemed in the best interests of peace, good government, or imperial authority to do so. These Agreements formed one of the basic foundations for the application of indirect rule as an effective policy of governing subject peoples.*

Indirect Rule as the Basis of Constitutional Development

Successive British Governments have stated that the object of their imperial rule was not only to benefit themselves through trade and commerce but also to better the conditions of subject peoples. They claimed that imperial rule existed to serve a dual purpose for themselves and for those they ruled. According to Lord Lugard, the British exercised a dual mandate:

> Civilized nations have at last recognised that while on the one hand the abounding wealth of the tropical regions of the earth must be developed and used for the benefit of mankind, on the other hand an obligation rests on the controlling power not only to safeguard the material rights of the natives, but to promote their moral and educational progress.[30]

The method the British chose in attaining this dual mandate, as Lugard wrote just before Uganda formally became a British Protectorate, was "to rule through its own executive government. . . . the Resident should rule through and by the Chiefs." [31] His reasons for this policy were clearly put: "as a cardinal principle of British policy in dealing with native races . . . . institutions and methods, in order to command success and pro-

* A relatively recent development, no doubt devised to mitigate the unsatisfactory nature of these Agreements, was the device of promulgating an Order-in-Council to give legal force to some portions of native Agreements: e.g., The Buganda Agreement 1955, S.I. 1955, No. 1221, S. 2 (2), where "the Governor may declare by Proclamation that any part of the Buganda Agreement, 1955, shall have the force of Law and, upon the making of the Proclamation, that part of the Agreement comes into force on such later date as may be specified in the Proclamation."

mote the happiness and welfare of the people, must be deep-rooted in their traditions and prejudices." [32]

It is this method of British authority exerting itself in a dependent territory through the established indigenous systems of government that is called "indirect rule"—the British not ruling the masses of the people directly but indirectly through their chiefs or kings.*

As a practical measure its great facility commended it.[33] For Buganda there was an elaborate kingship, whereby the Kabaka ruled through a hierarchy of chiefs who had a chain of command down to the smallest area in the kingdom. Similar rule prevailed in the western kingdoms of Ankole, Bunyoro, and Toro; the "principalities" of Busoga practised the same method.

Some writers contend that if indirect rule was based on kingly societies, then it could not be indirect rule when the method of governing through chiefs was extended to those tribes of the Northern and Eastern Regions which had no established central authority of kingship.[34] But in African society, be it based on kingship or chiefs or elders of the family, recognition of authority is inherent in its midst. Dr. T. O. Elias has accurately observed, "Whether the society is a monarchy or a gerontocracy one common denominator is the constant aspiration towards the democratic principles in constitutional government." [35] He observed that in the non-monarchical society (such as the tribes in the east and north of Uganda), "a council of elders wields the powers of the supreme chief in chiefly societies." In fact, it is because this is true that when the monarchical system, or ruling through chiefs, was exported from Buganda to these other areas, it became so completely understood and acceptable to them that some claimed it to be their own tribal order of government.[36] This is because they had equal recognition for the place and function of authority in society. They too recognized central authority, and because of this Major MacDonald could easily

---

* "Indirect rule" also provided a means whereby the imperial power was not required to invest vast amounts of its own manpower and treasure in the development of an infrastructure to sustain its overrule. The colonizing power was, therefore, able to administer often remote and uneconomical territories with a minimum number of administrators resident in the territory. This was certainly true of Uganda.

make thirty treaties in the late 1890s with chiefs northeast of the Nile.[37]

But there was another reason for indirect rule, a reason that bred the greatest misunderstandings and acute friction between Protectorate authorities and African nationalists, a reason that has been well put by Low and Pratt: "Many administrators regarded it as most desirable that patriotism should remain tribal, and that administrative efforts should be made to check any nascent nationalism." [38]

Whatever reasons led to indirect rule, by 1900 it was given official expression in the Buganda Agreement and, though to a less elaborate extent, in the Toro and Ankole Agreements of 1900 and 1901 respectively and later in the Bunyoro Agreement of 1933.

In Buganda the Kabaka was recognised as the supreme ruler of the kingdom.[39] For the purposes of administration the kingdom was divided into twenty counties,[40] with each county (saza) headed by a chief who would be selected by the Kabaka's Government but who had to be approved by the representative of Her Majesty's Government. The powers and duties of such a chief were not left undefined. He was to be entrusted by the Kabaka and Her Majesty's Government with responsibility for administering justice among natives in his county, assessing and collecting taxes, the upkeep of main roads, and general supervision of native affairs. Her Majesty's Government had power to demand his dismissal by the Kabaka and the appointment of a new chief. He was given, among other rewards of office, enjoyment of usufruct accruing from eight square miles of land.*

Above him were the three "Native Officers of State": the Premier (Katikkiro), the Chief Justice (Omulamuzi) and the Treasurer (Omuwanika).[41] These were the Kabaka's principal ministers. He appointed them with the sanction and approval of Her Majesty's Government. They were charged, *inter alia,* with the

---

* In January 1963, this evoked considerable feeling as the "Commoners" (Bawejere) demanded that this privilege be abolished, and that the usufruct go to the general revenue of the kingdom and not to individual chiefs. The chiefs resisted this demand vigorously.

responsibility of transacting most of the business between the Kabaka's Government and the Protectorate Government. It was to them that the county chief had to report, and it was from them that he had to take his instructions. The insistence that chief and minister alike had to have the approval of Her Majesty's representative before taking office was a most effective method of ensuring the paramountcy of British authority.

The kingdom's legislature, the Great Lukiiko, bore the characteristics of feudal rule. It was to consist of the three ministers and the twenty saza chiefs (or their personal representatives in their absence). There were also "three notables" appointed from each county by the Kabaka at his pleasure; he could also appoint a further six "important persons". The powers of this "Native Council" were quite extensive and rather all-embracing. It was "to discuss all matters concerning the native administration of Uganda and to forward to the Kabaka resolutions which may be noted by a majority regarding measures to be adopted by the said administration." But this power was deprived of its force when the Agreement stipulated that "The Kabaka shall further consult with Her Majesty's Representative in Uganda before giving effect to any such resolutions noted by the Native Council, and shall, in this matter, explicitly follow the advice of Her Majesty's Representative." [42] Finally, to complete the structure and nature of the Government, it was required that religious belief was not to count in considering the appointment of chiefs.

It was through this framework in Buganda that measures of the Protectorate Government achieved ready acceptance by the masses—most of the time. Although the agreements with Toro and Ankole did not set out elaborate composition of councils in these kingdoms, they did recognise the status of the rulers.[43] Furthermore, they divided the kingdoms into counties which, as in Buganda, were to be headed by county chiefs and, though not yet written but only understood, were to be part of the machinery of administration.

For the rest of the Uganda Protectorate legal form was given to indirect rule with the promulgation of the Native Authority Ordinance in 1919.[44] It defined "chief" to mean "any officer of an African local government recognized by the Government as a chief" and included "any body of chiefs exercising collective authority". A tribal chief or "Council of Elders" was included in the definition of "Native Court".[45]

The purpose of the Ordinance was to define more clearly the authority of the African chief, his duties and powers, and his privileges and rights.[46] It was his duty to maintain order in the area within his jurisdiction, and for such purpose he was empowered to exercise jurisdiction and powers stipulated in the Ordinance apart from those he might enjoy by virtue of native custom. He was empowered to employ any person subject to his jurisdiction to assist him in carrying out the duties imposed upon him.[47] He was given power to arrest any offender and had to do everything he could to prevent the commission of crime.[48] Subject to any orders of the Provincial or District Commissioner, he could direct any African within the local area of his jurisdiction to attend before him or any native court or before another government official; refusal would mean arrest.[49]

A variety of his powers was defined;[50] they included, among other things, power to issue specific orders for obedience to native custom, prohibiting or restricting the carrying of arms, requiring able-bodied male Africans to work in maintaining projects of a public nature for the benefit of the community. But he was completely subordinate to the authority of the Protectorate Government—which in practice meant Provincial and District Commissioners.[51] These officers had powers to countermand his orders; they could require him to accompany male Africans anywhere they were required to work.[52] More important was their power to fine, to imprison, or to dismiss a chief who defaulted in carrying out his duties.[53] Indeed, the Provincial Commissioner and the District Commissioner had magisterial powers to try chiefs for noncompliance with their orders.[54]

The limits and control of chiefs were thus considerable, but as has been pointed out, "It was nevertheless the hope of indirect rule supporters that the chiefs would accept these limitations and work under them without a deep sense of grievance." This certainly became the case. "In time, the interests of the chiefs and the Government became more closely interwoven. They collected government taxes, heard cases that involved statute law as well as customary law, received fixed salaries and promoted centrally initiated policies. More and more were they associated in the public's mind with the administration and more and more did they also associate their own interests with those of the ruling power." [55]

It is of interest to note that even as late as 1949, when the African Local Governments Ordinance was enacted, while constituting an improvement on the general constitutional set-up of local administrations, it was still basically rooted in the concept of indirect rule. The policy of keeping Africans isolated and each tribe effectively separated from any other tribe, and then running the country through them, was still very much alive.[56] That is why, when introducing this Ordinance as a bill in the Legislative Council, the Chief Secretary had this to say:

> The most important factor in that policy is the development of Local Councils and their functions, to enable Africans themselves to take a greater part, or progressively greater part I hope, in the administration of their own local services and local affairs generally, which affect their community.[57]

It was, however, an improvement in indirect rule. For the first time District Councils were established by law.[58] The Governor had power to establish such councils by proclamation anywhere in the Protectorate. He could determine their constitutions, including the election or appointment of their members; he decided what powers they were to exercise, including the power to enact by-laws with legal validity, although, as under the African Authority Ordinance, such by-laws would first have to be approved by the Provincial Commissioner. And so local governments were established in each district, consisting of chiefs and a District Council.[59] Under such councils were to be the minor councils (saza level); these councils would have no power to enact by-laws.[60] The Protectorate authority, as before, reserved the right to control the chiefs in no uncertain terms. They were to be "appointed by the Governor or by such other persons as the Governor shall authorise."

A chief was charged with the duty to "administer such Protectorate Laws as he is legally competent and to administer the provisions of the African Authority Ordinance and any by-laws lawfully made by any District Council." For the first time it was stipulated that, at his discretion, the Governor could establish a Provincial Council in any province to consider matters affecting the whole province. But such Provincial Councils would have no legal power to make laws or by-laws. In effect, they fulfilled the role of consultative bodies and represented the coordination of provincial policy. Yet, while the structure of government was thus outwardly improved in form, the powers exercisable by those councils were still very limited. Not until the early 1950s was it suddenly realised that to develop these councils as the basis of local governments they had to have far more power. Over this basic structure of local government a 1902 Order-in-Council established the overall Protectorate Government.[61] A Commissioner, who was also commander-in-chief, was to be at its head; this title was changed to Governor in 1907. He was the direct representative of the British Sovereign and, in this way, Uganda started on the well-trodden path of political evolution under British rule. The Order also established a High Court for Uganda "with full jurisdiction, civil and criminal, over all persons and over all matters in Uganda." [62] It further defined the type of laws applicable in the Protectorate.

In 1921 the Legislative Council had been established with powers to "establish such ordinances, and to constitute such courts and offices and to make such provisions and regulations for the proceedings in such courts, and for the administration of justice, as may be necessary for the peace, order and good government." [63] Limitations on the powers of the Legislative Council were those common to other colonial legislatures. Broadly speaking, these were of three types.

First, any law enacted was void if it was repugnant to any Act of the imperial Parliament extending to its territory whether by express words or necessary intendment.[64] Second, laws passed by it could be disallowed by the Crown at any subsequent time.[65] And third, by comparatively modern usage the Governor was empowered to reserve bills for the signification of the pleasure of the British Crown instead of himself assenting to them.[66]

Such, then, was the basic structure of Uganda's Constitution. No sufficiently positive measures were taken to transform indirect rule into a unifying instrument of nationhood. As the years passed, the need for greater participation of Africans in government became more and more apparent. As the Wallis Commission—appointed to review local government—observed at the time, "There is scarcely any feeling yet among Africans for Uganda as a unified country with a sense of common interest and common purpose." [67]

Indeed, Wallis further observed the confusion in the minds of British rulers: "There are in Uganda two constitutional ideas about local government. The first is the idea of building up an efficient and democratic system of Local Government. The second idea is that of native states. . . . These two ideas are mutually exclusive; yet they are both in the field." [68]

Even the new, relatively more comprehensive legislation on local government which resulted from this report in 1955 did not basically alter the fundamental constitutional doctrine of British colonialism: indirect rule.[69] Nor did the new Buganda Agreement of 1955, which redefined Buganda's Constitution and the position of the Kabaka, leave any doubt as to the continuance of indirect rule.[70]

Indirect Rule in Retrospect

That indirect rule provided a comparatively attractive method of governing indigenous tribes cannot be open to serious challenge. The traditional rulers and chiefs secured ready obedience from their people—obedience to orders of Protectorate authorities, which the chiefs were committed to administer. The smooth working of its machinery, as we have outlined, is testimony enough. As a long-term policy, however, it is possible to regard it as one of the greatest shortcomings of British rule in Uganda. It ensured with great consistency and continuity that tribal organisation remained predominantly concerned with its internal affairs, that any spirit of national consciousness beyond the tribe which might emerge had no outlet, and certainly all national, as opposed to tribal, institutions remained exotic to the indigenous masses and to their rulers.[71] As scholars have accurately noted,

"Only through these methods could the development of African interest and participation in the Legislative Council and in the institutions of the Protectorate Government be ignored." [72]

Although the Legislative Council was established in 1921, it was not until 1945 that the first few Africans made an appearance there. At its inception it was only the Indian community that clamoured for political representation, and the saying "Let sleeping dogs lie" was applied to the Africans for more than twenty years. When the Africans did participate, they were not elected but nominated. At such a stage of development this was not unusual, but it is probable that it was fortified by some in authority who shared Sir Donald Cameron's views about elections in native political development: "As far as I am concerned I would leave [election] to their genius. I would not force it upon them. . . . Whether the native will turn to a western system of Government with the vote and the ballot I do not know. That must be left to his own genius." [73]

As early as 1898 the Subcommissioner of the Uganda (Buganda) District had suggested that there should be established a Central Council for Uganda consisting of delegates from the tribes south and west of the Nile. This would have been invaluable for building a nationalist outlook and improving intertribal feeling. The idea came to nothing, but the British administrators did not stop there. In 1925 the Governor vetoed a proposal from the rulers of all the kingdoms and Busoga for holding regular meetings. This, too, was a discouragement of a logical, constructive approach leading toward a national identity.[74]

True, a number of reasons were offered for keeping the African out of national institutions; some have been already noted. It was a common argument for a long time that the African was not "ready", that he had not yet attained the stature of being worthy of belonging to national institutions like the Legislative Council. But Professor Ingham writes of a delegation that made representations to the Joint Committee on Closer Union in 1931:

> The Committee was particularly impressed by the authority and skill with which the African witnesses led by Mr. Serwano Kulubya, Omuwanika of Buganda, stated their case. . . . the good sense

and intelligence of their arguments . . . shone through the whole of their evidence and convinced their hearers that the British Government in the past had tended to underestimate the abilities of the leaders of African opinion.[75]

The fact remains, indirect rule did not help the multifarious tribes of Uganda to understand one another better, or at all.[76] It was, therefore, to a large extent responsible for the strains and stresses that Uganda went through in its final phase of development; it was responsible for giving Buganda continuous encouragement to secede from the rest of the country;[77] it was the basis for demands by the western kingdoms and Busoga for federal status and extravagant powers; it was the foundation of the belief among many Africans that the Central Government was not so much their own as was their local council or assembly, or not their own at all, even when Uganda had only a short period to go before attaining independence. To this extent it was a fundamental shortcoming in British policy and, to the same degree, ultimately negative in terms of encouraging the African to become more familiar with the practice of nationalist, parliamentary democracy at an earlier date. This basically remained the state of affairs until after the Second World War; in fact, until the 1950s. It was on this foundation that the legal system, the local governments, and the Legislative Council evolved and were based.

3. The Development of the Legislative Council

The Growth and Influence of the Legislative Council

We must now examine what had become of the Legislative Council established in 1921. In the prototype of Crown Colony government the Legislative Council was always the heart of constitutional development.

Examine the composition of a colonial legislature at any given stage in its development and you will at once know how advanced or backward that territory was by the ratio of appointed to elected members and by whether it had representative or responsible government. It was in this forum that nationalist elements launched their vigorous attacks on colonial rule and demanded their inalienable right to govern themselves.

But the Uganda Legislative Council was different from the standard Legislative Council for a considerable period of time, and the reasons for its delayed development account, in no small degree, for this Protectorate's delayed date of independence.

It was the leading private bodies in Uganda, such as the Uganda Chamber of Commerce and the Uganda Planters Association, that raised the first cries for constitutional development and for the establishment of a Legislative Council.[1] We have noted how it fell upon Sir Robert Coryndon in 1921 to establish the Council with only four official and three unofficial members, nominated by himself. When the Asians in Uganda were given one of the three unofficial seats they showed active interest in Uganda politics for the first time. They rejected the seat on the grounds that their numbers entitled them to more; they protested and wrote petitions to the Governor; but, after protracted struggle, they had to accept what had been offered them with a promise of possible future increase.[2]

It was this period—the year 1921—that witnessed the birth of what was to become Uganda's sovereign Parliament in 1962, but the Protectorate Government committed a fundamental error in policy by not including Africans in this Legislative Council. It has been argued that it would have been possible to find Africans of the right calibre to fill some vacancies on this Council, no matter how few they might have been. It was an omission that has filled subsequent British scholars with remorse. Professor Ingham had to admit, "It is a matter of regret that an opportunity was not taken at this time to forge a national link between the African population and the Central Government by including Africans in the Legislative Council." [3]

At the same time it is also regrettable that while the Asian community fought for constitutional rights, they made the great mistake of not appealing to Africans for support. Had they done so, they would probably have forged an indissoluble link in the protracted struggle for ultimate sovereign power. Consequently, instead of living side by side with the African as they do today, they would have been completely integrated and accepted in African society, and would not constitute the minority problem that the Uganda of today faces. It may, however, be a bit too harsh to judge the conditions of the 1920s by the standards of what has obtained since the "Winds of Change" or since the rapid growth of nationalistic feeling in Asia and Africa after the Second World War.

We have observed how the energies of Africans, because of the policy of indirect rule, were channeled only into tribal institutions: the Lukiiko in Buganda, the kingdom councils and administrations in the western kingdoms, and the district administrations throughout the remainder of Uganda. It was largely because of this method that through all the 1920s and the 1930s—in fact the whole interwar period—the African in Uganda felt very unconcerned with the Legislative Council.

But the Legislative Council carried on its functions all the same. As usually happens at this stage of development, the Governor, in practice, meant the whole institution. We have examined what powers were conferred on him by the Order-in-Council of 1920; how he was to consult an Executive Council;[4] his power to summon an extraordinary Member to attend its meetings if he felt the man's advice essential.[5]

He was not bound to consult the Executive Council, however, "in cases which may be of such a nature that, in his judgement", the service of imperial authority "would sustain material prejudice by consulting the Council thereupon", or when the matter to be decided upon was too unimportant to require their advice, "or too urgent to admit of their advice being given by the time within which it may be necessary for him to act in respect of any such matters".[6] Having taken action on his own in such circumstances, he was only required to inform the Executive Council of his conduct as soon after his action as possible. Even in times when no such urgent circumstances prevailed, the Governor could still act contrary to the advice of the Executive Council if he deemed it "right to do so", although he was required to inform the Secretary of State of his grounds for not taking their advice.[7]

To complete his extensive executive power, he was required to attend and preside at all meetings of the Legislative Council,[8] in which he was vested with both an original and a casting vote.[9] In fact, at this stage, he admirably symbolised Sir Andrew Cohen's vivid description.[10]

FETTERS ON THE GOVERNOR'S AUTHORITY

But the Governor was not without legal limitations on his vast powers. The draft instructions prevented him from assenting to a fairly wide range of legislation. Such legislation, in the form of bills, he had to submit to Her Majesty's pleasure for assent, which in practice meant one of Her Majesty's principal Secretaries of State. Instances of such bills were:

(1) Those concerning commerce:
  (a) any bill affecting the currency of the Protectorate or relating to the issue of bank notes;
  (b) any bill establishing any banking association or amending or altering the constitution, powers, or privileges of any banking association.
(2) Those relating to external affairs; any bill the provisions of which appeared inconsistent with obligations imposed upon the British Crown by treaty.
(3) Those which affected security and defence; any bill or measure interfering with the discipline or control of the British Crown's armed forces—land, sea, or air.
(4) Finally, those provisions that touched the realms of personal law, instances of which were bills for the divorce of persons who had been joined together in holy matrimony.[11]

Within these fairly well defined limits the Legislative Council continued to pass laws affecting all fields of development in the country. But it did so without any of those dramatic moments of heated debate characteristic only of elected representatives of the people; during this whole period it was the colonial civil service machine that facilitated the execution of all imperial policy.

ENLARGEMENT OF THE COUNCIL

We have seen how revolutionary the consequences of the Second World War had been, especially with regard to subject peoples in Asia and Africa. It was in 1946 that, for the first time in Uganda's history, Africans were nominated to become Members of the Legislative Council. As we mention elsewhere, there were no political parties in the modern sense, and therefore these first African Members of the Council were non-party Nominated Members.[12]

One was nominated from among the Kabaka's ministers, another from the Katikkiros (premiers) of the western kingdoms, and the third from among the Secretaries-General of the Eastern

Province District Councils.* In 1946 the number of Europeans and Asians on the Council was increased from two to three each, so the number of Unofficial Members came to nine. Official majority was ensured by the addition of three more heads of various departments.[13]

The wheels of progress were at last in motion. The Protecting Power had been compelled by events and persuaded by its conscience to initiate Africans into the Legislative Council, if not immediately, yet with certainty. Indirect rule, which had been practised for so long, was now bound to end.

It became desirable—in fact almost compelling—that the wishes, hopes, and fears of the African masses should be communicated to the Government. In the same year a violent disturbance had swept Buganda, a disturbance one root of which was political discontent, for it cannot be said there was an efficient channel for communicating the people's grievances to the central authority.[14] A speech by the Governor to the Legislative Council demonstrated this awareness:

> Ignorance by the people of what their Government is doing or attempting to do for them, and for what object, and ignorance by the Government of what the people are wanting, saying, and thinking create misunderstanding, suspicion and discontent. . . . the Government may set about what it is doing in the wrong way, but once satisfied that it is wrong it will endeavour to remedy the fault of concept or application, and the sooner it learns that fault the better for all concerned. It cannot learn that fault unless it is in close and continuous contact with the thoughts and wants of the people." [15]

But then His Excellency proceeded to pin-point the people's ignorance: "Few of them have any understanding of what the Government is doing and why it is doing what it is." With indirect rule it is difficult to visualise what better knowledge of the Central Legislature they were expected to have.

The year 1950 witnessed yet another enlargement of the Legislative Council. In a Communication from the Chair during the

* The Report of the Constitutional Committee, 1959 (hereinafter called the Wild Report), p. 15. The announcement on these nominations was made by the Governor on 23 October 1945: The Uganda Argus, 24 October 1945; also Ingham, The Making of Modern Uganda, pp. 230–31.

twenty-ninth session in 1949, the Governor announced the details of this enlargement. Provincial Councils were established in each of the provinces, and each was to elect two Members to the Council. For Buganda, the Lukiiko was to elect one and the Kabaka to nominate the other. Europeans and Asians were increased from three to four each. The grand total of Unofficial Members was now sixteen.

The Official Members were also increased by six. The Provincial Commissioners, together with the Buganda Resident, were, in addition, brought in "to provide the Council with the accumulated wisdom and specialised knowledge" they were supposed to have. The full strength of the Council had thus been increased to thirty-two.[16] In 1954 there were still more changes.* The number of Unofficial Members was increased to seven Asians and seven Europeans nominated by the Governor and fourteen Africans, of whom eleven were to be indirectly elected, one by each district (except Karamoja) and three by the Buganda Lukiiko. Undoubtedly efforts were being made, though belatedly, to bring the African more and more to share legislative responsibilities.

Meanwhile, in 1952, an event of great political and constitutional significance had taken place. The first national political party, the Uganda National Congress, was born under the leadership of Ignatius Musazi with the slogan "Self-Government Now".[17] The fortunes of this party are dealt with elsewhere, but suffice it to say here that whatever shortcomings beset it—and they were quite a number—it kindled the fire of nationalism; it converted contented and politically inert Africans into agitators for greater constitutional rights; it did, therefore, together with its subsequent off-shoots, keep the Protectorate Government alive to the need for rapid changes.

Sir Andrew Cohen, then Governor, was one of the greatest of modern British Governors. He was dedicated to the destruction of indirect rule. He was able to respond to the challenges of swift development. In 1955 he introduced the ministerial system of

---

* The announcement of these changes was made on 11 August 1953—*The Uganda Argus*, 12 August 1953; also Ingham, *The Making of Modern Uganda*, p. 261.

government.[18] His speech to the thirty-sixth session of the Council in 1956 set out its composition quite clearly:

> Now we have a Legislative Council of sixty, of whom half are Africans. Of the thirty Representative Members, eighteen are Africans elected either by the District Councils or by other means. Of the thirty Members on Government side, there are seventeen Official Members of whom seven are Ministers or Parliamentary Secretaries drawn from the public; the remainder of the thirty are back bench members drawn from the public who are free to speak and vote as they like except on an issue of confidence.[19]

The composition of the Council had changed, as well as its temperament. The Governor had to remark, "The extension of the Council has been accompanied by an increase, most encouraging to me, in the liveliness and vigour of the debates."

The Executive Council had been developed into a ministerial system. There were five Ministers drawn from public life and appointed by the Governor; three of them were Africans. In addition, there were two Parliamentary Secretaries. But changes are seldom without criticism. To some people, the old school of Europeans—exponents of indirect rule—it seemed as if the Governor was moving too fast for the African. It is certainly doubtful that Sir Donald Cameron, once Governor of Tanganyika, would have endorsed these reforms.

Cohen, however, was not lost for words nor was he wanting in justification for his actions. He listed the needs for the introduction of the ministerial system on four grounds.[20] First, a purely official form of government he considered completely out of date. Second, it was essential that "men drawn from the public should take part in the formation of policy at the highest level." Third, there was obvious merit in introducing the ministerial system now: the administrative organisation involved could be progressively improved in the light of experience rather than delayed until political developments took place in the future. The fourth reason, he argued, was that the ministerial system made it easier for the Government to take a general view of all fields of activity which formerly could receive only limited attention from a senior officer of the Central Government.

By now reforms were being effected in almost every field of the Protectorate Government's activity. When Cohen said that "great political reforms both at the centre and in the different parts of the country" had been made, it was not without foundation and so was deserving of gratitude.[21]

But the key to the contribution Cohen made to Uganda's development lay in his systematic endeavour to rid the country of indirect rule. Indeed, at the end of his term of office, when reviewing the progress made, he admitted freely in his last address to the Council:

> In my judgement, the most important achievement of the country during the last five years has been the real progress made in giving responsibility to Africans in all the main spheres of public life. A new atmosphere has been created in the country. The aim of all our efforts, the building up of the country towards the goal of self-government in the future is now clearly understood.

With this, he had brought a new approach to all concerned in the task of nation building. He fostered a new sense of cooperation between British civil servants and the indigenous masses. Seldom has a colonial governor reminded the elite of British authority in a protectorate, as did Cohen, publicly, of their proper responsibilities.

Having restated that the aim was self-government, he enunciated two fundamental principles:

> . . . all who have come from outside the country to live and work here must identify themselves with this aim, this goal and this task in what they say and do, in their attitude to public affairs and in their personal dealings with individuals—they have as part of their duty—and it is a most important part—to join in the great work of helping the people of this country to prepare themselves for self-government in the future.

His second point was a challenge to the African population:

> The responsibilities which are being progressively given to the people of this country place on them a special obligation.

The people, in their handling of their affairs, would be judged by their actions. The rate of progress in the country, both political and general, would depend on the way in which everyone carried out his responsibilities. Although the aim of political progress was clear, the rate at which it advanced would depend not just on the effectiveness of government policy but on the actions and attitudes and sense of responsibility of the people.

All this had been said and done through the Legislative Council. True, in 1953 Cohen had committed a great error of political judgement in exiling the Kabaka, but it remains equally true that, because of his vigorous reforms, the majority of the Africans still admired him. Various influential people behind the scenes undertook whispering campaigns to make him the Governor-General of Uganda at independence, although it never materialised. The African Members of the Legislative Council found him the stimulus they had lacked. They accordingly began to rise to their calling. Meanwhile, not only was the Legislative Council now expanding in membership, but its powers and functions were also assuming new proportions.

It had long ago become the practice of British colonial policy to empower colonial legislatures to enact laws determining their powers and privileges. This practice, which applied to West African dependencies[22] and the Caribbean,[23] was now extended to East Africa. In 1954 the Uganda Legislative Council was vested with similar powers, but with the standard proviso that such laws, immunities, or powers did not exceed those of the House of Commons in the United Kingdom.[24]

The Legislative Council Becomes a Platform for Political and Constitutional Demands

It is not intended in this examination of the Council's influence on constitutional changes to consider its day-to-day business in legislating for the general peace, order, and good government of the Protectorate, but it deserves particular mention that an increasing number of Africans took the floor and demanded

greater constitutional rights and a faster pace for such development. As yet there was no directly elected membership, but even
those who were turned out by the District Councils or the Buganda Lukiiko were not lacking in the growing sense of African
nationalism. The strands of single-nationhood started to show.
Thus in one debate George B. Magezi had to make an appeal for
unity which was met by spontaneous approbation from every
African Member in the Council chamber: "Mr. President, our
intentions as Africans are not to widen the gap [between our-
selves] but to close it up. Whether it be Buganda, Ankole, or
Bakiga, our struggle is one." [25]

The date 20 April 1957 was of historic significance in the life
of the Council. For the first time in its history a motion was
made—by an African Member—urging the British Government
to grant self-government to Uganda in 1958.[26] It was made
partly in protest against a despatch from the Colonial Secretary
which, in effect, stated that Her Majesty's Government, having
accepted the recommendations of the Namirembe Conference,
had decided that there should be no major constitutional
changes in Uganda for a period of five years.[27] Bamuta, elderly
and silver-haired but tenacious and patriotic, made the motion
with an appeal so passionate that it could be likened to Machiavelli's exhortation to the Italian princes for the liberation of
Italy: "I beg, I appeal, I bow before the Government to permit
us to rule ourselves." [28]

It was not in dispute that Bamuta's demand was unrealistic.
Africans on the Government benches, such as Z. C. K. Mun-
gonya, then Minister of Land Tenure, had to stage a most vigorous defence for the Protectorate Government's pace of constitutional development: "What I have seen in these vernacular
papers, that it is far better for the people of the country here to
rule themselves badly rather than to be ruled well by another nation . . . is something I very much deprecate." [29]

Even African Members on the Representative side were not
fully convinced that Uganda could manage self-government by
1958. G. B. Magezi, for example, had to oppose the proposal in
no less certain terms: All I can say is that whilst tribalism is still
acute in this country, it would be very wrong, wrong to throw

these people on the mercy of God and let civil wars start raging.[30]

The Government itself, of course, rejected the motion, stating that what was being done was most appropriate—namely, not introducing major changes until 1961.

Yet the defeat of the motion did not detract from its prophecy. Professor K. Ingham, a Nominated Government backbencher and a historian, grasped its significance when he stood up to say: "Today has been a great day in Uganda's history . . . and I do not feel that the introduction of this motion to the House has done more harm than good. I think it has done a lot of good." He continued, saying that the motion constituted "a challenge to the Government":

> The challenge is this: it is not enough to show a merely friendly sympathy for movements towards self-government. Everything that the Government does from this day forward—*I repeat, in everything they do or say from this day forward*—the Government must show quite clearly that they are moving towards self-government".[31]

It is no surprise that his speech was punctuated by spontaneous applause, most particularly from among the African Members.

The motion had additional consequences. Once again the Chief Secretary reiterated British policy in Uganda. He quoted a policy speech made by the Secretary of State for the Colonies in 1954.* The long-term aim was once again to build the Protectorate into a self-governing state, but Her Majesty's Government would wish to be satisfied that "the rights of minorities who are residents of Uganda were properly safeguarded in the constitution", although this was not to detract from the primarily "African character" of the country. The question of minority rights had thus become a pronounced issue in Uganda's constitutional evolution. It should be noted that the Legislative Council witnessed many occasions when its African Members debated the issue of minorities with great feeling and not without justification.

* Made on 23 February 1954.

The year 1957 also witnessed one of several debates on the demand for greater constitutional reforms. Leading among them was the demand for reform of the electoral process. In November of that year the chief of the Uganda National Congress, and at the time unquestionably the leading nationalist, made a motion that the Council "request Her Majesty's Government to make the necessary constitutional provision in order to have a House three-quarters of whose Members are Elected." [32]

If there has been any distinctive feature of political development that distinguishes Uganda from the vast majority of British dependencies on the African continent, it has been its relative lack of bitterness or extreme nationalist feeling, even up to the moment of independence. The militant spirit of Nkrumah's Convention People's Party in the Gold Coast, for instance, the dynamism of Dr. Azikiwe's National Convention of Nigeria and Cameroon, and even the Action Group in Nigeria,[33] were significant political movements to which the Uganda nationalist could look for inspiration but which he could never marshal his forces to emulate effectively. Reasons for this are to be found in Uganda's comparatively peaceful history, which we deal with in our discussion on political parties.

It is not, therefore, surprising that when making his motion, Musazi could go very near to Lord Lugard's postulate of the "dual-mandate" of imperial rule:

> The strands of history have brought our two countries together. We, the Africans of this country, have provided much material benefit to the British people at home and to our brothers the Asians, residing in the country, a country in which some of them wish to stay. The British people through their agents here, have in turn taught us many good things.[34]

During this period it was never, in fact, open to serious doubt in Uganda that Uganda was eventually to have self-government. Indeed, in the course of his speech Musazi summarised the constitutional doctrine of British imperial rule with remarkable accuracy when he said:

> Of all the Imperial systems of colonial administration in Africa, that of the British provides the greatest possibility for dependent

people to attain self-determination along constitutional lines. All political parties in Britain, Socialists, Conservatives, Liberals, are in Fundamental agreement on the main political objective of Imperial policy which is to guide the colonial territories to responsible self-government within the Commonwealth.[35]

Despite these tributes to British rule, the motion was a pointer to a very genuine grievance. If population was to have any effect on representation on the Council, there is no doubt that the Africans were grossly under-represented. We have observed how during the whole interwar period the Council was regarded as an exotic institution by the overwhelming proportion of Africans. For this reason Musazi pleaded: "I feel that this Honourable Council should support this motion, so that the Africans of this country may look upon Uganda's Legislative Council, not as an alien one but as their own Council." [36]

The demand for increased African support was upheld by all the African Representative Members. From the Eastern Province, C. J. Obwangor asserted; "It is our birthright that we should have adequate representation." J. Lwamafa and J. Babiha from the Western Province gave equally enthusiastic support.[37] But the motion was lost. The Chief Secretary reaffirmed the Secretary of State's despatch of July 1955, which precluded any major change until 1961.

African leadership had, however, come on to the stage and had come to stay. It delighted in and drew inspiration from successes of other freedom fighters in the world. In his motion for self-government Bamuta had cited Burma, India, Ceylon, "and now Ghana" as precedents for his argument.[38] On 6 June 1957 Musazi made a motion of goodwill to Ghana on the attainment of her independence.[39] In March 1958, making another motion for self-government, Bamuta had a wealth of precedent to draw from: "You gave [self-government] to Ghana—but what is Ghana?—it is not Uganda. You are going to give it to Azikiwe of Nigeria. Why not Uganda?" Undoubtedly, the African Representative Members of the Council had now discovered new levels of strength and found fresh grounds for hope from events happening elsewhere.

THE APPOINTMENT OF A SPEAKER

We have noted how extensive were the powers vested in the Governor by the Orders-in-Council of 1902 and 1921. Although the composition of the Council started to change fairly rapidly after the Second World War, it never brought with it a reduction or constitutional limitation on his authority. Legally, of course, even in 1958 Uganda did not have a representative legislature based on the prerequisite that at least half of its membership must be elected by the people.[40]

But 1958 saw the beginning of limitations on the Governor's authority, although it started with relatively small matters. The Governor was no longer to sit in, and preside over, the Legislative Council. In his last speech to the Council as its President, he stated that the reason for this change was the steady growth in the business of the Council. It needed a full-time person to guide its affairs and deliberations. But also it seemed to him "and to many Hon. Members of this Council" that a stage had been reached in Uganda's constitutional development when it was no longer appropriate for the Governor to be a Member of the Council, "equipped with an original and casting vote and to preside over its meetings." [41]

This, as we shall see later, was a period of Buganda's renewed separatism. The Baganda had agreed with the British Government to participate in the Legislative Council after the Namirembe Conference of 1955, provided no major constitutional changes took place until after six years.[42] Seeking a ground, however feeble, on which to base their nonparticipation in the Legislative Council, the Buganda Government claimed that the appointment of a Speaker was a major change before the six years had elapsed; that it was a breach of the agreement and consequently the Baganda were not bound by this agreement to fill the seat of one of their Members who had resigned.

When announcing the appointment of the Speaker the Governor rejected their claim: "It cannot be accepted however that this change in the machinery, as it were, of the Legislative Council is a major constitutional change." This argument was later to be upheld by a court of law.[43]

But the Governor took care not to alter the voting power in the Council lest it lend force to the Buganda claim; his original and casting votes were to be replaced by two Nominated Africans on the Government side. The rest of the Protectorate welcomed the change. The African Members of the Council viewed it with satisfaction and gratitude, although they always demanded more.

The Royal Instructions of 1958 gave legal force to the proposed change.[44] The Speaker was to be a person who was not an ex-officio, Nominated, or Representative Member of the Council; he was to be appointed by the Governor, by instrument, under the public seal. He did not, for instance, as in British Honduras in 1953, exercise any voting rights.[45]

MEMBERSHIP OF THE COUNCIL UNDER THE ROYAL INSTRUCTIONS OF 1958

In his last speech as President of the Legislative Council, Sir Andrew Cohen claimed that posterity would recognize the year 1958 as a year of major importance in the constitutional development of Uganda.[46] The comprehensive Orders-in-Council and the Royal Instructions of 1958, making room for the first direct elections ever held, left no doubt about this.

The composition of the Council was to be as follows:

(1) the Governor, still also called the Commander-in-Chief;
(2) the Speaker;[47]
(3) the ex-officio Members—the Chief Secretary, the Attorney-General and the Financial Secretary (locally called the Minister of Finance);
(4) the Nominated Members—these were to be:[48]
    (a) persons holding office in the public service,
    (b) such persons not holding office in the public service as the Governor is satisfied will support Government policy in the Council when requested to do so;
(5) the Representative Members—these members, the embryo of democratic government, were divided into two groups:[49]
    (a) such persons not holding office in public service and not being Nominated Members as the Governor, in pursuance of instructions from the Secretary of State,

may from time to time appoint by instrument under public seal;

(b) Elected Members returned through electoral districts.

In addition, the Instructions reaffirmed the Governor's power and also laid down the qualifications for membership of the Council.

INCREASED DEMANDS FOR SELF-GOVERNMENT

Even before the first direct elections, the African representatives on the Council sustained the demands for greater constitutional rights and at a faster pace. In March 1958 Mr. Y. S. Bamuta once again made a motion demanding a time-table for self-government. Speaking for the motion, the Member for Bunyoro, G. B. Magezi, did not fail to justify his case by external events: "I think that the Sudan had a time-table. Why is it impossible for Uganda? I do not care if the time-table is for twenty or fifty years—but it has to be definite." [50]

By this time a new rising star, A. M. Obote, had come to the Council as Member for Lango. Supporting the motion, he asserted what was—most particularly in Buganda—a consuming belief that "Uganda as a Protectorate cannot be considered as part of the British Empire":[51] a conception, as we noted earlier, destroyed in practice by a consistent chain of judicial decisions from the Privy Council, but one that gave Uganda politicians, in their view, greater claim for political rights and more constitutional powers.

Indeed, by this time the most thrilling debates in the Council chamber were by African politicians demanding self-government. True, disunity in the country and among the politicians was still prevalent. But the spirit of striving for unity and nationhood had come to stay. Thus, in fortification of his plea, Obote continued: "We want to know whether the Government is aware of the fact that there is a wide demand in the country for self-government. The Hon. Bamuta comes from Buganda. He has moved this Motion. I am from the North and that should prove to the Government that there is a wide demand." This enthusiasm of the African Members was not shared by other Members! European opinion in the Council was against a rigid, more clearly defined time-table and preferred, instead, taking carefully selected steps one by one with flexibility and caution.

The motion, like those before it, was rejected by Government. In his opening remarks the Chief Secretary had a plausible argument for this course: "A time-table for self-government would be unrealistic and unpractical because its formulation would require knowledge of future progress and development in various fields which we cannot foresee at the present time." *

In fact, the pattern of these demands had almost become stereotyped: first came a demand for constitutional reform, argued with the greatest conviction and eloquence, and then came the rejection of each demand by the Protectorate Government, followed by a restatement that the policy of Her Majesty's Government in Uganda was leading it toward self-government. The country still lacked the vanguard of a truly nationalist party embracing all tribes and with a specific programme of development, other than demanding "Self-Government Now".† Even after the first direct elections in 1958, parties had still the same failing as before; and, as we consider elsewhere at some length, it is because of their lack of disciplined, systematic and extensive drive that the Protectorate Government could afford to reject African demands—for the time being at least.

One of the most significant events in Uganda's constitutional history took place in February 1959. It was the appointment of the first Constitutional Committee in the Protectorate's history, which came to be popularly named the "Wild Committee", after its chairman. The Council was absorbed in debating its terms of reference and, once again, reasserting greater constitutional demands.

The composition of the Legislature in 1959–1960 was:

(1) The Executive Council, which consisted of seven European civil servants (Ministers) and the Resident of Buganda; one Asian and three Nominated Africans. Five of the Ministers were drawn from the public. Only six Official Ministers were ap-

---

* *Proceedings of the Legislative Council,* Pt. I, p. 108. But it must be submitted that part of the reason (which was never stated) was the lack of clarity and finality as to the precise form of government Uganda was to have on self-government.

† Low, in *Political Parties in Uganda*, demonstrates this.

pointed. The Executive Council now had an Official Majority, but it also contained a few Elected Members of the Legislature.[52] In 1959 it had attained the status which its counterparts in Gibraltar[53] had attained in 1950, and those in Singapore[54] and Sierra Leone[55] in 1951.

(2) The Legislative Council, which had not changed materially since 1958. It consisted of a Speaker and

(a) A Government Side: This was composed of all Members of the Executive Council, except the Resident, three civil servants (all Europeans) and three Parliamentary Secretaries (all Africans, two Nominated and one Elected). In addition there were fifteen Nominated Members, of whom ten were Africans, three Europeans, and two Asians. Finally, there was

(b) The Representative Side:[56] This consisted of twelve African elected Members from the Northern, Eastern, and Western Provinces. All were directly elected except for Ankole, where the District Council served as an electoral college.* There was also one Nominated African Member from Bugisu, the District Council there having declined to participate in the 1958 elections on the grounds that it needed more representation. Buganda was entitled to its quota of five Members under the 1955 Buganda Agreement, but it had boycotted the 1958 elections and its seats remained vacant. There were also six Nominated European and six Nominated Asian Members. Karamoja was the only area not represented.

The final figures were: Government side thirty-two, Representative side thirty (including the five Buganda vacancies), giving the Government a majority of seven. Ex-officio plus Nominated Members outnumbered those elected by forty-five to twelve, but there was a majority of Africans over non-Africans, of non–civil servants over civil servants. There were also five female Nominated Members of the Council. Since 1945 the Council had made considerable progress, although certainly much still remained to be done.

* Ankole had declined to hold direct elections because the ruling Protestant group heading the local government feared that if they opted for direct elections the predominantly Catholic electorate would defeat them. Election of a Representative by the District Council, where the Protestants held a majority, would ensure the election of their own candidate.

Representative and Elected Members' Organisations

As the Council enlarged, Members, either Nominated or Elected, set up two respective organisations. It was largely those who were nominated by the Governor and only a few who had been elected by District Councils that formed the Representative Members' Organisation. It was, so to speak, a group of moderates.

On the opposite side were those who were elected the representatives of the people.* They tended to regard those in the other organisation as being mere puppets of imperial policy. They were a small, militant, self-confident group who formed the "Heart of Uganda Nationalism"—being its most vocal and most able advocates.

The purpose of the two organisations was to discuss Government business and formulate views on its policies. Unlike most of the Representative Members, the Elected Members were not on Government benches. They filled, at the time, the role of what came to be the Opposition.

Qualifications for Membership of Council

Although the Legislative Council (Elections) Ordinance of 1957 laid down the detailed provisions relating to the direct elections to the Council of 1958, the Royal Instructions of 1958 repeated the qualifications which by now had become a standard form for British dependencies.† Every Member had to be either a British subject or a British "Protected Person".[57] Acknowledgement, adherence, allegiance, or obedience to a foreign power was a disqualification; so was being an undischarged bankrupt, as declared so by a competent court. If a person was convicted of a criminal offence under certain circumstances he was dis-

* When the author was elected by the Eishengyero (State Assembly) of Ankole in May 1960, he joined the Elected Members' Organisation.

† Buganda boycotted the 1958 elections because of the resurgence of its separatism and a renewed apprehension that further cooperation with the Legislative Council would be supporting the very body that she felt would be responsible for her eventual destruction. This factor is discussed in greater detail under "Buganda Separatism".

qualified.[58] But the Nominated Members held their seats only at the Governor's pleasure. Both Representative and Nominated Members would lose their seats if, among other reasons: (1) they died; (2) they ceased to be British subjects or British Protected Persons; or (3) they absented themselves from sittings of the Council for a period of twelve consecutive months or absented themselves from two consecutive meetings of the Council without appropriate permission from the Governor.[59]

THE COUNCIL'S ACTIVITY IN PUBLIC AFFAIRS

Until dissolution just before the general elections of March 1961, the Council continued to gain influence, and its African Members sustained their efforts for greater African participation in public life. There was no field of Government endeavour in which the African Representatives did not either ask Parliamentary questions or make motions to achieve the improvement of agriculture, animal industry, and trade. They demanded a greater and faster rate of African participation in all government jobs in the civil service.* When the pace of education slacked, they staged vigorous protests and demanded more and higher education.† They demanded improvement in medical attention. In short, they brought their needs to Government notice. Above all, they laboured to get recognition of their demands for constitutional reforms.

When Buganda separatism revived, they opposed it with resolution and fortitude.‡ They demanded to know Uganda's future

* Hon. Y. B. Mungoma, in Question No. 229 of 1960, demanded to know, "What avenues of promotion are open to African dispensers and stores assistants employed in Government hospitals?" In the Committee of Supply, in a debate on a vote for the Ministry of Information, Hon. A. G. Bazanyamaso demanded to know "the racial break down" of programme organisers for the Uganda Broadcasting Service. *Proceedings of Legislative Council*, 1960, Pt. III, p. 1203.

† *Proceedings of Legislative Council*, 1960, 40th session. Hon. J. Babiha made a motion for adjournment, demanding that B. Sc. (Agric.) be introduced in Makerere College (p. 2003).

‡ An instance is the demand by Members of the Council that the Protectorate Government should not pay travelling expenses for Buganda delegates abroad, who were in pursuit of their secessionist ideas: *Proceedings of the Legislative Council*, 1960, 40th session, p. 1893; also Question No. 421/1960.

form of government.* If Government eluded their pointed demands and won the day, they resumed them the next day with equal zeal. Indeed, they had come to realise that in their hands the salvation of their country lay. This is borne out by a plea from an Elected Member from Bunyoro in a debate concerning disorders in Buganda:

> I still believe that those who are charged with the task of leading either Local Governments or township authorities or municipal authorities, or churches, would have the sense to realise that this country has a future and that future lies in their hands and they have got to contribute to build a modern, happy, peaceful democratic society.[60]

On 19 September 1960 the Governor, in a great ceremony, opened the new Parliamentary Building, which he described as "one of the finest in Africa". This opening ceremony was graced by the presence of the Secretary of State, The Rt. Hon. Ian Macleod, who made a moving speech to Members exhorting them to seek unity rather than division and giving stern warning to those (in Buganda) who were intimidating people to prevent them from registering for the coming elections.

With regard to the life of this Council, it is important to note that the Representative Members, especially the elected ones, had by this time adopted one political party or another. The Democratic Party, formed in 1954, had only one Member.† On 9 March 1960 a new political force was born—the Uganda Peoples Congress, which had been formed as a result of a merger of

* Hon. G. B. Magezi made a motion for adjournment on 4 May 1959, demanding to know Uganda's future form of government. *Proceedings of the Legislative Council*, 1958, Pt. II, p. 42.

† The general public, and most academics, have usually assumed that the Democratic Party was founded by Mr. Matayo Mugwanya in 1954. However, recently compiled Democratic Party documents suggest that Mr. Joseph Kasolo, a retired Makerere-educated civil engineer, was the Founder-President of the party in 1954. When Mr. Matayo Mugwanya, a leading Roman Catholic politician, was rejected by the Kabaka for the post of Katikkiro in 1954, he joined the Democratic Party; in 1956 he succeeded Mr. Kasolo as President-General. Mr. Benedicto K. M. Kiwanuka, now Chief Justice of the High Court of Uganda, succeeded Mr. Mugwanya as President-General in 1958. Mr. Kiwanuka later became Chief Minister during the internal self-government era.

two other smaller political parties. Although relatively new, it claimed the majority, if not all, of the Elected African Members. For the first time a political party with a large following was represented in the Council, where its followers would present its views effectively. The Protectorate was poised for substantial change—the first direct elections of the greatest number of Legislative Council Members on a political party basis and, after a consistent and sometimes controversial evolution of the electoral process, on a much more widened franchise.

The Evolution of the
Electoral Process

The direct elections that took place in March 1961, which brought with them, for the first time, a measure of responsible government, were a result of protracted demands by African Members of the Council. We have noted how, when the Legislative Council was established in 1921, the Governor had the power to nominate its entire membership. There was no form of election; there was no franchise. During the interwar years, even when the Council's functions and responsibilities were gradually enlarging, the power to choose its membership lay exclusively with the Governor. True, he always took care to nominate persons for their representation of racial groups and business interests, but it was done at his absolute discretion. This was always the standard pattern of constitutional development when the legislatures of British dependencies (Colonies or Protectorates) were still in the elementary stages of development.

But the postwar years brought great changes. In Uganda, however, even after 1945, when the beginning of African membership in the Council began to expand, nominations did not cease. In due course a method was introduced whereby African Representatives were elected by District Councils and nomination was left for some African Members on Government benches and Representatives of the Asian and European communities. For Buganda this right was given to the Lukiiko under the 1955 Buganda Agreement, which, however, due to Buganda's separatist propensities was never effectively exercised.[61] The demand for direct elections started anew early in 1956. In January 1956 the issue was debated in the Council. It was generally agreed that the aim of the Protectorate Government should be to introduce direct elections. Yet the majority of Members, including those on the Representative side, voted against binding themselves to the introduction of direct elections throughout the Protectorate in 1957.[62]

On 24 April the Governor, addressing the thirty-sixth session of the Council, stated the policy thus: "The objective of our policy must be to introduce direct elections on a Common Roll for the Representative Members of the Legislative Council from all parts of the Protectorate." [63]

Having stated this fundamental objective, he went on to qualify it in a manner that was to unleash most lively debates and vigorous protests from African opinion at a later date.

"Time was required," he said, "to study the implications of this novel method of election and consequently it would be impossible to introduce it in 1957. But if it was the desire of the country, it should take place in 1961." But he offered a concession to Buganda. Its method of election under the 1955 Buganda Agreement,[64] he proposed, should be changed by a joint review by the Protectorate and Buganda Governments. As if to induce the Baganda, he offered them direct elections for their Members to the new Legislative Council scheduled for 1958, an offer not extended to the rest of the country. Indeed, in doing this he was fulfilling the desire so eloquently expressed by the Baganda delegation to the Namirembe Conference, which drafted the 1955 Agreement, but a desire which they subsequently dropped and rejected in their pursuit of separatism.

It was the Governor's advocacy of the common roll, however, that was most problematic and contentious:

> Before agreeing that a Common Roll should be introduced, Her Majesty's Government will require to be sure that the system includes provision which will secure adequate and effective representation of the non-African communities on the Representative side of the Legislative Council under the Common Roll, whether by reservation of seats or in some other way.

As for the rest of the country, they had to wait until 1961 because they "will be able to watch the results of the 1957 experiment in Buganda if that is introduced." There was no doubt that the statement just made was an important one. Besides being a clear objective of policy, the Governor promised, "If direct elections on a Common Roll are introduced in 1961, this will be a positive step forward towards self-government." [65]

The thirty-seventh meeting of the Council offered opportunity for a full-scale debate of this exposition on elections. In spite of the Chief Secretary's lengthy explanations, African Representative Members dismissed the idea of "adequate and effective" representation on the Council for the non-African minorities as unwarranted.[66]

As they saw the problem, the best safeguard was not by legislation but by goodwill and good faith. It is this that prompted I. K. Musazi to make this eloquent appeal: "The urgent need in this country is to change, it seems to me, the psychology of the African people from suspicion to trust. Change it from antagonism to goodwill. Change it from resistance to co-operation." [67]

It seemed to sum up the case for the African Members, and was followed by the apt and wise conclusion by C. J. Obwangor, Member for Teso, when he said, "I believe in this country no legal provisions will safeguard forever or for all times representation of non-Africans in this Honourable House." [68]

The problem, however, was not decided, but was left for future finalization. The preferential treatment of giving Buganda, alone, the right to direct elections in 1958 had evoked so much protest from the rest of the country that the Government felt it necessary to set up a Committee of the Legislative Council, under the chairmanship of Mr. J. V. Wild, to assess the extent of the demands for direct elections in the rest of the country.

Its report was introduced to the Council in this session, with approval by the Chief Secretary, who summarised its recommendations as follows:

(1) that for the next Legislative Council direct elections of the African Representative Members should be introduced in all areas that wanted them, except Karamoja;

(2) that for the election of African Representative Members

in 1958, the qualifications and disqualifications of voters and candidates throughout the country should be as set out in the appendix to the report; and

(3) that in districts which return two or more African Representatives, the district should, for the purpose of 1958 elections, be divided into separate constituencies, each constituency returning one Member.[69]

The reaction of Members to Government's granting direct elections to all in 1958 was one of satisfaction. In the words of one of their ablest spokesmen: "So far we have acquitted ourselves well in our march by reaching free elections by negotiation and not by revolution and bloodshed." [70]

But there was demand for universal adult suffrage.

It is against this background that the reform in the electoral process was launched. The Uganda (Electoral Provisions) Order-in-Council of 1957 [71] was passed to enable the existing legislature of Uganda to make provision for the election of Members to the new Legislative Council and also to enable registration of electors in pursuance of any such electoral provisions as were to be enacted.[72]

Consequently the Council enacted the Legislative Council (Elections) Ordinance of 1957. Many provisions were dealt with by this law: the machinery of registration of voters;[73] the officers running the elections;[74] and the actual process of voting. Provision was made for the punishment of those guilty of corrupt practices such as impersonation, threats of undue influence, and bribery.[75] Methods were also set out for the avoidance of elections on election petitions by those candidates who felt discontented.[76] The High Court was to determine such cases.

Of particular interest were the qualifications of voters, the franchise, and the qualifications for candidates.

THE FRANCHISE.

Voters were required to register only in one polling division, and it was made a punishable offence to register and vote in more than one polling division and more than one time; each voter was given one vote.[77]

We have seen how, during the early stages of constitutional

development in British dependencies, qualitative franchise plays a prominent role. Uganda was no exception; these were the first direct elections ever held. The Protectorate Government therefore did not wish to open them to every adult and, consequently, as if it were on a trial basis, limited it to persons with specified qualifications. Of course enlightened African political opinion, both in Council and outside of it, protested and popularly branded it as a technique of prolonging imperial rule by denying the vast number of Africans the vote. Anyone would be registered as a voter if:

(1) he was twenty-one years of age or over;

(2) he was resident in the electoral district; and

(3) he

    (a) was the owner of freehold or mailo land in the electoral district, or

    (b) for the two years immediately preceding his application for registration had occupied land on his own account for agricultural or pastoral purposes in the electoral district or for such a period had paid "busulu" or rent for Crown Land in the electoral district or had been lawfully exempted from paying such busulu or rent, or

    (c) was able to read and write in his own language, or

    (d) had been employed in the public service of the Protectorate for a continuous period of seven years and his employment had not been terminated with dismissal, or

    (e) had been in regular paid employment in agriculture, commerce, or industry during seven years out of the eight years immediately prior to his application for registration, or

    (f) had a cash income of Shs. 2,000/– or more per year or owned property worth Shs. 8,000/– or more.[78]

For the purpose of this section a person was deemed to be resident in an electoral district if:

(1) he owned either freehold or mailo land in the district; or

(2) he held a "kibanja" in the district; or

(3) he was entitled to right of occupancy over land in the district; or
(4) he had lived for not less than three years since his eighteenth birthday in the electoral district in which he was situated, and was living in the electoral district on the date on which he applied for registration; or
(5) he owned a business in the district; or
(6) he was and had been for the six months prior to applying for registration employed in the district.

The Ordinance also prescribed certain limited conditions for disqualification of electors, such as unsoundness of mind and, under certain circumstances, being sentenced to death or imprisonment. Although it was a limited franchise, the African populace embraced it with great enthusiasm; and after registration 626,046 people had been written on the roll of voters.[79]

QUALIFICATIONS FOR CANDIDATES

It is interesting to note the broad similarity of qualifications for membership with other dependent territories on the African continent. In the Gold Coast and Sierra Leone, age, fluency in English, property ownership, and employment in public office were requirements common to all.[80] While the Gold Coast provided specific and different qualifications for specified interests (mining areas, municipalities, and provincial areas),[81] Uganda had one overall set of specified qualifications.

The Uganda law required that a candidate:
(1) be twenty-seven years of age;
(2) have the ability to speak, and unless incapacitated by blindness, to read and write the English language with a degree of proficiency sufficient to enable him to take an active part in the proceedings of the Council;
(3) be registered as an elector in the administrative area in which the electoral district for which he is standing as a candidate is situated; and
(4) have an annual income of not less than Shs. 4,000/– of property belonging to himself or property belonging jointly to himself and his spouse worth Shs. 14,000/–.[82]

The disqualifications were similar to those for voters: bankruptcy, unsoundness of mind, conviction and sentence for a criminal offence under certain circumstances. In addition, participation and holding office for conducting elections was also disabling.[83]

As the report on the elections held under this law states, they were very successful and seemed to indicate that Uganda had been overdue for such a measure. In preparation for the general elections of 1961 an amendment to this Ordinance was tabled in the Legislative Council on 13 June, 1960.[84] It was an improvement on its predecessor, although it still left much to be desired. By far its most important provision was the extension of the franchise to more people.

The requirement of a cash income, which the Principal Ordinance[85] had laid down, was reduced from Shs. 2,000/– to Shs. 1,500/–; the property value was also reduced from Shs. 8,000/– to Shs. 6,000/–. A new, alternative qualification was introduced in the form of the prospective voter being required to be forty years of age.

Moreover, one was enabled to vote if one:

(1) was able to read and write one's own language; or

(2) was or had been employed in the service of the Protectorate Government, the Kabaka's Government, a District Council, or an African Local Government for a continuous period of five years and his employment had not been terminated with dismissal; or

(3) had been in regular paid employment in agriculture, commerce, or industry during five years out of eight years immediately prior to his application for registration; or

(4) was at the time of his application for registration, or at any time had been, the holder of one of the offices specified by the Ordinance.

With regard to residence, it was stipulated that:

Any person who is temporarily living in an Electoral District at the time of a General Election, if he can satisfy the Registration Officer of such district that his name is entered on a Register of Electors for another Electoral District which has been published under the provisions of S.15 of this Ordinance shall on application to the Registration Officer be entitled to have his name entered for the purpose of such General Election only in the register of the Electoral District within which he is living.[86]

For the purposes of this provision, a person would be deemed resident in an Electoral District if he was living in such District on the qualifying date and had lived there for a period of not less than six months.[87]

These, together with what had been laid down by the Principal Ordinance, led the Attorney-General to speak of "the qualifications for voters which . . . cover practically every man and woman in the Protectorate who has any real stake in the country, who has any real right to vote." [88]

In spite of this, however, the legislation did not go as far as most of the African Representative Members would have wished; it did not even fulfil what the Wild Report had recommended on the issue. For instance, the report stated, "We also recommend that any person who is a citizen of any country (other than a citizen of the United Kingdom and Colonies) should not be an elector."

In making this point the Wild Committee stated their reason simply and clearly: "With regard to the exclusion of citizens of other countries, it is our intention that persons who are citizens of India or Pakistan or of the Sudan, for example, should not be entitled to vote in elections in Uganda." [89]

Government was reluctant to deny thousands of resident people a franchise, most of whom had a definite stake in the Protectorate and many of whom were Uganda-born. Members of the Asian community had built the economy of the country; the vast numbers of African foreigners had largely supplied labour— the handmaiden of economic development. It was therefore reasonable for the Attorney-General to contend:

. . . it would be indeed a shame if the many thousands of Banyarwanda who have lived in this country for many years were by the strict laws of citizenship deprived of the vote, and if one realises the large percentage of the population that they are in certain provinces in the Protectorate, I think all would agree that it would be unjust that they should not be able to vote as to who should represent them in the Legislative Council.[90]

African opinion in the Council was divided. Those who were Nominated, moderates or conservatives, welcomed the reform of the franchise with gratitude and contentment. In the words of one of them:

> Sir, the franchise is very wide, I agree, and I am happy with that, but I would like to have a very high qualification, that the men who have stakes in the country can select people who can sit here and govern their country wisely. You cannot have a democratic system of Government without creating a middle-class first.[91]

But their Representative, elected counterparts did not share their sense of satisfaction. On the contrary, they vigorously opposed most of these qualifications as appendages of colonial rule, which had outlived their time. C. J. Obwangor symbolised their feeling in these words:

> I take another important point which we on this side of the House vehemently hate. There should be no restriction of any sort on the franchise in this glorious paradise of Uganda, other than on the principle of universal adult suffrage.[92]

The qualifications for a candidate were also amended. It was now provided, in addition to the existing requirements, that every candidate had to pass an appropriate test in the English language unless he had previously been a Member of the Council, or held a university degree or had passed the Cambridge School Certificate examination with a credit in English or with a pass in oral English.[93]

The object of this measure was, obviously, as the Attorney-General stated, to ensure that those who were to be elected would be able to understand and participate in the proceedings, since English was the Council's official language. Yet few measures had received such a hostile reception in the Council from the African Representative Members. Being sitting Members themselves, there was no doubt that they would qualify, but the objection was to the emphasis on "learning" that the new provision imported; previously there had been no such requirement.

The Members' irritation was probably caused or increased by the fact that, although they were certainly able men, only a few among them had the qualifications of a university degree or a diploma.

It was because of this that B. K. Kirya, in a parallel not wholly in context but certainly quite illustrative, questioned Government amid prolonged applause from his side: "I would like the Attorney-General to give us some information about the education of Mr. Churchill, whether he has any university degrees, and, if so, how many he has." [94]

The seriousness with which African Representative Members debated this bill was marked by their dramatic call for a division at the end of the debate.[95] Note the solemnity of one of their concluding speeches:

> Sir, we intend to fight this Bill, if need be, line by line, so that it will go down in the record of our Parliamentary Archives that this was something which was imposed against the will of all of us. . . . it is a fact that it took England about 117 years before it attained universal adult franchise. . . . The reason is this, that you were pioneers in England and I admire you for it. You may have had tramways and buses which may never have existed before; but for us it is different, the environment is different, temperament is different, and I must reject this idea of having us adopt a constitutional development in an Oliver Twist manner, stage by stage, dose by dose.[96]

Meanwhile, a delegation of African Representative Members, led by A. M. Obote, had flown to London to put demands to the Colonial Secretary; prominent among these demands was the implementation of the Wild Report, recommending a Chief Minister and a wider franchise—but limited in scope to exclude all non-British subjects and non-British Protected Persons—for the coming elections. The Colonial Secretary seemed unable to offer them any firm commitments.

While it can be said that in the evolution of British dependencies the electoral provisions of various territories have borne similar features, it becomes exceptional when specific stringent legislation is enacted to prevent the intimidation of the electorate from either registering as electors or from casting their votes.

But such was the case in September 1960. For some time now Buganda had been a disturbed area; its Government, relentlessly yet blindly following its policy towards secession or separatism, had come out firmly and ordered its subjects not to participate in the forthcoming elections to the Legislative Council. They backed their commands with the sanctions of intimidation, arson, bodily harm, and like acts. It is against this background that the Elections, 1961 (Prevention of Intimidation) Bill of 1960 was introduced in the Council by the Chief Secretary.[97]

Seldom in the history of the Council had such a measure of legislation introduced by a British civil servant been so warmly embraced with singular unanimity and vigour by all the Members, particularly the African Representatives, as was this bill. The country was getting impatient with Buganda's fears and separatist tendencies. By now two main political parties had emerged, both committed to the swift attainment of independence, to be preceded by direct elections throughout the whole country. Although the U.P.C. was dominant in the Council, D.P. had a few spokesmen as well. The political parties united to support the Protectorate Government.

We thus find G. Oda expressing D.P.'s endorsement:

> This Bill has my personal support and also the full support of my party. . . . Sir, anyone or group of people who do not give support to this Bill, want to take the country back to the dark ages of a hundred years ago. . . . Whether it be a colonial government or an independent state, the government must rule. This is unquestionable. We are now living in a new democratic age where individuals have a right to choose their own government and a right of say in the affairs of the public. This Bill aims at nothing else but to protect individuals in exercising these rights freely without fear; to choose their own government in the new age of Uganda, in 1961.[98]

M. M. Ngobi expressed the view that was to be on the lips of every U.P.C. member when he said, "Mr. Speaker, Sir, in view of what is happening today and the terms of the Bill, one cannot possibly take any other line but to support it." [99]

But Buganda Lukiiko opinion was also represented. Kawalya-Kagwa, a distinguished veteran Nominated backbencher, had to confess, "If I were not a Backbench Member I would not have supported a Bill of this nature."

The legislation was unquestionably an arbitrary measure. It gave the police unusual powers of search and detention; it empowered the Governor to order the detention of a person if he were satisfied by evidence on oath that such a person was a danger to public security;* it further empowered him to make rules under which such a person could be detained. The Chief Secretary himself admitted, "The powers sought in this Bill are unusual and extraordinary."

There was an outcry by the press that it was an infringement of individual personal freedom and an eclipse of the rule of law.[100] But voters had to be protected, and in the words of one Member:

> It has been said by a celebrated English judge that "the life of the Law is not logic, it is experience." We cannot afford to indulge in theoretical considerations of the Rule of Law when we are faced with a very practical problem and the only way to meet it is in the light of past experience.[101]

To mitigate the offensiveness of the legislation, it was to operate only during the period of registration of voters and elections. Although in Buganda the boycott of elections was almost complete, Government nonetheless made an effort to guarantee the free exercise of this franchise to the electorate.

The movement towards greater constitutional participation by Africans was therefore on almost all major fronts. It is not surprising that the evolution of the franchise was closely tied to the development of the Legislative Council, since it was in this Council that more constitutional rights were unyieldingly solicited by its African Members.

* "Public Security" was defined in law.

4. Towards Political Awakening

The Tide Turns
against Imperialism

It would be misleading to suppose that all the forces that engineered constitutional progress in Uganda, or for that matter in any other dependency, were exclusively internal. The savagery and inhumanity of the Second World War had brought a change in the values that guided the world community of nations. Although reluctantly, Great Britain had to accept the fact that its non–Anglo-Saxon "empire" in Asia and Africa had to be liquidated.

The greatest single forum where pressure mounted for the liberation of imperial dependencies was the United Nations organisation, formed at the end of the Second World War. Its charter reaffirmed "faith in fundamental human rights, in the dignity and worth of the human person, in the equal rights of men and women and of nations large and small." The Commission on Human Rights, an organ of the U.N., drafted the Universal Declaration of Human Rights which was adopted by the General Assembly. This became the "Universal Magna Charta" for reasons evident in the speech the President of the General Assembly made when the declaration was being adopted in Paris:

It is the first occasion on which the organized Community of Nations has made a Declaration of Human Rights and Fundamental Freedoms, and it has the authority of the body of opinion of the United Nations as a whole, and millions of men, women and children all over the world, many miles from Paris and New York, will turn, for help, guidance and inspiration to this document.

The declaration, significantly, did not discriminate between sovereign and dependent peoples. Besides, the Charter of the U.N. itself imposes specific conditions to safeguard the interests of dependent territories, and clearly states that the ultimate obligation of imperial powers is to bring them to self-government as soon as possible.

The presence in the U.N. of diverse "great powers" like the U.S.S.R. and the United States, which did not subscribe to the kind of imperialism practised by European powers in Asia and Africa, was another outstanding contributory factor in forcing the reluctant hand of British imperial rule to yield to the cries of dependent territories for freedom. Indeed, several resolutions were passed by the U.N. General Assembly for the betterment of conditions in colonies, and in 1960 the Assembly adopted a declaration on the granting of independence to colonial countries and peoples.

Great Britain accepted and responded to the challenge of the times. Many of her leading statesmen made public declarations about it, such as this one by the Leader of the Labour Party, C. R. Atlee: "Labour . . . repudiates Imperialism. We believe that all peoples of whatever race have an equal right to freedom and to an equitable share in the good things of the world."

The casual and timeless pace of colonial administration had therefore to give way to the more rapid and planned development of colonies for independence. This had to begin with reviews of outstanding problems, which needed committees, commissions, or boards of enquiry to examine outstanding problems and to propose measures for their solution.

Sir Andrew Cohen has claimed that constitutional development in British dependencies has been a result of the interaction of local politicians and the initiative of British administration, and not a result of only one of these two.[1] Although there is considerable truth in this claim, it is not open to challenge that the strength and influence of political parties in British dependencies was the dominant force in pushing the often reluctant hands of British proconsuls to let go of political, sovereign power.

Political organisation of the subject peoples by their leaders was a cardinal signpost on the road to independence. This was very spectacular in the non–Anglo-Saxon parts of the British Empire—Asia and Africa. The will to be free was engineered by a multitude of reasons: the realisation and assertion of human dignity by the intellectual leaders; the belief that happiness and prosperity could come only when a colonial was master of his own house; the desire to share in the councils of the independent, sovereign nations of the world with an equal and respected voice; and in many cases the bitter memories of human degradation forced by an imperial power on its subject peoples, such as slavery and the slave trade.

In Asia and Africa the champions who fought for and won freedom for their countries were generally not the reactionary, traditionalist elites but the new educated elite, which organised the masses and inculcated in them the sense of revolt against foreign rule, however benevolent that rule may have appeared to be. As Mansur quotes Hodgkin to have said:

> The decline of the chiefly interest, and the growing prestige of the "young men", the western-educated, the *évolus,* the new middle class, is a common theme of British, French, and Belgian literature. This is the class to which the new representative institutions of British and French West Africa and the Sudan . . . have presented political opportunities.[2]

To this dynamic brand of new political forces belonged such parties as the Indian National Congress in India, the Convention People's Party in Ghana, the National Congress of Nigeria and Cameroon and the Action Group in Nigeria, to cite only a few.

If this was the general rule, there were certainly a few exceptions. There were dependencies in which the urge to struggle for sovereign power was, at times, nonexistent, sometimes slow, and often long-delayed or executed with relatively slow and unimpressive speed and vigour. To this category Uganda belonged.

Uganda's Delayed Political Awakening

We have noted that it was not until after the Second World War that the Uganda African started to participate in national institutions, such as the Legislative Council, and that this was, in the beginning, a very insignificant participation. The reasons for this lack of interest or indifference towards political oneness were largely historical. Foremost among them was the effect of the doctrine of indirect rule.

We have seen how indirect rule was made the basis of British policy in Uganda's constitutional development. Administrative units, called districts, were drawn to ensure that in most cases each tribe composed a district by itself. The few educated Africans looked at the service of their tribal local government as most worthy of their highest ambitions, and they were encouraged by British officers to think so. Consequently they worked their way up to the pinnacle of power in their respective districts with satisfaction and contentment.[3] There was almost no need for them to look beyond the tribe, to view any issue as a Ugandan. The Africans who found their way into the machinery of the Central Government went there as civil servants to earn their bread; and to ensure promotion they had to be "nice chaps" in the eyes of their British masters, which inevitably meant noninvolvement in political activities against the established order.

Perhaps this aspect of seeking satisfaction in tribal organisation found its fullest expression in the Kingdom of Buganda.[4] We have outlined the structure of government in this kingdom. Referring to the top posts in this government—Katikkiro, Omuwanika, and Omulamuzi—Low has rightly observed, "These positions presented a pinnacle of unusual power, influence accessibility and autonomy, and the activities of those who held them were as a result always the subject of intense scrutiny by those with political interests."[5]

They were targets of the relatively enlightened, educated Baganda. Others aspired to become chiefs, either saza or gombo-lola, for the prestige, the favour at the Kabaka's court, and the perquisites attached to such positions. It followed that the most enlightened Baganda, by seeking positions in their tribal society, nullified the prospects of an all-embracing Uganda conscious-ness.

Buganda's position made this approach inevitably felt throughout the country. It had always been the focus of Ugan-da's development in almost every field. What happened or what did not happen there, as Low has pointed out, "was bound to in-fluence what was to happen or not to happen in the other three provinces of the Protectorate." [6]

In the attainment of positions in these tribal hierarchies, reli-gion and tribal or clan affiliations—and not political organisa-tion—played the leading role. Of the significance of religion in politics we shall speak later, but we should note here that the Protestants and the Catholics formed contending blocks as a means of capturing political power, the only requirement for de facto membership being adherence to the relevant religious com-munity.

It must also be admitted that Low's observations about this class of political leaders was an accurate analysis:

> They never established a formal political organisation; they never had presidents or secretaries, committees or branches. They were not concerned to advance programmes for the general good of so-ciety. Nor did they represent any distinct social economic or politi-cal groupings. . . . After the first generation when adherence to one or other mission station had been established, recruitment was mainly an accident of birth. If born of Protestant parents and therefore baptised in a Protestant church, an aspirant was edu-cated at a Protestant school and thereafter automatically formed himself a member of the Protestant party.*

The case was similar for a Roman Catholic; this remained the position from 1900 until just a few years before independence, although even then it still survived in a modified form.

---

* Low, *Political Parties in Uganda*, p. 17. Even when they purported to form a political organisation before Independence, "Kabaka Yekka," they strenuously denied that it was a political party.

We have said tribalism was also an instrument used in the pursuit of positions in these tribal governments (district administrations). Instances of this were the sharp conflict between Teso's two major halves, the Issera and the Ngaratok,* and the Bairu/Bahima conflict that existed in the Kingdom of Ankole. The use of tribalism and religion in this kind of struggle for positions accentuated tribal and religious differences and consequently eliminated any unifying political concept. It is also important to recall in this connection that since the 1920s, Buganda had opposed participation in the Legislative Council, when it was the only component of Uganda during this period which possessed the manpower that might have led the way towards forging national consciousness. It had to follow, therefore, that the Legislative Council together with other Uganda-wide institutions remained alien to the Africans of the whole Protectorate.

Even after political consciousness had begun to grow, a new, more astute class of neotraditionalists established their mastery in Buganda beginning in 1955, and ensured the impotence of political parties in the modern sense until the day of independence.

ABSENCE OF SOME DEFINITE
THREAT FROM BRITISH RULE

On first view it may seem strange that a subject people should have felt and lived in contentment under their foreign rulers from 1893 until the 1950s. Yet this was true of Uganda Africans until very recent times.

In the colonies or protectorates where there has been swift mobilisation of the masses, it was the result of some tangible objectionable or oppressive policy administered by the British authorities. In what were then the Rhodesias and Nyasaland or in Kenya, for example, it was the need to mobilise and fight against the domination of a white settler minority.

In Ghana and Nigeria it was the existence (at a relatively early stage) of an educated class that first objected to the presence of a colonial power in their mother country because of its

* See *Report of the Commission of Enquiry into the Management of the Teso District Council*, March 1958. It is true that in almost every district or kingdom there were tribal frictions.

obvious shortcomings and the bitter memories of certain evils, such as the slave trade.

On the other hand, the British Protectorate had ruled the indigenous tribes of Uganda with a benevolent hand, if the short-lived memories of their military or quasi-military conquest of some areas in the Protectorate can be discounted.

The comparatively few enlightened Africans who could have been in the vanguard of mass mobilisation found full satisfaction in the pursuit—as we have seen—of offices in the local governments of their respective tribes. They never felt, and the British never gave them reason to believe, that their status and dignity were lessened by being under foreign rule. The accorded respect and pomp that the tribal societies attached to their positions continued superficially undiminished, although in reality the British authorities were unquestionably masters of both the ruler and the ruled.

There were no political or economic issues of the magnitude essential to arouse massive opposition to foreign rule. There was no land problem such as that in the Kenya "highlands"; if the average African was poor, he was not destitute. In fact, he had most of the necessities to enjoy the simple life he and his next of kin lived. He had land where he could grow enough food for his dependents and, when necessary, a cash crop to bring in money for the payment of tax and the purchase of the basic necessities of a simple household. There had been no large populations uprooted from their tribal setting and relocated in new and bewildering cities. This is one reason why the Asians could amass enormous wealth while the African looked on with little or no concern. Legislation was passed to exclude non-Africans (Asians and Europeans) from acquiring freehold title to land. It could happen only with the consent of the Governor—which was seldom given, and even then only after thorough scrutiny.

The political problems that arose internally were those of tribe versus tribe or religion versus religion, and there was no one to charge that such problems were created by the British. They could not have formed a basis for objection to foreign rule on the part of the Ugandan African population. On the contrary, such problems absorbed the full attention of the Africans involved in them, and never permitted them sufficient time to think and appreciate that—beyond religion or the tribe—there was a geographical or political expression called Uganda, which was still under foreign rule and ultimately committed to remaining a united state. There has been no district or kingdom without some sort of tribal conflict within itself; such conflicts have, however, differed in intensity and magnitude.

The Indian community did not constitute a threat strong enough to warrant positive mobilisation of the Africans against it. True, the British gave every encouragement to the Indian businessman to prosper. Indians created a second-class strata for themselves, while the Africans were automatically relegated to the third, and lowest. The Africans, by virtue of their contentment, bought by ignorance and indirect rule, never seriously thought about this situation as a problem or a threat to their own well-being. Those who did, and sought to redress the position through an organised trade boycott of Indian shops, were limited only to the Kingdom of Buganda and, in any event, they lacked a more intelligent, effective approach for redress.

ECONOMIC BACKWARDNESS AND POVERTY

It would be wrong to underestimate the degree to which economic backwardness or poverty played a role in hampering the rapid evolution of vibrant political parties in Uganda. Up to the time of this writing Uganda possesses an agricultural peasant economy. The main sources of income, cotton and coffee, are cultivated by peasant farmers on relatively small holdings scattered all over the countryside. There has been no industrial revolution resulting in the rapid growth of large towns with concentrated populations readily accessible to politicians in their pursuit of mass conversion. The bulk of the population has been scattered all over the country, covering vast distances. We have noted how the economic power of the Protectorate was vested in the hands of the Asian minority who, it should be said again, had no interest in politics except when it came to safeguarding their enormous wealth. The African politician who emerged in the 1950s was generally poor. He did not have an independent means of livelihood that would enable him to work full time as a politician. Consequently he had to take a regular job for a living and to do politics as a part-time job after office hours. He belonged to the category Dr. Nyerere, President of Tanzania, called "week-end politicians".

Handicaps attached to a politician in such an environment are obvious and considerable. He could not afford to buy a car as a quick means of transport to cover a widely scattered population; if he was lucky enough to have one, the expenses for fuel and maintenance were prohibitive. Moreover, the majority of those with a fair amount of education, if they were not absorbed by their tribal local government, sought employment with the Protectorate Government and, as we have seen, had to refrain from political activity at the pleasure of their imperial masters. The number of those who could actually participate in politics or who took it up as a vocation was correspondingly small and ill equipped to produce visibly dramatic and vibrant political activity among the masses.

We have noted that the average, indeed the vast number of politicians were poor. It was essential, if their political organisations were to succeed, that they have the means to carry out their programmes. It was natural that some of them should have levied contributions from their followers or gone abroad to sympathetic independent nations for financial assistance. Enough money was obtained from both these sources to run the political parties these men led.

It is a matter of deep regret that most of the funds collected in this way were pocketed by several of these leaders and used for their personal comfort. This exercise started with the beginning of political parties, and the consequences could not have been other than discouraging. Some enthusiastic and honest followers, dissatisfied with such corruption, either became indifferent to the nationalist cause or dropped out in disgust. Top positions in some party hierarchies became the focus of the most intricate struggle for those who wanted to use them as their predecessors had done. Occasionally this caused splits or pressure groups in a party that was otherwise ideologically completely united. This remained a legacy in Uganda politics until independence, and even beyond.

As a by-product of economic backwardness it is proper to add the absence of a properly educated class—versed in political organisation as known in the more advanced countries—as contributory to the delay of political and, consequently, constitutional progress. We have seen that Makerere, the only local place of higher learning, attained university-college status in 1949. Its products, being few and subject to great demands in Government service and industry and themselves having no other means of income, submitted to the easy lures of a certain career in preference to the hazards of pioneering a political organisation in a British protectorate. Before 1955 the number of Uganda Africans who had been overseas was negligible. Consequently there was an absence of imported, external experience or knowledge among Uganda Africans. Had they been more educated and more widely travelled abroad, the situation would have been different.

RELIGION AS A BASIS OF POLITICAL ACTIVITY

The influence of the Christian missionaries, both Protestant and Roman Catholic, has been enormous in Uganda since 1888. This influence was institutionalized and structured at the advent of formal British overrule in 1893. The imprint of religious consciousness was very visible in Uganda up to the time of independence, and even beyond independence.

The Committee of Members of Parliament, consisting of Government and Opposition Members, recommended as an appropriate motto for the Uganda Coat of Arms, "For God and My Country", and this was accepted by an African government. The words of the national anthem reflect not only dedication to the state but also a recognition and acknowledgement of "Providence". An illustration of this is a verse of the anthem:

Oh Uganda! May God uphold thee,
We lay our future in thy hand,
United, Free,
For Liberty
Together we'll always stand.

This is symbolic of the influence Christian missions had during the whole era of Protectorate rule.

Both groups of missionaries led the way in introducing education to the African.[7] They built schools in every district and kingdom for a fairly long period without Government assistance, and at a time when Government took a negligible interest in education for the African. Right to the day of independence, the best schools in Uganda were mission schools: Kings College, Budo (Protestant), and St. Mary's College, Kisubi (Roman Catholic), stand out as excellent examples of this.

The missionaries took the trouble to visit the illiterate parents of a child, baptise him, then take the child to school. In their pursuit for more converts they waged a literacy campaign by establishing several weekly newspapers and magazines. So effective were their efforts that by the end of the Second World War an overwhelming proportion of the educated Africans were either Protestant or Roman Catholic.

In this search for converts to Christianity several very serious errors were committed by the missionaries; from the very beginning the French Roman Catholic priest and the English clergyman developed damaging rivalry, as each group wanted to get more converts than the other.*

The English Protestant clergyman and the French Roman Catholic priest attempted, each in turn, to convert the ruler or elder of the tribe in order to use him not only for the promotion of his faith but also for the suppression of the other. If the enlightened churchmen from Europe showed such visible hostility to one another, their African converts had no choice. The Africans also divided to follow their spiritual leaders, and for the first time the African population, first in Buganda and later in other regions, was badly divided on grounds of religion. Indeed,

---

* The zeal of the early missionaries in acquiring converts was not confined solely to religious considerations. The Protestants were English (Abangereza), or at least identified as such, while the Catholic missionaries were French (Abafaransa). The long-existing colonial rivalry between England and France—especially in Africa—went a long way towards each country giving maximum support to its own missionaries in order to assert its political identification with the widely accepted religious activities of its nationals—a factor not always in the best interests of the African.

the conflict between the Protestants and Catholics in 1893 led to an armed clash in Buganda between the two groups, with a consequent loss of life to many.[8]

The struggle was not limited to church matters; it penetrated the entire range of human activity. If the Protestants happened to be in control of a local administration, it was normal to expect that if a Protestant was competing for a post with a Roman Catholic, say the post of saza or gombolola chief, preference would go to the former. Where the Roman Catholics were in the majority they, too, practised the same discrimination.

A vivid illustration of this conflict was seen in Buganda, where for more than five years until 1900 there were two Katikkiros (Prime Ministers) simultaneously for Buganda: one Protestant the other Roman Catholic.[9] Although the 1900 Buganda Agreement specifically excluded religion as a basis of consideration in offering positions in government, that provision remained a dead letter up to the time of independence.

The struggle was made more acute by the general belief among the Roman Catholics, themselves having been converted by nationals of the competing French and Italian imperial powers, that the British in Uganda were giving preferential treatment to Protestants because Britain was a Protestant power that had revolted and seceded from papal domination. The Roman Catholics and Protestants tended to unite only for common objectives in their own respective camps; it became extremely difficult for the two groups to come together in the prosecution of a common design, such as the struggle for national independence.

On most occasions the struggle for religious supremacy or the pursuit of positions in local administrations on the basis of religious groupings fully occupied their attention. To these two groups belonged the country's African educated elite on whom, though unknown to them, ultimately fell the responsibility of building a united country moving towards independence. Even among those of the elite who in the early 1950s rose to this challenge, the use of religion as a basis for political action and organisation, either through conviction or as an expedient, was unmistakable. Appeal to religious feelings for political support was forcibly prevalent in the crucial general elections of 1961 and 1962.

The third religious group of consequence were the Muslims. The influence of Islam had penetrated the East African hinterland long before the advent of Christian missionaries. It came in the vanguard of Arab traders, but its spread was eventually arrested and then contained by the establishment of a British Protectorate over Uganda. Muslims were also at one time engaged in the struggle for converts, but by the beginning of the twentieth century they had settled down to accept a minority role. The Islamic leaders, like Christian missionaries, did not, apart from spiritual instruction, inculcate any dynamic feeling of nationhood among their followers; this concept was generally absent.

The Muslims, as a religious group, had been neglected from the point of view of education. Until the end of the 1930s there was no Government interest in education to speak of, and as we have noted, education largely depended on the efforts of missionaries; but, unlike missionaries, Muslim leaders lacked the interest, and certainly the means, to educate their followers. The Protestant (Anglican) schools, in contrast with the Roman Catholics, were willing to educate Muslim children without requiring them to be converted. Consequently, in the 1950s, when political parties emerged and appealed for religious support (among other polarities), the Muslims, almost en masse, withheld their support from the Roman Catholics and sided with the Protestants.* In this way religion became a hindrance to concerted political action and the constitutional issues that existed had to remain outstanding for a considerable time. Needless to say, the Protectorate Government kept silent and simply

---

* A definite anti-Catholic attitude existed among most of Uganda's Muslims, to such an extent that some Muslim leaders considered voting for the D.P. during the 1961 and 1962 elections as unacceptable as eating pork. This attitude was the result, not exclusively of Catholic resistance to Muslim development, but also of the fact that a leader of the Muslims was a member of the Buganda Royal House and obviously was associated with, and usually reflected, the political attitudes of the Buganda establishment—which was emphatically Protestant. The U.P.C./K.Y. Alliance ensured that Prince Badru Kakungulu, who was a powerful Muslim leader as well as an uncle of the Kabaka, would lend his support and following to the U.P.C. in its contest for ascendancy over the D.P.

watched as the African used religion as yet another tool to prolong Britan's imperial rule over Uganda.

GENERAL LACK OF EDUCATION

It must now be clear from the primary reasons outlined above
that lack of ample and suitable education for the Africans was
one of the reasons for delay in the realisation of Uganda's nationhood. To begin with, although missionary education had immense advantages, it had the defect of tending to turn out products who believed in a literal application of Jesus Christ's dictum
that if someone strikes you on one cheek you should turn the
other. In any event, without government aid and with limited
financial resources of their own, Christian missions had tremendous problems to contend with.* It is not surprising that the vast
majority of pupils acquired only elementary knowledge and that
only a tiny handful found their way into higher education.

When the Protectorate Government later intervened with economic assistance, their educational policy was geared towards
ensuring peaceful colonial rule, as had been the case elsewhere.
Nehru observed the effects of such British education in the following terms: "The British had created a new caste or class in
India, the English educated class, which lived in a world of its
own, cut off from the mass of the population, and looked always,
even when protesting, towards their rulers." [10]

This was substantially true of the educational product the
British turned out in Uganda. It was important that, like the
British, they should appear "thoroughly civilized" and "nice
chaps", and this attitude, of course, precluded their engaging in
movements that might (if need came) turn them against British
rule. But even then this class of educated men was, for the most
part—at least until 1950—too small even to create an effective
cult within itself. Almost without exception these men were absorbed into the Protectorate Government or local governments
as civil servants, leaving the political field vacant.

When in the 1950s political parties finally developed, they
found their rank and file without enough education to grasp the
essentials of the struggle for national liberation. Like their rank

* They also built hospitals and dispensaries; some of the best hospitals in
Uganda were built by the missionaries.

and file, the leaders, although educated, had not attained an intellectual calibre comparable to that of the men who led the struggle for freedom in the British dependencies on the African West Coast. Consequently, when men of high intellectual standing began joining in the general political effort, as they returned from universities abroad or from Makerere, they were suspect and thus cold-shouldered by those not so well educated. It was assumed that they probably wished to wrest leadership from them by virtue of their higher education. This naturally caused a lack of cohesion and trust, and even splits, in some political parties.

The Beginning of Political Awakening

Despite the many handicaps, the trend towards national consciousness could not remain perpetually dormant. We have mentioned the impact of the Second World War on colonial dependencies, which brought with it an almost undreamt-of determination in Asia and Africa to attain sovereign power. This was matched by a comparatively more willing response from the imperial power to concede it.

By 1950 this feeling of the need to strive for independence had found its way into Uganda, and in 1952 the first political party was formed; the party's avowed objective was attaining "Self-Government Now" for Uganda. We should now briefly examine the fortunes of this party—the Uganda National Congress (U.N.C.)—and its subsequent offshoots and rivals and what influence they had in shaping Uganda's constitutional evolution.

THE UGANDA NATIONAL CONGRESS

The name "Congress" derived its origin and inspiration from the Indian National Congress, which had steered India to independence; the first president was Ignatius Musazi. In the main, it drew its greatest support from among the Baganda, and it was only the militant elements in the other provinces of Uganda that joined it.

From its inception it was a truly nationalist party, with the leading slogan of "Self-Government Now". From the beginning it seemed to possess the answer to how to inculcate the concept of single-nationhood in the multifarious tribes of the Protectorate. Its failure to realise this, and indeed its merely nominal existence by independence time, was unquestionably due to the simultaneous interplay of the drawbacks we have briefly reviewed. Low has rightly ascribed its failure to its inability "to attract the more forward looking, better or best educated in Buganda." In consequence, it lacked even a pragmatic approach to sustain its virility. Unlike most nationalist parties, it produced no "manifesto". Instead, it depended on the exploitation of local issues on a district-to-district basis.

For example, when the headquarters of the Eastern Province was removed from Jinja in Busoga to Mbale in Bugisu, its branch in Busoga protested vigorously, while the transfer was welcomed with unreserved enthusiasm by its branch in Mbale. The play on local issues, while a means of establishing some support, was by no means the best way to foster unity among diverse tribes to whom the sense of oneness was still essentially strange and alien. Indeed, at times it tended to accentuate the divisions in the country rather than heal them.*

The lack of a planned course of action and the absence of solutions to outstanding constitutional problems drew indignation and discontent from Musazi's more enlightened followers, who led the first attempt to break away and form a different party. The rift was, for a while, healed by the installation of J. W. Kiwanuka as Chairman of the U.N.C. Executive in 1956.[11]

But the flame of discontent had been lit. In July of 1957 a group of intellectuals broke away in protest because Musazi, as Low records, "never showed any inclination for any positive programme". They formed a new party, the United Congress Party (U.C.P.). They were joined by two Members of the Legislative Council, Muwazi and Lubogo, formerly of the U.N.C.,

---

* In the embryonic days of "nationalist" parties, it might be more accurate to say that they were "national"; but once they became nationally established they evolved a more nationalistic platform parallel to the rise of national issues and, for the most part, became the vehicle for articulating these national issues "nationalistically".

who later resigned from the Legislative Council in protest against the Government's refusal to hold direct elections throughout the whole Protectorate in 1957.*

The third and major split in the U.N.C. occurred in 1959 when the more enlightened lieutenants of Musazi revolted and formed a rival party led by A. M. Obote as President and Abū Mayanja as Secretary-General. The absence of a coherent programme and the lack of discipline and integrity had destroyed the Uganda National Congress as it was originally conceived. There occurred expulsions and counter-expulsions of the leaders during this process of disintegration. Those who clung to Musazi's wing did so not because it remained a dynamic nationalist force, but either for some material benefit they might reap from such adherence or simply out of stubbornness in refusing to acknowledge their shortcomings.

So unpopular had the U.N.C. become by the time of Uganda's great constitutional changes that out of 81 Elected Members in the National Assembly it secured only one representative during the 1961 national elections. In most of the areas where it had put up candidates, these not only lost the elections but forfeited their deposits as well.[12]

In spite of this decisive decline, the U.N.C., at least in name, had something to say on the constitutional problems that existed in the country. They upheld the existence and the grandeur of monarchy. Indeed, since 1953, when the Kabaka was deported, they had striven relentlessly for his restoration. Whether or not it was because of its policy in championing local issues in various areas of the Protectorate is beside the point. The fact remains that the U.N.C. played a significant role in the return of Mutesa II to the Kabakaship of Buganda.

It is not surprising therefore that even in its last moments, when it was a mere shadow of its former self, the U.N.C. condemned Buganda's intention to secede from the rest of the country, while at the same moment it recommended federal status for the kingdom area to the Relationships Commission when the Commission came to make enquiries on what would be Uganda's ideal form of government.[13] As to the precise division of

* All the personalities mentioned in this chapter are well known to the author.

powers between the kingdoms and the federal Uganda Government, they remained—like most Ugandans at the time—imprecise.

The contribution of the U.N.C. must remain its kindling of the flame in Uganda Africans for national consciousness and the introduction, publicly, of the concept of self-determination. Of the obvious defects we have broadly noted, the most prominent must remain the failure to produce a disciplined programme for national liberation. Although the U.N.C. gradually disintegrated, it was the people who had been its members and who had derived their inspiration for nationalism from it that eventually formed the parties that made Uganda's independence a reality.*

THE PROGRESSIVE PARTY

In the opening months of 1955 a new party, the Progressive Party, was formed. Although it was largely Protestant in leadership, it would be incorrect to deduce that the Protestant clergy had instigated its formation. It drew its membership from schoolmasters, well-to-do farmers, and Baganda businessmen. It was overwhelmingly Baganda in membership and almost exclusively so in leadership. E. M. K. Mulira was its first president, and undoubtedly one of its primary objectives was to rival and supersede the U.N.C.

But it never made headway, and although unlike the U.N.C. it produced a "manifesto", its "leadership was not particularly imaginative"; by the late 1950s it had already lost its grip as a political force to be reckoned with.[14] Like the U.N.C., and indeed like most political parties, it experienced a phase of struggle for leadership. By 1961 Mulira had been replaced by a more vociferous president, Dr. Babumba, through whom ideas on the constitutional set-up of Uganda were channelled either to the public or to the two Constitutional Commissions which examined Uganda's constitutional set-up.

The Progressive Party proposed a federal constitution for Uganda, but went further with the bold and controversial prop-

* Such men included A. M. Obote, B. K. Kirya, J. W. Kiwanuka, and A. K. Mayanja.

osition that the Kabaka should be Uganda's Head of State.[15] But during the crucial moments between 1960 and 1962, when determining Uganda's future constitution, the Progressive Party did not have a single Member in the Legislative Council, nor was it ever represented at any of the London Constitutional Conferences.

We should now turn to the political parties that were more closely connected with, and more effective in, the last stages of Uganda's constitutional evolution, and whose manifestos and objectives were largely responsible for Uganda's constitution at the time of independence.

THE DEMOCRATIC PARTY

In 1954 the Democratic Party (D.P.) was born as a new force on the political scene. It has been correctly said that, at its inception and indeed in later years, it "was almost exclusively Roman Catholic in inspiration and membership".[16] We observed how the struggle of Catholicism versus Protestantism was a divisive force in Uganda's political development. There are a variety of reasons why Roman Catholics deemed it desirable to form a party of their own.

Discrimination in the Tenure of Public Office. A truly genuine grievance was the discrimination against Catholics in appointments for the holding of public office. Buganda, which even experienced religious wars, was for a long period a vivid example of this. Since the religious joint-Katikkiroship ended in 1900 there has never been a Roman Catholic Katikkiro.[17] Although the Catholics outnumbered the Protestants, it was a tradition that eight saza chiefs would be Catholics and ten would be Protestants. In the Buganda Government, whose crowning glory was victory in the struggle to return the Kabaka in 1955, there was only one Catholic and one Muslim, but four Protestant ministers. This was so despite a clause in the 1900 Buganda Agreement assuring no discrimination on religious grounds when it came to tenure in public office.

Outside Buganda the same general pattern was unmistakable; the Protestants held a general belief that, by and large, the Catholics could not rule. The population figures and the percentage of those who held top positions show that the Protestants had consistently held the ascendancy over many years. It could be argued that the Protestants may have happened to possess personnel of the required calibre. On the other hand, it is possible to retort that the Protestant ascendancy could not have been so systematic and long-lived unless it were backed by a partial imperial power whose national religion was also Protestantism. Apart from noting this fact, it is of no value to apportion the blame or to examine the weight of associated arguments, for it would serve no useful purpose.

Concrete instances of this state of affairs were also seen in the kingdoms of the Western Region. In Ankole, Toro, and Bunyoro not only was it a tradition that the kings should be Protestant, but also that no Catholic should ever become the leading minister (Enganzi or Katikkiro) in any of these kingdoms—they were always Protestants. In Busoga, the constitutional head, the Kyabazinga, was always Protestant. In the districts of the north and east the highest post, that of Secretary-General, was usually occupied by a Protestant. It should not be surprising that the Catholics reacted by forming a party whose objective must have been more related to the redress of these injustices than the immediate struggle for national independence based on African nationalism.[18]

Catholic Priests in Politics. It has been a distinguishing mark of the Roman Catholic Church that it should participate in a closer ecclesiastical interest with politics than the Protestant Church. In many states of the world, and for centuries past, the Catholic Church has sought to influence—if not to control—governments. It should be remembered that the Pope at one time exercised temporal power over Europe by means of ecclesiastical edicts in his role of spiritual leader.

Indeed, the Roman Catholic Church's political theory as articulated by Pope Boniface VIII (d. 1303), although superseded by modern developments, seems to be still operative here:

We are taught by evangelical words that in this power of his [St. Peter's] are two swords, namely *spiritual* and *temporal.* . . . Each is in the power of the Church, that is, a spiritual and a material sword. . . . The latter, indeed, must be exercised *for* the Church, the former *by* the Church. The former [by the hand] of the Priest, the latter *by* the hand of Kings and Soldiers, *but at the will and sufferance of the priest.* For it is necessary that a sword be under a sword, and that *temporal authority be subject to spiritual power.** [19]

The activities of Catholic priests, especially those coming from Italy, France, Quebec, and Germany, unquestionably complied with Pope Boniface's exposition. They constituted themselves not only spiritual leaders among their followers but also political advisers. They partially instigated the formation of the D.P. Once formed they sought to control it, although usually behind the scenes. By virtue of its rigid discipline, Catholicism in practice, unlike Protestantism, produced unquestioning followers, over whom the priests held extraordinary influence and control. But there may have been reasons that impelled them to intervene in politics other than seeking higher positions in public life for their followers or merely acting out the religious dogma we have noted. They felt it their duty to fight against any incursion of "communism" in Uganda, or for that matter, in the world.

It is true that some leaders of U.N.C. had, in the early 1950s, gone to Eastern European communist countries. In fact, they had procured substantial financial assistance to strengthen their party. In Uganda they used a language so intemperate in their public speeches—or so the priests thought—that U.N.C. members were not even called "uncommitted" but simply "communist". Consequently, Catholics had to marshal all their forces to fight what was branded "communistic"—the U.N.C.

The D.P. rank and file, and even their leaders, did not know what communism was. They could not intelligently and independently assess its defects and attributes. But they were taught to hate it; to oppose strongly any party that seemed to their spiritual leaders to be "communist". Indeed, when a new political party was formed in 1960, the U.P.C., which was more radical and socialistic, the D.P. also accused it of being "communistic". As to what role the Catholic priests played for the D.P. in the elections of 1961 and 1962 more will be said, but it was a dynamic and vital one.

* Author's emphasis.

Missionary work, be it Protestant or Catholic, has in the last seventy years bestowed many a blessing on the masses of Uganda Africans. But one of its worst legacies has been the intervention of its spiritual leaders into the realm of politics. Until very recently the vast majority of these priests were foreign nationals; their temporal allegiance was to foreign powers— France, Italy, Canada, Belgium, and the like. Most of these countries were themselves imperial powers in Africa with even less liberal colonial doctrines than the British. It would not have been very likely that they would support a political party and plan for it because they were concerned with securing Uganda's independence. Indeed, had this been so, missionary teaching would not have discouraged a pupil's interest in politics or his questioning of imperial rule. Had the missionaries been interested in preparing the African for independence, they would have encouraged the cultivation of political consciousness among their students. In fact, priests, both Protestant and Catholic, preached to their congregations in the churches that their primary concern should be with life after death—in itself a proper Christian concept but one that by itself tended to lend weight to the politicians' allegations that it was a device to keep civil power out of African control. It is difficult to see how this second aspect of the D.P.—the influence of a church manned by foreign nationals—could have helped to build a firm foundation for a nationalist party that sought to wrest sovereign power from the kith and kin of these same missionaries.

It must have been a hypothesis of those who founded the D.P. that—since the Catholics were more numerous in Uganda than those of any other single religion—if it was established as a Catholic party it could not fail to have a majority.* Paradoxically, what was the source of its strength—religion—was also the source of its weakness and, indeed, as we shall see, the cause of its decline. Those who belonged to other faiths, or who had no faith to follow, felt rejected and later came to form their own political parties; united, they constituted the majority in Uganda.

Constitutional Problems as the D.P. Saw Them. Despite its

* It was public knowledge at the time; some D.P. leaders, including its President, proclaimed this theory even at public meetings.

strong undercurrent of religious bias, the D.P.—more than any other party thus far formed—rose to the challenge of the times. Its leaders attempted to analyse the outstanding constitutional problems of the day and endeavoured to propose solutions for them.

In preparation for the 1961 elections they produced a "manifesto", which was both a testament of their political philosophy and a catalogue of solutions for the various problems confronting the country; we later discuss these issues.[20] We should record here that, although they were generally politically less astute and guarded than their U.P.C. opponents, they were unwilling to commit themselves to any specific view regarding the most controversial and sensitive issues of the day: the future form of government, the question of who would be head of state, and the "lost counties" problem. All the same, by their very existence, the D.P. played no small part in mobilising the country towards self-government and subsequent independence.

The Uganda People's Union

The closing months of 1958 and the beginning of 1959 saw the formation of yet a new political party, the Uganda People's Union (U.P.U.). It was different from existing parties in two fundamental respects. First, its leadership: those who formulated and launched its policy were almost exclusively Members of the Legislative Council.* W. W. Rwetsiba, its first President, had been indirectly elected by the Eishengyero of Ankole (later the Ankole National Assembly). Its Secretary-General, G. Magezi, had been directly elected from Bunyoro. From Busoga, W. W. Nadiope, elected in the 1958 direct elections with overwhelming support, abandoned the tottering U.N.C. and joined the U.P.U. Within two months after the first direct elections a party that had very recently been nonexistent now commanded the highest number of seats in the Legislative Council.† The reasons for this extraordinary momentum were not accidental. It

---

* Low, *Political Parties in Uganda*, p. 28. These men continued to play a leading role in the emancipation of Uganda, and they still hold leading positions in Government.

† The breakdown of the parties: U.P.U.—7 members; U.N.C.—3 members; D.P.—1 member; Independents—1 member.

owed its strength to U.P.U.'s fundamental characteristic of
being the first possible political avenue for the majority of the
politically conscious non-Baganda.

All the parties we have considered, except U.P.U., were not
only Buganda-based, they were also Baganda-led. Despite their
apparent appeal for national unity, they never made any progress in recruiting substantial membership from other areas of
Uganda. Most parties had a principle seldom expressed but
often practised—no one who was not of the Baganda could lead
them. This, indeed, was one of the major issues that caused
U.N.C.'s basic break-up. On many issues, especially those concerning the status of royalty in the kingdoms, the Buganda-
based parties invariably tried to project their Kabaka above any
other dignitary or ruler in the country—a claim they assumed to
be understood and accepted by everyone else. Furthermore, Buganda was too inward-looking, as its traditional government in
Mmengo had consistently sought to pursue the lonely policy of
separatism or had proposed to join hands with the whole of
Uganda only on highly particularist terms. What also hindered
unity in this connection was not only the British scheme of simply making Buganda *primus inter pares* but their convention of
listening to its demands, however extravagant or unreasonable,
with far greater patience than they were prepared to accord to
those of any other areas.

In more or less the same way as the Catholics formed the D.P.
to redress injustices, so did the non-Baganda form the U.P.U. as
an instrument not only to contain Buganda's extravagant
dreams or merely to demand more for their respective districts
but also to provide leadership where Buganda was visibly failing—the positive struggle for national independence.

It has been suggested that religion played a part in the formation of the U.P.U. Its founders deny validity to this claim. But
they had been elected to the Legislative Council, in the absence
of a unifying political philosophy, on the basis of a combination
of factors, including their personalities, religion, tribe, or even
clan. They owed their deportment, however, to their broad experience in life, many of them having been school teachers or public servants.

At the time of U.P.U. formation the personality of the individual leader mattered almost as much as, if not more than, the political views he might hold on outstanding issues. Although the U.P.U. was not as long established as the U.N.C., its potential support, especially in the western kingdoms and Busoga, the areas from which it drew its leadership, was impressive. It is appropriate to discuss its views on constitutional issues when we discuss the U.P.C., to show that it was the only dynamic, vibrant and nation-wide political party of the period.

THE UGANDA PEOPLE'S CONGRESS

What Uganda lacked in terms of a unifying nationalist movement was now to be provided by the formation of the Uganda People's Congress (U.P.C.) on 9 March 1960. A general feeling of frustration and anxiety had increasingly gripped the enlightened Africans as they saw neither the leader nor the party that could assume a stature sufficient to lead them toward independence. A multitude of political parties, many fraught with internal dissension, and all of them rather ineffective, were the order of the day; that day was now over.

The U.P.C. was the progeny of a merger between the U.P.U. and Obote's wing of the U.N.C. The two parties agreed to merge with the object of consolidating party politics in Uganda in order to present to the people a common programme for the immediate attainment of complete independence.

With the wisdom of hindsight and experience it is easy for armchair critics to condemn all those who participated in making Obote leader of this party. That the matter of choosing a leader did not get the attention it deserved is without question. The author, as one of the dramatis personae, can confirm that the principal yardstick of what made a good leader was fiery oratory and boldness in assailing the bastion of colonial rule.

Again, with the wisdom of hindsight, it is astonishing that none paused to consider with sufficient care the background and general suitability of the would-be leaders of Uganda. None seriously probed the antecedents of Obote or his close associates to determine whether they were the best available men to lead an independent Uganda nation.

The U.P.C. posed as the party of compromise and accommodation, which the country had long needed. Its aims and objectives were declared to be:

(1) to struggle relentlessly by all constitutional means for the
immediate attainment of complete independence;

(2) to uphold the dignity and prestige of hereditary rulers and
other heads of African governments; and

(3) to promote, secure, and maintain the complete unity of
the peoples of Uganda under a strong government conducive to stability and rapid progress.

The idea of struggling "relentlessly by all constitutional
means" was not a novel one in the literature of colonial emancipation. It was used in almost all former British dependencies. It
reflected a consciousness of the constitutional processes; disregard of such meant a direct warrant to the imperial power to
outlaw the nationalist movements and frustrate their objectives.

The specific, although brief assurance that the prestige of the
rulers would be maintained was an assurance that had to be
given if the monarchists—nurtured under concentrated "indirect
rule"—were to join, however reluctantly, in the struggle for national liberation. No one could have foretold that within four
years these promises were to be dishonoured and the kingdoms
abolished by Obote and his U.P.C. At the time these promises
were made, it seemed by all outward appearances that they were
genuinely intended.

The U.P.C.'s pledge of a strong central government was a
bold statement on the only form of government that could hold
Uganda together after independence, particularly since Uganda
had developed as a collection of various tribes with largely separate cultures over a long period of time. In the main, the party's
success lay in its genius for a combination of flexibility with
firmness and the maintenance of an optimum balance in political situations that were quite diverse and often conflicting.

OTHER PARTIES

Lest it appear from the foregoing that these were the only political parties in Uganda, we must add that there were several
others. One was the Uganda African Union, ruled by the vocif-

erous Godwin Kawombe, whom his witty opponents described
as its "sole Member, Secretary and President". The year 1960
saw the formation of the United National Party. Its leadership
had been entrusted to Apolo Kironde, one of the first Ugandan
lawyers, and its membership, small as it was, had the additional
handicap of being drawn almost in its entirety from only one
area, Buganda.

In the excitement that swept the country during the rapid constitutional changes from 1961 onwards, Kironde had first tried a
merger with Obote and the U.P.C.; later he was successful in
merging with the effusive J. W. Kiwanuka, who was now chief of
the U.N.C. remnants. One of the most dramatic and vivid illustrations of the instability of Uganda politics of this era is shown
by the fact that within thirty-six hours after these two party
bosses had merged to form a new party, the United National
Congress, they broke apart because Kironde alleged that Kiwanuka had used money to buy the votes that made him president of the new short-lived party.

This type of political party had become a common feature of
Uganda politics. It is as fair to say that these parties or types of
parties contributed more towards confusion than unity of purpose as it is to assume that their primary objectives were the
capture of high-sounding titles of leadership rather than the tax-
ing exercise of organising the masses for independence. The
leaders seldom left their comfortable Kampala offices when, in
fact, any effective organisation of an overwhelmingly rural
population required extensive travelling in the countryside.

Nevertheless, it is legitimate to conclude that despite the confusing and sometimes divisive results of such a multitude of political parties, they had the positive effect of awakening the
masses of African people to rise and demand their fundamental
rights, foremost among them being the right to self-government.
The various parties could draw on all the forces at work to for-
tify their arguments, forces from both outside and inside
Uganda.

The Constitutional Committee of 1959 and Its Significance

The Protectorate had witnessed many committees since its inception; there had been committees on education, economic development, agriculture, and local government. The Constitutional Committee, whose membership was announced to an excited Legislative Council by the Chief Secretary on 4 February 1959, was the first in the field of country-wide constitutional developments dealing with a central legislature and, therefore, of distinct significance.

In 1958 Governor Crawford promised, with the agreement of Her Majesty's Government, the appointment of a Constitutional Committee with the following terms of reference:

> To consider and to recommend to the Governor the form of direct elections on a common roll for representative members of the Legislative Council to be introduced in 1961, the number of representative seats to be filled under the above system, their allocation among the different areas of the Protectorate and the method of ensuring that there will be adequate representation on the Legislative Council for non-Africans.[21]

In addition to these strict terms of reference the Governor had gone on to say that during the course of their work and hearing of evidence this Committee would, no doubt, receive expressions of views regarding the size and composition of the Legislature and also possibly of the Government.

But he warned, "I must make it clear that these are matters on which a very special responsibility lies directly with Her Majesty's Government and cannot be settled here in Uganda." He nevertheless agreed that he would "value any advice the Committee may wish to offer" him on these subjects, although they are outside their strict terms of reference, because it would assist him, he admitted, in advising the Secretary of State not only on the Committee's recommendations arising from their terms of reference but also on any other related issues that might be brought before the Committee.

On February 1959 the Chief Secretary in a Statement to the Legislative Council announced that the Governor, with the agreement of the Secretary of State, had appointed the following to be Members of this Constitutional Committee:

The Hon. J. V. Wild, O.B.E.—Chairman
Lt. Col. The Hon. A. A. Baerlein
The Hon. Professor K. Ingham, M.C.
The Hon. I. B. Bazarrabusa
The Hon. H. K. Jaffer, C.B.E.
The Hon. C. B. Katiti
Mr. Erisa Kironde
The Hon. B. K. Kirya
The Hon. G. B. K. Magezi
Mr. Balamu Mukasa, O.B.E.
The Hon. W. W. Kajumbula-Nadiope
The Hon. A. M. Obote
The Hon. C. J. Obwanger
The Hon. G. Oda
The Hon. C. K. Patel, M.B.E., C.B.E., Q.C.
Mr. F. K. Kalimuzo—Secretary[22]

The general excitement in the Council did not detract from its criticism of the terms of reference from the moment the Governor issued them. To the African Representative Members, especially to those among them who were directly elected, it was high time a comprehensive review should be undertaken covering all the important issues of the future machinery of the Uganda Government. They saw no reason, consequently, why such things as the composition of the Uganda Government should not have formed part of their terms of reference. Equally irritating and objectionable to them was the need to include consideration of ensuring adequate representation on the Legislative Council for and by non-Africans.

It was not surprising that in the debate that followed the Chief Secretary's announcement there were heated exchanges on the Committee's terms of reference. Rejecting the special place accorded to non-Africans, Obote put his proposition in the following terms:

Is it the intention of the Government to introduce racial politics into Uganda? We know very well that non-Africans living in Uganda have always been claiming that this is their country of adoption; and if this Committee is going to consider the question of the common roll for Representative Members in the Legislative Council, and also the number of such seats to be filled by such a method, why is it that the reservation here should be made of "adequate representation"? [23]

We have noted how in its early stages the Legislative Council contained Members drawn from the three main racial groups. This was secured effectively with the Governor's powers of nomination. But we have reviewed the pattern of constitutional development in British dependencies as well: the Governor progressively loses his powers of selecting the Members of the Legislature. The question the Committee was to answer, then, was whether, when elections replaced nominations, racial minorities should still continue to have representation as of right.

The limited scope of the terms of reference did not quite escape unchallenged. "No one on this side can agree", Magezi asserted, "that we should treat the matter of commenting on the composition of Government as something optional. I regard it as obligatory that we should definitely give Government a very clear and vivid picture of what the country wants in regard to the composition of that Government." [24]

These criticisms from Members, however, did not diminish the enthusiasm with which the Committee faced the magnitude of its work. They were specifically instructed to tour the whole Protectorate, having been given the widest publicity, so that the views of every shade of opinion could be recorded and known.

In Buganda the Committee met a temporary discouragement. By this time the Buganda Government had firmly settled on the policy of noncooperation with the Uganda Government; above all, they would have nothing to do with the Legislative Council. It is not surprising that the Lukiiko refused to give evidence to the Committee.

Ministers of the Buganda Government wrote to the Governor stating their grounds for boycotting the Committee.* They ar-

* The letter was dated 13 February 1959.

gued that the introduction of the common roll was tied up with citizenship and that since such an issue as citizenship could be settled only by Uganda Africans, it was wrong to introduce elections on the condition that there be a common roll.

The Governor quickly replied, correcting the Ministers' view and pointing out that they had misunderstood the purpose of the Committee; he hoped they would express their views to it.* Although regrettable, it was not unexpected that the Governor's appeal would have little effect; Buganda's views were never expressed through the Lukiiko.

The Committee's findings and recommendations were dealt with under the following major headings.

EXTENT OF DIRECT ELECTIONS

The Constitutional Committee reviewed the extent and method of the direct elections which had taken place the previous year; elections had been held in nine out of thirteen districts. As we have noted, indirect elections were held in Ankole, where the Eishengyero acted as an electoral college; there was no Representative Member from Karamoja. Since opinion in this district was divided on the question of elections, "and since the argument for treating the whole country alike was a very strong one", the Committee recommended that direct elections should be introduced in Karamoja.† They traced the vacillating opinion on the question of elections in Buganda; if the Protectorate Government was lenient when Buganda boycotted the Legislative Council elections in 1958, the Committee came out firmly on the issue.[25] They noted that by virtue of article 7 (3) of the Buganda Agreement it was mandatory that direct elections be held in Buganda in 1961 if such a system was not already in operation; their report ran in the following terms:

* The Governor's reply was dated 27 February 1959.
† Wild Report, para. 40. This, however, did not prevent future governments from treating Karamoja as a special case in order to hasten its overall development. This had been recommended by the Munster Commission: Ch. 20, *Report of the Uganda Relationships Commission*, 1961; also, para. 29, *Report of the Uganda Independence Conference*, 1962. Comd. 1778.

In all these circumstances, we make the following recommendations in the interests of the unity of Uganda in accordance with the wishes of the very great majority of the people of Uganda:

(i) that direct elections should be held in *all* parts of the country on the next occasion;

(ii) that no option should be offered to the alternative of indirect elections.*

In his despatch containing Her Majesty's Government views on the report, the Secretary of State for the Colonies accepted this recommendation.[26] An assurance had been secured that, with or without the Buganda Government's consent, direct elections were to take place in Buganda in 1961.

THE COMMON ROLL

We have already noted objection to the common roll as an equitable electoral arrangement; we have further considered it in the context of the problem of constitutional safeguards for minorities. This system was considered ideal for Uganda; it offered equal opportunities to all who sought membership in the National Legislature. Above all, it created an atmosphere "whereby one stops thinking in terms of different communities and thinks in terms of individual worth." [27] It would enable the inhabitants of the country to vote without any racial discrimination.

It was recommended that the next elections should be fought on a common roll.† To meet the fears of those who saw it as a step towards claiming citizenship, it was further recommended that "Her Majesty's Government should be asked to give an assurance on the introduction of the common roll" and that "there will be no question of a claim to citizenship or land rights being established by those admitted to it." It was considered premature to enact a law dealing with citizenship.

* But although there was no indirect election for the 1961 elections (because of Buganda's demand for it and partly because of the prevailing wish to persuade Buganda from the pursuit of separatism) the system was re-introduced in Buganda for the 1962 general elections. *Report of the Uganda Relationships Commission*, 1961, para. 123 (vi). (Author's emphasis.)

† Wild Report, paras. 51, 52. In fact, the Munster Commission also drew a distinction between citizenship and land rights and warned against failure to distinguish them. *Report of the Uganda Relationships Commission*, 1961, paras. 169, 190–93.

These recommendations met with support from the Secretary of State. It was in anticipation of such recommendations that the Legislative Council (Elections) (Amendment) Ordinance of 1960 had been enacted. The Secretary of State further assured the Africans of the protection they still enjoyed—for instance, the limitations imposed on non-Africans in respect of land acquisition under the Land Transfer Ordinance.[28]

THE NUMBER OF REPRESENTATIVE SEATS AND THEIR ALLOCATION

We have noted how in 1959 the composition of the Legislative Council was constructed; the Committee now received overwhelming evidence for an increase in the Council's membership. The case for a large increase in the number of Elected Members rested on four factors: the need for proper representation of the people of Uganda in the Legislative Council; the relatively poor communications; the large areas involved; and the difficulties experienced by Members in maintaining contact with their constituents. Absence or scarcity of information services in most of the rural areas (vernacular newspapers and radio) was another point in favour of a large number of Elected Members together with the need for maintaining closer contacts between the constituents represented and the Government. Indeed, the Committee had to admit: "The case for a very substantial increase in the number of directly elected Representative Members is understandable, and we believe unanswerable."[29]

It then recommended a substantial increase in the number of Elected Members, which "should be based on representation primarily on a population basis, one member to represent approximately 90,000 people, save in areas where population density is less than 50 to the square mile, where the proportion should be one member to approximately 70,000 people."[30]

The allocation of representatives was as follows:*

1. Buganda Province 20
2. Eastern Province 22

* Wild Report, para. 66. These constituencies remained in operation even after independence was achieved.

    (a) Bugisu 4
    (b) Bukedi 4
    (c) Busoga 8
    (d) Teso 6

3. Northern Province 15
    (a) Acholi 4
    (b) Karamoja 2
    (c) Lango 4
    (d) West Nile & Madi 5

4. Western Province 18
    (a) Ankole 6
    (b) Bunyoro 2
    (c) Kigezi 6
    (d) Toro 4
    Total 75

In addition there was a strong argument for urban constituencies, which were allotted seats as follows:

    (i)   Kampala (Capital and the largest town) 3
    (ii) Jinja (a Municipality) 1
    (iii) Mbale (a Town Council) 1
    Total 5

This was the first demarcation of constituencies for a direct election. The ordinary African, even in the remotest area of the Protectorate, was going to participate in the election of his Parliamentary Representative for the first time. The Secretary of State accepted these recommendations.[31]

QUALIFICATION AND DISQUALIFICATION OF VOTERS AND CANDIDATES

Voters: The Committee reviewed the existing provisions under which a person would be qualified to vote.[32] Of paramount consideration was that anyone who was to vote must have a stake in the country. It was for this reason that they recommended the denial of a vote to all aliens: "Any person wishing to be an elector must either be entitled to a right of occupancy over land in

Uganda or have lived in Uganda for five years out of the eight years prior to registration." [33]

It was further recommended "that any person who is a citizen of any country (other than a citizen of the United Kingdom and Colonies) should not be allowed to be an elector." [34]

Universal adult suffrage was recommended as a replacement for the wide range of alternative qualifications. We have examined elsewhere how a number of these recommendations were rejected and the reasons why. The Secretary of State limited himself to saying that his objections to universal adult suffrage and his reason for extending the franchise to aliens had been well argued in the Legislative Council when the Legislative Council (Elections) (Amendment) Ordinance, 1960, was being enacted.*

Candidates: A review was taken of the existing law relating to the qualifications and disqualifications of candidates. In the light of the evidence the Committee recommended, among other things, a reduction of the qualifying age to twenty-one;[35] they further recommended that a person need only be registered as an elector in Uganda to be entitled to stand for any constituency in Uganda, provided he was otherwise qualified and, of course, not disqualified.

It was recommended that special arrangements should be introduced to allow bona fide candidates to be registered beyond the time limit. It was also felt unnecessary and cumbersome that there should be property qualifications for candidates, and their removal was recommended.[36]

The Secretary of State dealt with these detailed recommendations summarily and entrusted the entire responsibility for incorporation of these recommendations into the Electoral Law of 1960 to the Protectorate Government's discretion.[37] A few of the recommendations were rejected, but the majority were accepted and enacted into law.

The Committee had dealt within its strict terms of reference; it had tackled complex problems with simplicity and penetrating understanding. The result was a straightforward, understandable

---

* Universal adult franchise was later adopted for the pre-independence elections. See *Report of the Uganda Relationships Commission,* 1961, para. 169.

and workable basis for Uganda's future constitutional reforms. It was in their comments concerning the potential form of government, which had been excluded from their strict terms, that the Committee members showed their masterly grasp of the problems involved.

COMPOSITION OF THE LEGISLATIVE COUNCIL

The Committee confirmed what was already a well-known but regrettable fact, another aspect of indirect rule:

> At present the Legislative Council is not regarded as belonging to the people of the country. . . . We think, in the circumstances, that there is a great deal in the argument which was put before us that unless the Legislative Council is transformed so that it contains a large proportion of Elected Members, there is a real danger that the present tendency towards withdrawing within district or provincial boundaries and securing from the Central Government more and more powers for the authorities within those boundaries, will become even more marked.[38]

Against the background of these ugly probabilities they recommended that the party which gained a clear majority of Elected Members should be invited to form the basis of the Government side of the Legislative Council, and that the remainder should form the Opposition. But in order that the new Members of the Legislative Council not handle all the responsibility of Government before being experienced with it, it was recommended that the three ex-officio Members, the Chief Secretary, the Attorney-General, and the Minister of Finance, should be retained on the Government side.*

At the time the Committee was reporting, it was difficult to foretell within any reasonable margin of certainty which political party would win in the event of a country-wide election; the possibility of there being no clear majority by a single party in the Council was considered.

It was recommended that if no party secured a clear majority the Governor should invite the leader of the party with the

* Wild Report, para. 152. It has always been the practice in British dependencies that these three officials are the last of the imperial hierarchy to disappear from elected Colonial or Protectorate legislatures.

greatest number of seats to form a coalition with another party or other parties which could form the basis of the Government side. If he could not succeed, the Governor would invite another leader to attempt to form such a coalition. In the event of this failing, the Council was to be dissolved and fresh elections held after an interval not exceeding six months; during the interregnum the Governor would rule with the advice of a Nominated Executive Council.[39]

It had long been felt within the Protectorate that Nominated Members of the Council, even those who were Africans, were not representing the people; certainly they did not command the confidence of the public, and they were often regarded as mere mouthpieces of the government. But on this question the Committee was divided. The majority recommended that the system of nomination be abolished. They suggested the alternative method of having six seats for Specially Elected Members, with the whole Council acting as an electoral college for the purpose of this election. They also recommended that the size of the Council should be fixed at a definite number of seats. In contrast, the minority view, which was held exclusively by the non-African Members, preferred to have the Governor retain the power to nominate more than fifteen additional Members of the Council in consultation with the Leader of the Majority Party.*

The Secretary of State upheld the majority recommendation for specially elected seats. The Governor was to have the right to propose five of the candidates for the six special seats. But because he placed considerable value on these seats, the Secretary of State increased their number from six to nine. To meet the demand of the minority view, he acceded to their wish that the Governor should retain the power of nomination, provided, that "having regard to the decision that there shall be an unofficial majority in the Council, the power of nomination would not be used to frustrate the result of the elections and would, accordingly, be used sparingly." [40]

The despatch further stated that in Her Majesty's Government's view it was necessary and important to retain the power

* *Ibid.,* paras. 154, 156. The minority recommendation was from the Chairman, A. V. Wild, Col. Baerlein, Prof. K. Ingham, Hon. Jaffer, Hon. C. K. Patel.

of nomination for use in some or all of the following circumstances:

(1) to permit the appointment of additional civil service or other Ministers who were not Members of the Legislative Council;

(2) to permit the appointment to the Council of persons of any race who, although not elected to the Legislature, may be especially well suited by experience or knowledge to speak on some subjects coming before the Legislature. Such Members would not be nominated on racial grounds but purely on grounds of merit;

(3) to secure a workable majority if that should be necessary.[41]

We deal with the representation of special interests elsewhere, but it is enough to state here that no entrenched or special arrangements were recommended for them by the Committee; the Secretary of State accepted this in principle.

There had never been an elected Speaker in the Legislative Council. The Committee felt it appropriate to recommend that he should continue to be appointed by the Governor. They felt, however, that during the lifetime of the next Legislative Council, at an appropriate moment, there should be a Speaker elected by the Council.*

While sympathising with this recommendation, the Secretary of State left it open and promised its further consideration during the lifetime of the next Legislative Council.

TITLE OF LEGISLATIVE COUNCIL

The Committee had been showered with overwhelming pressure demanding the change of the Council's name "because of its colonial associations". They felt that this fundamental change in the character of the Council, which they were recommending, could properly be marked by a change in name, and accordingly they recommended "National Assembly".

* *Ibid.,* para. 165. We have noted the first appearance of the Speaker in the Legislative Council. The election to this post was first made under the Uganda (Constitution) Order in Council, 1962, S.I. 1962, No. 405 2nd Schedule, S. 40.

It has been a phenomenon in the constitutional evolution of British dependencies that as they approach self-government the standard nomenclature of "Legislative Council" has changed to what the colonial territory itself considered commensurate with its impending or newly acquired and enhanced status. But the Secretary of State was unable to accept this recommendation on the ground that it should properly be left to the Relationships Commission, soon to be appointed, to designate the name.*

THE OPPOSITION

Having been under British rule for a considerable time, it is not surprising that the Committee recommended "the creation of a leader of the Opposition, elected by the Elected Members of the Opposition and paid a special allowance".[42]

They also recommended the creation of an Opposition Whip, a person to be elected by the Elected Members of the Opposition, and the provision of the necessary funds for an Opposition Whip's Office in the same way that funds were provided for the offices of the Elected Members' Organisation and Representative Members' Organisation.

These recommendations were accepted by the Colonial Secretary, and he promised their implementation when the next Legislative Council met.

COMPOSITION OF GOVERNMENT

Even the bulk of evidence from the public suggested that the retention of the three ex-officio Ministers was desirable. The majority opinion of the Committee considered that the choice of the remaining Ministers should be extended to include Specially Elected Members, but should not extend beyond that. The minority view, having preferred that the Governor's power of nomination be retained, considered that the choice of Ministers should be extended to include Nominated Members also.

But it was a bit surprising that, rather than recommend the

* Despatch No. 1461, para. 16. This was recommended by the Relationships Commission and adopted in the Protectorate's first comprehensive constitution, which brought internal self-government: S.I. 1962, No. 405. The Uganda (Constitution) Order-in-Council, 1962, 2nd Schedule, S. 28.

British practice whereby the Sovereign acts on the advice of the Prime Minister in the choice of Ministers, the Committee recommended that the Governor should appoint the Ministers and allocate portfolios in consultation with, not on the advice of, the Leader of the Majority.

It was recommended that there should be Parliamentary Secretaries or Assistant Ministers to help the Ministers. But their choice, like that of Ministers, was entrusted to the Governor acting in consultation with the Leader of the Majority.

The Secretary of State had reservations on this matter. While he agreed that after the next elections there was to be a majority of non-officials on the Executive Council, "it would be premature to lay down [before the results of the election were available] the number of Unofficials and Officials who will comprise the new Council." [43] Regarding the requirement of consulting the Leader of the Majority Party the despatch made it clear to the Governor that this would only be consultation, "and you will of course not be bound by any advice that may be offered."

Executive Council

For the same reasons that led the Committee to recommend a change of name for the Legislative Council it was recommended that the Executive Council should be called the Council of Ministers.[44] The Committee was, in fact, seeking to recommend some form of responsible, internal self-government. They felt it was high time the Governor stopped attending, and presiding over, the meetings of what was now the Council of Ministers; the Majority Members recommended that the Council of Ministers should have collective responsibility to the National Assembly and should not be advisory to the Governor.

When they recommended that the Governor should have reserve powers to veto the decisions of the Council of Ministers without limitation and should be allowed to legislate over the heads of the National Assembly, they denied themselves—at a single stroke—by their recommendations the status of internal self-government. Even if, as they recommended, the Leader of the Majority should preside over the Council of Ministers with the title of Chief Minister, it was a conferment of title without much substance, since authority would be retained by the Governor.

We have observed that in British dependencies, even when there was internal self-government, the Legislature of a territory, and consequently its executive government, was still subject to limitations and subordination to the imperial Parliament. The Governor, for instance, retained powers of reservation which he might use to stifle the enactment of what he considered to be undesirable legislation. But, at this juncture he did not preside over the Council of Ministers or the Cabinet, and his right to withhold assent to bills was limited to a specified field—foreign affairs and the Armed Forces of the Crown.

At this stage he had no powers to nominate any Member of the Legislature; if, in unusual cases, he had such power it was extremely limited power.

Even when the Executive Council (Council of Ministers) consisted of both Official and Unofficial Members, when the latter were in a majority the Governor was bound to act with their advice and consent, save in limited spheres.

What the Constitutional Committee recommended was not internal self-government or full responsible government but rather Representative Government. It was a most anomalous position to have accepted collective responsibility in a Council of Ministers when, at least technically, the Governor had the right to veto a measure which might provoke censure of the Ministers if they did not promote the measure in the Legislative Council, especially when they had been appointed by the Governor—regardless of the fact that they were appointed only after consultation with their Leader.

The Secretary of State accepted the name change to "Council of Ministers" as recommended; the recommendation that it should be "advisory" to the Governor was also accepted.[45] It was declared impossible to accord greater responsibilities to the Council of Ministers, as they "would have no experience"; the post of Chief Minister was rejected as being a premature idea.

The Minority recommendation, which had suggested that the Council of Ministers should be only advisory to the Governor, was also met. In fact, the Secretary of State's view weighed more in their favour.*

The despatch went on to mention aspects of the prevailing political situation in Uganda:

> I am conscious, however, that there are misgivings in many quarters in regard to the decisions that have been rejected. I am aware that there is a body of opinion which considers that the decisions fall seriously short of the political needs of the Protectorate at this juncture and views to this effect were expressed to me forcibly when I had my discussions with Representative Members in June.[46]

In spite of this more demanding set of attitudes, the Committee's report was a landmark in Uganda's constitutional history. It predominantly expressed the aspirations of the African nationalist leaders and the bulk of their enlightened followers. The constitutional set-up in Uganda had previously been clouded in vagueness because of the fear to state what it really was, lest those who believed in extravagant devolution of power would rise in protest. Now, firmly, the Committee established the foundations of a united Uganda with a unicameral Parliament having responsibility for, and drawing membership from, every part of the country—kingdom and district alike; the emphasis now was on unity and equal treatment. It was a sound foundation for the future Commission charged with defining the distribution of powers or, as it was called, of "relationships" between the various local authorities and the Central Government.

In retrospect it is difficult to see the wisdom of the Secretary of State's accepting more than what he did accept of the Committee's recommendations. While it is true that people cannot know how to exercise responsibility unless opportunity is given them to exercise it, it is equally true that it is hazardous and uncertain in the extreme to suddenly entrust great responsibilities to people who have never previously exercised governmental responsibility.

We have noted that for a long time political parties were not

---

* The composition of the Minority Committee was: The Chairman, Col. Baerlein, Bazarrabusa, Prof. K. Ingham, and Jaffer.

involved with the Legislative Council; as a result, only a few of their leaders at this time had any experience with parliamentary business. Of those Africans who were either Ministers or Parliamentary Secretaries and, therefore, had some governmental experience, only a few, if any, could ever hope to become Ministers in the event of an election. The probability was—and it turned out to be true—that those who were elected to Parliament would have no experience in parliamentary government. The opportunity for exercising such responsibility should have been offered much earlier; but that is a separate argument. The fact remains that, under the circumstances, the recommendations of the Committee as accepted were realistic and wise. The Government that was formed after the March elections in 1961 was based on them. As we shall see later, it was a great step forward in our constitutional development.

5. Constitutional Problems on the Eve of Independence

We have noted the constitutional and general development of the Protectorate; we have observed the deep penetration and impact of indirect rule and its enthronement by British authority in the minds of its willing, recipient practitioners—the African chiefs. We now review the constitutional problems the Protectorate was faced with as a result of, among other things, the impact of "Western" ideas of government—problems that were bound to arise in forging a nation from a collection of tribes with different social systems plus the immense difficulties brought about by the permanent settlement of a minority Asian community that controlled the economic life of the Protectorate. In short, the problem of immigrant minority communities, the question of Buganda separatism, the contest between kingdoms and districts over a federal or unitary form of government relative to the Relationships Commission (designed to resolve the issue).

To speak of Asians as the minority group that warrants most of our attention should not detract from the reality that there are also African minorities, either small indigenous tribes of the Protectorate or immigrants now settled in Uganda who came in search of a better life.* These African minorities have not posed

* See the tribal breakdown in the census figures of 1959, which shows a number of immigrant tribes in Uganda.

the same problem, and it has been generally taken that they are part and parcel of the majority group—the Africans; any strains they may have caused in the process of political evolution have been of a different type. Fortunately, the European community is relatively too small to constitute a problem.

A Brief History of the Asian Minority Problem

The contact between the Indian subcontinent and the east coast of Africa (Kenya, Uganda, and Tanganyika) goes back centuries, long before the advent of British rule. Indians traded for a long period with, and even settled, the islands off the coast, although they never appreciably penetrated the hinterland.

The majority of the first Asians—Indians and Pakistanis—to venture into the hinterland were soldiers under British rule. Regular Indian troops were employed in Uganda in 1897 when a mutiny broke out among Sudanese soldiers in the northern areas.[1]

During the initial stages of the establishment of British rule in the hinterland, Asian soldiers played an indispensable role in the maintenance of law and order. Even in the First World War these troops saw active service in the East African territories and, on occasion, sustained heavy casualties. When they were finally withdrawn from East Africa they had served for more than a quarter of a century.[2]

But it was not the Asian soldier that later settled in East Africa; it was the civilian. The construction of the railway to Uganda could not be completed with African labour alone. Consequently, "coolies" were shipped from India by the thousands to assist this project. Although the majority of them returned to India after the completion of the railway, a few remained permanently in various capacities, largely as labourers, on the Uganda Railway.

A third category of Asians, the traders, were to become the bulk of Uganda's Asian settlers. Even before completion of the railway a few Asian traders had already found their way by the old caravan route to Uganda, and by 1903 they had taken control of most of the retail trade in Uganda.[3] When the railway reached Kisumu on the shores of Lake Victoria in 1901, access to Uganda from the east coast was made much easier, and by 1911 there were already 2,000 Asians in Uganda. Conditions at this time were difficult for the success of British adventurers and traders and, in any case, their numbers were negligible. The industry and astuteness of the Asian trader, on the other hand, allowed him high esteem in the eyes of the British administrators, who were anxious to start and develop East African trade and commerce.[4] Sir Harry Johnston, Special Commissioner for Uganda (1899–1901), believed strongly in giving the Asian traders maximum encouragement.[5]

Indeed, the committee set up by the Colonial Secretary to report on "Emigration from India to the Crown Colonies and Protectorates" received overwhelming testimony from most British administrators that Asian traders were indispensable. It was then firmly believed that all trade depended on them. We are told that even the Commissioner for Zanzibar felt that if the Asian traders were driven out, the British might as well "shut up the Protectorate".[6]

In Uganda they turned to cotton, controlling its ginning, and by 1907 cotton had become the Protectorate's leading source of revenue. They established their mastery in all spheres of trade and general commercial life in the Protectorate, while the African was still contented with his old ways of life; their number continued to increase. The East African hinterland presented to many Asians a fresh ground where they could earn a better living or even make a fortune, and quite a number came to do so. From the very beginning the Indian was regarded, in the words of Johnston, as a "middle place" between the African on the one extreme and the European on the other.

THE ASIAN DOMINANCE OF TRADE

For many years African and Asian lived happily together in the Protectorate. The African farmer worked and tilled the soil and provided the labour for the agricultural produce which the Asian bought cheaply, processed, and sold overseas at very handsome profits. The result of this economic imbalance was to place the economic power of the Protectorate in Asian hands. They built and owned practically all the towns and important institutions in Uganda, except those constructed by government effort. In addition, they lived an isolated communal life, they never mixed with Africans, and their interracial dealings never went beyond business matters. Social intercourse between the two groups was almost nonexistent. Beyond commercial concerns the Asian knew little about his country of adoption or its people; there was a completely separate existence of the two races in this Protectorate.

On the other hand, despite the fact that the British were the "master race" in Uganda, it was undeniable that to a relative degree they mixed more freely with the Africans than did the Asians; however, there were no real conflicts or strained relations between the races. Until the end of the Second World War the African was generally contented with his traditionally inferior status, although unquestionably he was potentially the master.

THE BEGINNINGS OF AFRICAN CONCERN

We have seen how World War II brought great changes. The importance of wealth in modern terms became vividly evident to the Africans; together with other parts of the Empire, Uganda was hit by hard times as its resources were collected and utilised to fight the war. Uganda soldiers abroad not only saw active service but also witnessed and experienced different and better standards of living among the people in whose countries they served. They returned to a home country where economic life was still firmly in the hands of an alien minority community with whom they had almost nothing in common.

By the second half of the 1940s and early 1950s Uganda's educated African element rapidly increased. The inequality in wealth struck them with stark force. They became aware that the Asians, because of their wealth, could send their children abroad for higher education, whereas the Africans, in contrast, were hampered in doing so by lack of financial means.

The winds of change which brought independence to many subject countries also began to blow over Uganda, and the African politician was not insensible to its redeeming mission. A sense of injustice, in fact of protest, was for the first time beginning to show. It suddenly became humiliating that all the towns in the Protectorate should be inhabited and owned by Indians; that they should be the people with the money, the big cars, and the mansions. When a nationalistic stranger from an African dependency fighting for independence visited Kampala and expressed disgust that the future capital of independent Uganda was more like Delhi, the Uganda politician and, indeed, any sensible, proud Uganda African experienced intensified discontent at the established order.

The sum total of these forces brought a new wave of discontent and protest, not only against the Protectorate Government, which must have been largely responsible for the order of things, but—more directly—against the Asian.

In Buganda, where the Africans were relatively more economically conscious, attempts were made at different periods, with varying impact, to wrest trade from Asian hands by force. Unquestionably, the most widespread and largely felt attempt was the trade boycott which the Africans in Buganda imposed on Asian traders from 1959 to 1960. It was accompanied by large-scale sanctions of violence and intimidation against any African who, instead of buying from or selling to fellow Africans, dealt with an Asian.

Government had to take drastic measures by deporting or restricting the leaders of the boycott movement—after banning it. The whole Asian community was terror-stricken. The economy of the Protectorate was severely shaken. It was a dramatic eye-opener to the Government that the future of the Asian minorities after Uganda attained independence was a situation for them to safeguard. Its rank as a problem, social, economic, political, and constitutional, was unquestionable.

POLITICAL RIGHTS OF THE ASIAN MINORITY

Despite this short-lived reign of terror, the vast majority of Uganda Africans, and certainly responsible African politicians, did not wish to victimise Asians or wrest economic power from them by violent means.

To African politicians the solution lay not in violent action but in a successful demand for greater constitutional and political rights and sovereign power in whose exercise they could redress the economic imbalance without violence. Their struggle was against any governmental measure that sought to vest the Asian minority with political power that might prolong or perpetuate this economic imbalance.

The Asian minority had participated and had been represented in the Legislative Council long before the African ever was. After the Legislative Council was established in 1921 the Asians rejected the one seat allotted to them and demanded representation equal to that of Europeans, claiming they were numerically superior.[7] They persisted in this protest until 1926, when they accepted their one seat on the understanding that their representation by a single Member would not prejudice their having a second Member in the near future. After a fresh protest in 1929 a second Member was appointed in 1933.[8] We are informed that Her Majesty's Government made it clear that Unofficial Members of the Legislative Council were appointed in their personal capacity and the Uganda Constitution did not provide for the representation of different sections of the community on the Council.

We have noted the development of the Legislative Council and the increase of its membership. In the Council's reforms of 1946, when the African representation was increased, the number of European and Asian representatives was increased from two to three each.

In the changes of 1950, when the basis of African representation was changed to Provincial Councils, the number of Asians was also increased, like that of Europeans, from three to four.[9] 1954 saw another expansion, when the Africans were increased to fourteen and the Europeans and Asians increased to seven each.[10] The changes of 1955 brought a reduction in the number of Asian and European representatives by one each.

All along Asians had taken part in the government of the country; some of them were also in the civil service. Until the mid-1950s they participated in the Council, not because they were elected but because they were nominated by the Governor, who still possessed the powers of nomination. The issue in question was whether they would continue this participation after the Governor's powers to nominate them disappeared, when Uganda attained sovereign status.

The existence of minorities has not been unknown in the history of the British Empire. In South Africa, while under British rule, political power had been systematically vested in the white minority; in Southern Rhodesia the white minority was similarly vested with political control. In the West Indies the problem of minorities became largely extinct through interracial marriages and the consequent comparative homogeneity of society; in India, Pakistan, and Burma no special provisions were entrenched in the constitution for the representation in their legislatures of minority groups as such; in Malaya and Nigeria the problem of minority safeguards had been disposed of by constitutional entrenchment of fundamental human rights. Which method was Uganda to follow?

An authoritative statement was made by the Secretary of State for the Colonies in the House of Commons on 12 March 1954; having stated that government in Uganda was to be mainly in African hands when self-government came, he went on to say:

> The Advancement of Africans, and the economic development on which that advancement depends, cannot take place without the other races. When the time of self-government eventually comes, Her Majesty's Government will wish to be satisfied that the rights of the minority communities resident in Uganda are properly safeguarded in the constitution, but this will not detract from the primarily African character of the country.[11]

Confirmation of this came three years later in a Communication from the Chair on 24 April 1956 from Governor Cohen:

> Before agreeing that the Common Roll should be introduced, Her Majesty's Government will require to be satisfied on all these points, and will wish to be sure that the system includes provision which will secure *adequate and effective representation* of the non-

African communities on the Representative side of the Legislative Council under the Common Roll, whether by reservation of seats or in some other way.* [12]

On 10 October 1957 the Secretary of State made a statement in Uganda on the introduction of direct elections, in the course of which he said:

> Her Majesty's Government is also convinced that the non-African communities have a valuable contribution to make to the life of this territory, a contribution which will benefit all the inhabitants and, therefore, considers that it will be necessary to preserve to such communities a proper part in the Government of the country. Indeed Her Majesty's Government regards it as its duty to see that this is done.[13]

It was now clear to the Africans that the British and Protectorate Governments were determined to devise a method that would ensure Asian participation in the Government before and after self-government. But what method, precisely, had not been decided. As the Secretary of State said in 1957, "The precise method of ensuring this need not be determined now." It was to be the subject of study and discussion during the life of the next Legislative Council (1958–1961).

In 1957 and 1958 the African politicians had opportunity to express their opinion on this exposition of Government policy during several Legislative Council debates. The Chief Secretary revived the whole topic when, in 1957, he introduced a debate on the common roll and direct elections—recalling Governor Cohen's recent statement. He spoke with clarity on the merits of the common roll and rejected the idea of communal representation for the minority communities.[14]

The shortcomings of communal representation were lucidly pinpointed by Martin Wight when he said that communal representation "crystallizes and perpetuates differences, and though superficially an attractive solution of racial differences and to some extent the line of least resistance, [it] will be fatal to the emergence of that unquestioning sense of nationhood which is essential to the exercise of full self-government." [15]

The African Representative Members could not embrace the

* Author's emphasis.

policy of providing "adequate and effective representation" for non-African minorities—in this case the Asians. They expressed unquestionable hostility towards the idea. First, it was never explained how this policy would be implemented. Secondly, it was never stated what number of representatives would ensure "adequate and effective representation". If their representation was allowed as stated in this policy, then it followed that they were bound to have a controlling hand in the direction of governmental policy—a thought violently distasteful and, indeed, inconceivable to the African mind.

Small wonder that this idea of minority safeguards was rejected with spontaneous and widespread unanimity. From the Eastern Province C. J. Obwangor put his argument thus:

We have been brought up in a democracy whereby we will not refuse any-body who possesses concrete human ability to be a representative in the future National Assembly. . . . I believe in this country no legal provisions will safeguard forever, or for all time, representation of non-Africans in this Honourable House.[16]

From the east P. C. Ofwono echoed almost what Martin Wight would have counseled:

In trying to get reserved seats for non-Africans, the future of non-Africans is being jeopardised, rather than ensured. The time will come when these two Governments (the British and Protectorate) will not be there to ascertain that the number of seats are reserved or filled.[17]

From Buganda, Musazi, after rejecting the policy for safeguards, postulated perhaps the best safeguard of all, "goodwill":

The urgent need in this country is to change, it seems to me, the psychology of the African people from suspicion to trust. Change it from antagonism to goodwill. Change it from resistance to co-operation.[18]

What emerged from these debates was that no formula had been devised to achieve the policy desired by the Protectorate Government; and G. B. Magezi, Member for Bunyoro, had ample justification to claim that Government had "failed, completely failed, to interpret what those words mean." [19]

It was against this background—after examining the problem —that the Constitutional Committee recommended that

adequate representation on the Legislative Council for non-Africans should be secured by their full participation in the Common Roll arrangements, and we are satisfied that this is the only way in which adequate (in the sense that we understand it) representation can in the long term be achieved.[20]

The late 1950s was a period of Buganda's revived separatism. The Baganda seized on the issue of an electoral common roll to justify their recurrent aversion to the Legislative Council. They claimed that granting such a franchise to the Asians automatically entitled them to Uganda citizenship when the time came to enact a citizenship law. And, although we have noted how the Constitutional Committee proposed a policy toward the problem, it was boycotted by the Buganda Government.

Their concern over the common roll is well illustrated by a letter the Kabaka's ministers wrote to the Governor on 13 February 1959, which stated:

Your Excellency, we still hold the view that the question of the Common Electoral Roll is tied up with the question of citizenship, and in all fairness, the right time to consider this matter is after the Uganda Africans have attained independence for Uganda, for this is not a matter which can be decided by the British who are in a position of Trustees to Uganda Africans.

They then rejected appointment of the Constitutional Committee, claiming it could not serve a useful purpose.

On 27 February 1959 the Resident communicated the Governor's reply, explaining that the purpose of the Constitutional Committee had been misunderstood, and urged them to suggest Buganda representatives to the Committee and also to give evidence to it.[21] This failed, and Buganda officially boycotted the Constitutional Committee.

For the Asians too the problem still remained—the question of their future status and their rights and place in the society of an independent Uganda. Fears for their wealth, anxiety for their personal safety and, what could not be written in a constitution but what was vital, their future social relationship with their new

African masters. These were the problems for which the Relationships Commission and the Uganda Independence Constitution Committee were to provide solutions, consistent with the spirit of British policy toward the Asians' future—although this policy had to a significant degree been modified by the preponderance of negative African opinion towards the overall British policy for Asians after Uganda gained her independence. It is important to recall that Asians were precluded from freehold. This ensured that land rights were in African hands and must have, to some degree, ensured the relatively long spell of non-aggressiveness on part of the African against the Asian.

Buganda Separatism—The Demands and Fears of a Premier Tribe

Much of Uganda's written history is concerned with various aspects of the turbulent Kingdom of Buganda, which, since European contact with Uganda, has been the kingpin of almost every sphere of human endeavour and the focus of the Protectorate's progress; it has also been the womb of Uganda's political and constitutional problems to the time of independence—and beyond.

It is not intended to recount the complete history of this kingdom; we concern ourselves with the factors that made it the most intractable constitutional problem in Uganda's history, and we touch on other aspects of its history only so far as they may bear relevance to the topic of our concern, namely, Buganda's persistent demands to secede from Uganda.

GEOGRAPHICAL AND HISTORICAL REASONS FOR SEPARATISM

The Kingdom of Buganda occupies a central position in the area the British eventually carved out as Uganda. Largely at the expense of Bunyoro—once a far greater power than Buganda but now on the decline—Buganda increased its size throughout the seventeenth and eighteenth centuries.[22] Through its southward expansion it made contact with Arab traders from the eastern African coast long before the advent of British rule. Arabs were frequent visitors to the Kabaka's court, exchanging firearms for salt, ivory, and slaves. By the early nineteenth century Buganda had established its position as the most powerful kingdom north and west of Lake Victoria. Its social order had become one of the most advanced systems in Africa south of the Sahara.[23]

When British explorers came to this kingdom they were highly impressed, especially since they had been through vast portions of the continent and encountered numerous other indigenous tribes of lesser calibre. One explorer, the famous H. M. Stanley, had something to say of Mutesa I, the king then ruling Buganda. Having described him as "a powerful emperor, with great influence over his neighbours," he recorded:

> I saw about 3,000 soldiers of Mutesa nearly civilized. . . . I saw about a hundred chiefs who might be classed in the same scale as the men in Zanzibar and Omman, clad in rich robes and armed in the same fashion; and have witnessed with astonishment as much order and law as is obtainable in semi-civilized countries.[24]

It is true to say Mutesa I "invited" the British to establish a Protectorate over his kingdom which at the time was called Uganda by the British. The Uganda Protectorate was formally established in 1893 by a treaty concluded between Mutesa I's successor (Mutesa I died in 1884), Mwanga II, and a representative of the British Crown; however, the British made Buganda their base of operations for a variety of reasons. It was geographically strategic, giving command of the source of the River Nile and providing favourable access to the Lake Albert region, the White Nile, and the Katwe Salt Lakes;[25] *Buganda also offered the hand of friendship to the British.*

Its social order and system of government was the best existing in the environs of Lake Victoria, and indeed far beyond. It was a virile, young, rising power—with ambition to expand.[26] Additionally the British administrators, very few at this stage, needed—more than anything else—the alliance of a friendly and, preferably, powerful tribe. Buganda truly and fully answered these requirements, and so it became the base of British rule in what was eventually to become the Uganda Protectorate. From then on the history of Buganda was characterised by territorial expansion and the growth of royal power expressed in a feudal, centralised government through appointed chiefs. At the time of Lugard's arrival in 1890, Bunyoro's decline had been arrested by its ruler, Kabarega, who began to regain his control of the country west of Buganda. Kabarega was anti-British, and consequently the rise of his power conflicted with the British vested interest of controlling the whole Nile basin. With the aid of Buganda the British set out to conquer Kabarega, leading to the annexation of his territory. This was later to constitute part of the well-known "Lost Counties" dispute between Bunyoro and Buganda.

We have noted how the doctrine of indirect rule was made the basis of constitutional development and how it was based on the Buganda system of chiefly government. Baganda were recruited in large numbers and used to export this system to the surrounding areas, which later composed almost three-quarters of the Protectorate. As the British held themselves to be a civilising influence on the "barbaric" Africans, so did the Baganda regard themselves in relation to their neighbouring tribes; admittedly, others did not have as elaborate a system of government as the Baganda. The Baganda became the chiefs or main agents of the Protectorate Government during the period of Uganda's consolidation as a precise, administrative geographical expression. History must justly record that in this respect Buganda made a positive contribution to the consolidation and general development of the Protectorate. Even their close neighbours, the neighbouring kingdoms of Ankole and Toro, had to copy and accept its method of administration and to employ Baganda chiefs for a considerable time.[27]

Among these western kingdoms there was no such elaborate social system or sophisticated elite as had come to terms with the British in Buganda. Toro and Ankole had also been strikingly enlarged and consolidated by British intervention. The ruling class of Bahima in Ankole for the most part were wandering herdsmen who had "war lords" rather than stabilized territorial chiefs.[28]

Buganda became the base of almost every development in the Protectorate; as the country settled down to orderly development after its consolidation it became the focus of commercial activity, the centre of learning, and the area with the best medical facilities. Kampala, the principal town in Buganda, became the commercial centre of the whole Protectorate. As all roads led to Rome, so now did all roads in the Protectorate converge on this growing metropolis. Indeed, the Baganda became not just *primus inter pares* in relation to the rest of the tribes but also —with British encouragement—"culturally superior" in attitude. They did not need much encouragement to assert their position as "the chosen tribe" of Uganda. Not unnaturally, it seemed as if fortune had decreed that they should be the premier tribe to lead the country.

We have noted the late development of national political consciousness throughout the Protectorate and how this suited the designs of imperial authority; indirect rule took root and flourished. There was never any need for the Baganda to look beyond their tribe, or to conceive the image that the other tribes were, by fate, tied to them. This negative idea of each tribe thinking it was a nation unto itself prevailed everywhere in Uganda, but it received its fullest expression in the Kingdom of Buganda.

The interaction of all these forces brought, regrettably, considerable conceit to the Baganda. They looked upon other tribes much as the Romans viewed the "barbarian" tribes. They evolved phrases or words like "Munyoro", "Mukanyabulo", which bore contemptuous connotations when applied to anyone not of the Baganda. Many developed such a degree of intolerance that anything not done their way could not be right, that every African custom or mode of behaviour that did not conform to their own standards was not deserving of any respect. In this manner Buganda isolated itself from the rest of the country, and the British helped to maintain this false and transitory pinnacle of isolation. Buganda became, relatively, the most highly developed province in the Protectorate and consequently the most politically conscious. The Kabaka and his Lukiiko (Parliament) took a leading role in the 1920s in opposing the creation of an East African Federation, or, as it was called in 1931, the Closer Union of East African Territories (Kenya, Tanganyika, and Uganda). The lesson learned at a later date—the creation of the Central African Federation—shows Buganda to have taken a proper stand; otherwise the interests of the European settler minority in Kenya would have dominated and eclipsed those of the Africans throughout the Federation.

However, it should be noted that the Baganda were not fighting this issue in terms of Uganda as a whole; their paramount interest was the preservation of their own kingdom and its associated prestige. So far as the Baganda were concerned they were a distinct, superior nation, tied to the rest of the Protectorate only by British overrule.

THE DUNDAS REFORM

Governor Mitchell, who was succeeded by Sir Charles Dundas, had already initiated, but not completed, the evolution toward more responsibility for the Lukiiko. Dundas decided to push ahead with this reformation of Buganda administration much according to the doctrine of indirect rule. He was committed to strengthening the indigenous method of government.[29]

Nothing speaks more eloquently of his views than his own speech delivered to the Kabaka and an expectant Lukiiko on the role of the Resident:

> His duty is not to direct affairs or to control your officials but to advise your Government and to advise me in the exercise of my authority. But since he cannot direct and control, he cannot assume responsibilities for the actions of your Government and its servants. That responsibility lies with your Highness acting on the advice of your Ministers and Council subject to the Governor's over-riding powers. In the past it was necessary for the British Administration to go beyond these limits and to take a direct part in detailed inspections of the work of your chiefs. That meant, however, that the chiefs were under two masters and the people, particularly in more distant parts of Buganda, looked to the District

Commissioners as much as to your Government for adjustment of their affairs. In consequence there has been a dual administration within Buganda. As I say, such was perhaps necessary, but the stage has now been reached at which it should no longer be necessary for us to go beyond the scope set by the Agreement in the way of supervision of your administration. . . .

Accordingly I wish the Resident and his staff to confine themselves to advice and guidance, leaving inspection and control to your government and its agents.[30]

This increase of administrative responsibility constituted a great strain on the Lukiiko's administration, which was not, whatever its grandeur, sufficiently experienced in modern government systems to shoulder it. In fact, with the arrival of Sir John Hall to succeed Dundas, the old order of greater control of Buganda administration by Protectorate officers was reinstated; all the same, the feeling remained in Buganda that the Baganda were entitled to manage their own affairs with a minimum of supervision from the British authorities.

Deportation of the Kabaka

Although it is not intended to fully discuss the events that led to the deportation of the Kabaka, it is essential to note that it was the first major political crisis after the Second World War; Buganda, conscious of her autonomy, sought to defend it.[31] There were three fundamental factors that led to the deportation of the Kabaka:

(1) Buganda's opposition to the concept of an East African Federation;

(2) the demand for transfer of Buganda affairs from the Colonial Office to the Foreign Office; and

(3) a time-table for Buganda's evolution toward independence.

The Kabaka demanded the last two points, although he outwardly accepted the British Government's assurances on the first; his refusal to retract when required by the Governor to do so led to his swift deportation. It was worth noting that the Kabaka suffered this martyrdom while fighting for Buganda's interests alone, as opposed to Uganda's interests as a whole.

The swift and just sympathy he received was not only from Buganda; it was wide-spread. The "republican" north and east and the kingdoms in the west all joined with Buganda to express their indignation at the disgrace visited on a leading African ruler; they all demanded his immediate reinstatement.

Eventually the Kabaka was restored, and his position and that of his kingdom were redefined and given effect in the Buganda Agreement of 1955.

THE BEGINNINGS OF FEAR

So far Buganda had weathered the storms of political fortune well; the Kabaka emerged from the crisis of 1953 with enhanced prestige and love among his subjects. His kingdom by the Agreement of 1955 secured even greater administrative powers than under the Dundas reforms. However, the fears that brought about the crisis when the Kabaka was deported still remained and were soon to increase. Since 1900 Buganda had always defended herself and the position of her ruler against the British or other colonialists, but the conclusion of the Second World War unleashed a tremendous sense of nationalism that soon swept across the continents of Asia and Africa.

On the African continent politics and constitutional development took a new, swift, and radical turn. The Federation of Rhodesia and Nyasaland had been imposed against the will of the majority of Africans there. In 1957, Ghana opened the gates of freedom for African British territories. What became alarming to Buganda was the allegedly unceremonious and harsh treatment the Ashanti king had received at the hands of the first African government in Ghana.[32] Suddenly it dawned on everyone in Uganda that it was merely a matter of time before Uganda got independence. This prospect brought into prominent focus the anxieties that had always been latent in Buganda. What would be the position of the Kabaka after independence: would it be the same, lower, or higher than it was under British protection? What would be Buganda's role and place if left without any arbiter except its neighbouring African tribes; was it to remain the first among equals, or was it to deteriorate as a result of the envy and "retaliation" of the other tribes, all of whom Buganda assumed had old scores of one sort or another to settle? As the Buganda Lukiiko saw it, there was only one answer: secession from the rest of Uganda before the British left and bequeathed sovereign power to an independent Uganda Parliament overwhelmingly non-Baganda in its composition. Every effort in Buganda was now to be directed to securing fully autonomous status for the kingdom. In doing so a great variety of schemes were to be attempted.

The first approach was to cripple and eliminate any political parties in Buganda; during this endeavour all the forces of the kingdom's history were in favour of the secessionists. By 1955 the traditionalist elements in Buganda had consolidated their forces and acquired new and more vigorous leadership in people like Sempa and Lutaya.

The conflicts that led to the Buganda riots of 1945 and 1949 between the chiefs and the peasants had been wiped out, if only for a short period, by the deportation of the Kabaka in 1953; from this juncture they all united in one single, formidable tribal force. After the reinstatement of the Kabaka in 1955 public opinion in Buganda was influenced and directed by the tripartite force of the Kabaka, the chiefs, and the "people".*

They now turned on the politicians in order to liquidate them. E. M. K. Mulira, President of the Progressive Party, was prevented from attending the Lukiiko. A fictitious charge was leveled against J. W. Kiwanuka, one of the leading men of the U.N.C., for not only insulting the Kabaka but having plotted to assassinate him. M. Mugwanya, the President of the Democratic Party, was prevented personally by the Kabaka from taking a seat in the Lukiiko which he had won at a by-election. There is no doubt that the grounds on which these political leaders were silenced were deliberately fabricated. By these successive blows political parties and the influence of political leaders in Buganda were, for all practical purposes, eliminated. The traditionalists could now claim to speak for Buganda without fear of dissent.

The case for Buganda's opposition to rule by political parties was eloquently put in a Memorandum by the Lukiiko to Her

* This seems also to be the view of A. Low, in his *Political Parties in Uganda, 1949–62*, p. 41.

Majesty the Queen seeking the termination of British treaties of "protection" over Buganda:

> It would be asking too much of the Baganda to entrust the destiny of their country into the hands of political party leaders whose experience has not been proved by time. This could be extremely risky in the light of recent history, which has shown clearly that politicians in emergent countries use parliamentary democracy as a spring-board to virtual dictatorship.[33]

Having thus silenced effective political activity in Buganda, they turned to the Legislative Council; the Council was of vital significance if their plan was to succeed, as it was the embryo of Uganda's sovereign legislature. It might, after independence, be used to whittle away at Buganda's grandeur. It was imperative that the Council be destroyed, or at the very least, its powers considerably reduced.

Buganda's opposition to the Legislative Council dates back to the 1920s. It was always regarded as somewhat alien and as a definite rival to the Lukiiko. So long as it was in British hands its threat remained relatively theoretical, and consequently only latent. Because there was no immediate fear from the Council, Kintu, the Katikkiro (Prime Minister) of Buganda, demanded for Buganda direct elections to the Legislative Council for 1958, while the 1955 Buganda Agreement was still being negotiated. But the sudden prospect of independence threw the whole question into a new and vivid light. The Baganda responded by sharply recoiling into their tribal shell and renewing, with greater vigour, their opposition to the Legislative Council.

The traditional government in Mmengo had to apply all its available ingenuity to frustrate the holding of direct elections to the Legislative Council in 1958; they succeeded.* The heart of their opposition was that the natural heir to British rule was not the Legislative Council but their Lukiiko, and for the other king-

---

* The case *The Katikkiro of Buganda v The Attorney-General*, Uganda (E.A.L.R.), 1959, was eventually lost by Buganda, but by the time it was disposed of elections had already been held in 1958 in the other provinces, though not in Buganda.

doms and districts, their traditional governments—the district and kingdom councils. The force of this argument can only be demolished by practical and political constitutional considerations on a wider (East Africa–African) plane. There is little doubt that their formula would have provided the logical conclusion to indirect rule as it had been practised in Uganda, as the concept of a unifying African authority had never been developed.

The view the Baganda took was well put in their Memorandum seeking the termination of agreements with Britain:

> The Lukiiko would like to stress the fact that it is not opposed to parliamentary democracy as such, but it views with apprehension any induced democracy which is only strengthened by the desire for independence. To the Lukiiko, parliamentary democracy ought to suit the local conditions, because there cannot be such a thing as international parliamentary democracy. Independence should be a means to an end and not an end in itself. Buganda cannot sell all her heritage for the purchase of Uganda's independence; nor is Buganda willing to sacrifice everything at the altar of Uganda's unity.*

In an attempt to diminish the potential sovereignty of the Legislative Council the Buganda Government took the initiative of forming the Katikkiro's Conference (heads of the local governments of the kingdoms of Ankole, Toro, Bunyoro, and Buganda), which was subsequently widened to include the Secretaries-General of all districts. We discuss the character of these conferences elsewhere, but it should suffice to say that Buganda had originally envisaged that all these various leaders from the Protectorate might support her demand to increase the degree of power for the various component districts and kingdoms at independence. This would have resulted in a weak central government. It is ironical that ultimately, after the politicians infiltrated and influenced these conferences, they then made them an effective tool for opposing Buganda's extravagant demands and, in

---

* Quoted from the pamphlet *Buganda's Independence*, p. 30. In these demands Buganda had veteran support from retired missionaries in Britain, such as H. M. Grace; also Conservative M.P.s and Members of the House of Lords.

the end, condemned Buganda with unanimity when she eventually passed her own resolutions to secede.

THE BID TO SECEDE

Against this background Buganda launched her campaign to obtain independent, sovereign status by seceding from the rest of the Protectorate. On 16 December 1958 she sent a lengthy document to the Colonial Secretary: "A Memorandum from the Buganda Lukiiko for submission to Her Majesty the Queen being the desire of the Baganda to bring the Buganda Treaty of 1894 to an end." [34]

It was by this treaty that the Kabaka of Buganda had formally invited British protection for his kingdom, protection which was subsequently extended to the rest of Uganda.

The second article of the treaty clearly stated that Her Britanic Majesty Queen Victoria had been graciously pleased to bestow on Mwanga, "King of Uganda, the Protection which he requested".[35]

Since "protection" had been provided as the result of Buganda's "request", they now argued it could, and should, be terminated by notice at the pleasure of those who initiated the request for protection. What lent weight to their argument, in their view, was a further provision that seemed to give the Agreement the status of international law by stating, *inter alia,* that it would be carried out in accordance with the provisions of "any International Agreements arising from the same to which Great Britain is or may become a party".[36]

The Memorandum was a critical review of British administration and policy from inception to the time the Memorandum was submitted. It alleged that the 1900 Buganda Agreement had been negotiated and signed by the chiefs under "unsavory circumstances"—that the signatures of the chiefs "were purchased". The Lukiiko preferred to view the treaty as a "constitution" rather than an agreement.

The Lukiiko deprecated the 1955 Buganda Agreement as not having been freely negotiated, as the Kabaka's return from exile depended on the Agreement being signed by the chiefs: "Unquestionably, it was signed under duress, however harsh this may sound; yet it is difficult to gainsay".*

The legal standpoint was considered, and it was concluded that, however unjust it might seem, the law regarding these Agreements was clear. They had no legal force. Buganda, as part of a Protectorate, had no *locus standi* in the international community of nations. Any complaint on the propriety of certain treaties or agreements could only serve to arouse sympathy for political action among the Baganda as a premier tribe, wronged and cheated by the British Crown.

The Memorandum continued its criticism:

> In 1902, an Order-in-Council was passed with the sole purpose of ruling Uganda as a British Colony and subsequent upon that the affairs of Uganda were transferred from the Foreign Office to the Colonial Office and thereafter Uganda ceased to count as a Protected State but became a Colonial Protectorate in spite of its 1894 Treaty. The result was that the Supreme Court became the High Court and the Commissioner became the Governor, and finally Orders-in-Council obtained the force of an Act of State. . . .
>
> The direction which has been followed by British administration in Uganda has been confusing. This confusion has very much arrested political progress throughout the country. The British policy in Uganda started in the form of developing the country as a unitary state, for that is what it was by the 1894 Treaty, which treaty bestowed British protection not only over Buganda but also other neighbouring countries such as Bunyoro, Ankole, Toro, Busoga and other neighbouring territories.[37]

So far the Memorandum was factually correct. We will note later the controversy over the future form of the constitution—whether it was to be federal or unitary. An endeavour is made to show that at no stage of its history, contrary to popular belief, did Uganda ever have a federal constitution. Undoubtedly indirect rule, more than any other single concept, was responsible for this view. It was not surprising to find this claim in Bu-

---

* It is interesting to note that by international law, fraud may vitiate a treaty or agreement but duress does not affect its validity. See Oppenheim, *International Law*, Vol. I, *Peace*.

ganda's Memorandum: "Each tribe was encouraged by British Administrative Officers as an entity in itself and the foundations of a Uganda nation were destroyed. Tribal pride became the rage; until recently it has burst out into tribal jealousies, with its forum as the Legislative Council."

This complaint was understandable; it led to the Lukiiko's point of greatest concern—the Kabaka's position:

> The Baganda were therefore rightly moved to ask what would be the exact position of the Kabaka of Buganda in a self-governing Uganda. The British Government has replied that the position of the hereditary rulers in Uganda will be discussed by a committee composed of Legislative Council Members. The right of the Legislative Council to discuss the status of a monarch who was responsible for the introduction of British protection over the whole of Uganda is highly questionable. Pledges are pledges and they should be honoured.[38]

The Memorandum then recalled, with bitterness, the exile of the Kabaka in 1953, when he "was kidnapped and unceremoniously bundled into a military aircraft under an escort and was flown to England, not being provided with warm clothes, for England was in a severe winter spell".

Still convinced of the legal force of their treaties and agreements, the Baganda asserted, "We do not concede that in the Agreements we made with the British there is any proviso which gives to either party the right to arrest the other in the event of a breach of any section in the Agreements."

Buganda's grounds for termination of British rule, although extravagant and founded partly in ignorance, were historically understandable and concerned matters within the territorial limits of the kingdom's jurisdiction. But it was an extraordinary claim when the Memorandum asserted:

> By the 1900 Agreement the British changed their policy [of Uganda being a unitary state] and *Buganda was made to renounce her dependencies* in favour of the British. But these dependencies, although surrendered, still enjoyed that same protection for which King Mwanga paid the price. The three kingdom countries (An-

kole, Toro and Bunyoro) subsequently were each given a separate Agreement of their own.*

From this context one would inevitably infer that the "dependencies" referred to were the three western kingdoms and probably Busoga. This claim angered even the closest friends of Buganda, its fellow kingdoms in Toro and Ankole. It had no foundation in fact; Ankole and Toro were smaller kingdoms, both enlarged and consolidated with the help of the British—as was Buganda to a large degree.[39]

There had been tribal raids conducted by Buganda against Ankole in which the prizes were cattle and beautiful women.† But Ankole had long had its own separate and independent existence. It had never paid homage or tribute to the Kabaka; on the contrary, it had its own dynasty of independent rulers. The Kingdom of Toro, although comparatively young, having seceded from Bunyoro, was equally independent of Buganda.

It would be more accurate to say that when Bunyoro was at the zenith of her power and unequalled by any kingdom in what eventually became Uganda, it exacted recognition and tribute from Buganda, which was then much weaker. During the decline of Bunyoro and Buganda's corresponding rise and expansion at Bunyoro's expense, Bunyoro still maintained its independent existence.

It is true that Buganda's claim to these "other dependencies" was not a pretext for the Lukiiko of 1958 to secede; it was a claim staked out back in 1898 by the Buganda Katikkiro to the British administrators with a view to acquiring more territory for Buganda. The claim was thoroughly investigated, but it was found that there were no grounds for Buganda to claim its neighbouring tribes and kingdoms as dependencies. It was established that they had separate and independent existence.‡

* Author's emphasis.
† H. F. Morris, in "The Making of Ankole", *Uganda Journal*, Vol. 21 (1957), shows the creation of modern Ankole, but at no stage does he indicate Ankole to have been a province of Buganda.
‡ Ingham, *The Making of Modern Uganda*, p. 69. George Wilson, who investigated Buganda's claim, concluded that, although the claim over the western kingdoms of Ankole, Toro, and Bunyoro were theoretical and unreal, Busoga itself had been a tributary of Buganda for a considerable time.

But this claim on her neighbouring tribes, revived as late as 1958, was an error of judgement on the part of Buganda. At a single stroke Buganda had antagonised them by hurting their individual pride. Ankole vigorously denied Buganda's claim and with strong support from the other tribes dismissed the claim as just another example of Buganda's cultural arrogance. In turn, Buganda, now almost completely isolated, was driven more and more into believing secession was the safest course available. The lengthy Memorandum, which was signed by the Lukiiko, concluded:

> In view of the foregoing, and because we are convinced that the time has come for the handing over to us of our sovereignty, we urge that the Treaty and Agreements come to an end on the results of an understanding on the following points:
>
> (i) The manner of handing over to us of our sovereignty;
>
> (ii) The discussions on the future position of non-Africans in our country—to see how they can live amicably side by side after the Queen to whom they are responsible has surrendered her protection over us;
>
> (iii) It is evident that according to the terms of the 1894 Treaty, there are other territories in Uganda which obtained British protection by virtue of the Treaty, and that it follows that anything touching the Treaty affects those territories. It is, therefore, intended that discussions be held with a view to creating a workable formula between ourselves and those territories;
>
> (iv) The future relation between the Baganda and the British on matters affecting our mutual interests within the British Commonwealth of Nations.

It was a far-reaching demand to make, and it is not surprising that the British Secretary of State for the Colonies rejected it.[40] On 11 December 1958 he came to Uganda and held a meeting with the Lukiiko's Constitutional Committee. The Katikkiro, in his address of welcome, leveled a series of complaints against the increasing toughness of the Protectorate Government:

> Since 23rd May, 1959, when Buganda was declared a "disturbed area", the Protectorate Police and Officials have been making direct approaches to the people. The recognised procedure is that the

Protectorate Police and Officials act through and in co-operation with the chiefs who are responsible for law and order in their respective areas.[41]

It was an eye-opener for Buganda to see the extent of power the Protectorate Government had over it. There was never any legal provision requiring the procedure they were demanding. The Protectorate Government had the right, technically, to take the action it did to maintain order, peace, and good government. It is a most unfortunate result of indirect rule that a convention was established in Buganda which gave the Baganda a seemingly moral basis for claiming that Protectorate officials were constitutionally bound to act through Buganda chiefs only.

The British Secretary of State was not disposed to entertain their claims. He told them, specifically, that the Agreements could not be "torn up" by 1961, although it was possible to review some of their provisions.[42]

But the Lukiiko was given to assiduity; early in 1960 it sent another Memorandum entitled "A Further Memorandum from the Lukiiko to Their Memorandum Petitioning Her Majesty the Queen to Terminate the Agreements"; it was stated in the same tone as the 1958 Memorandum.[43] Once more it traced the history of Buganda's special position emanating from its Agreements with Britain, which were unlike the less elaborate and less sacrosanct Agreements with the other kingdoms of Uganda. It emphasized Buganda's anxiety on the position of the Kabaka if Buganda were to remain an integral part of Uganda. Finally, it asserted Buganda's claim of economic superiority and expressed considerable discontent:

> . . . it is well known that most of the Protectorate Government's revenue comes from Buganda and that those monies are spent in other parts of the Protectorate while Buganda receives back a mere pittance of what it subscribes, thus Buganda no longer sees the benefit of remaining in Uganda.[44]

Meanwhile, a Constitutional Committee of the Lukiiko was established which was charged with the task of pressing Buganda's demands before the British Government. In 1959 it met the Colonial Secretary in London and opened protracted negotiations with the Governor of Uganda in 1960, which never came to anything as both parties completely lacked a *modus operandi*.

It was the Lukiiko Memorandum of 8 October 1960 to the Colonial Secretary that removed any shadow of doubt in Uganda that Buganda intended to achieve what it meant. It was drawn up and endorsed by the Lukiiko after its Constitutional Committee had deadlocked in London, where the Colonial Secretary still firmly rejected its proposals to secede. The Memorandum highlighted more vividly Buganda's desperate need for complete autonomy. It left no one in doubt that fear was at the root of these demands.

The reaction in the rest of Uganda towards Buganda's demands to secede were swift, determined, and unanimous; Buganda seemed to be left by itself. It was for this reason that the Memorandum stated:

> If Buganda's legitimate constitutional demands have caused all these most unlikely reactions, while the Treaty relations are even still existing between Buganda and Her Majesty's Government, the Lukiiko's apprehensions as to what the future Uganda Government's attitude towards Buganda will be are greatly intensified. We cannot expect that Government to do much better than Her Majesty's Government as they are going to inherit this form of disguised dictatorship. *Public pronouncements made on various occasions by people likely to be leaders of a future Uganda are not conducive to the idea of unity as Her Majesty's Government envisages it.* In order to avoid another "Katanga" in this country immediately after Uganda's independence, Buganda has decided and is determined to go it alone.* [45]

There was yet another excuse for Buganda to take this extreme stand; it was the time-table the British Government had devised for Uganda's remaining constitutional hurdles before independence. While the protracted negotiations were still going on between Buganda and the British authorities in London, the Colonial Secretary announced the time-table:

(1)   There was to be registration of voters throughout the

* Author's emphasis.

whole Protectorate in 1960.

(2) Before the general elections in the following year a Relationships Commission would be appointed by himself to make recommendations as to the form of Government most suitable for Uganda (including Buganda).

(3) There were then to be general elections to the Legislative Council early in 1961.

(4) After the general elections there would be a Constitutional Conference, to be held in London in 1961, representative of all parts of Uganda, including Buganda, to consider the recommendations of the Relationships Commission. This Conference was to be attended by the Elected Members of the new Legislative Council.

The time-table was obviously bound to entail far-reaching constitutional changes. For this reason the Baganda opposed it strenuously. For the first time they publicly proposed to waive secession if the Colonial Secretary was prepared to state that, whatever the future form of government might be for Uganda, *Buganda was to have a federal relationship vis-à-vis the future central government of Uganda.*[46] They demanded that this commitment should be made before any of the stages in the time-table were fulfilled. The fear was, of course, that the directly Elected Members of the Legislative Council, the majority of whom would obviously be non-Baganda—some of them in Government—would endeavour to deny Buganda her claims at the Constitutional Conferences if no prior commitment was made by the British Government.

Alternatively, Buganda demanded that the Relationships Commission should submit its report before any of the other stages of constitutional change were implemented. Both demands were firmly rejected by the Colonial Secretary.

In concluding their Memorandum the Lukiiko saw no better alternative than submitting a *"plan for an independent Buganda"*. It is worthwhile to note the various powers demanded by Buganda for herself, as they not only show the extent of these demands but also present a sound perspective of the several problems the Relationships Commission and the framers of the Uganda Constitution had to meet in trying to reconcile Buganda with the concept of Uganda as one united sovereign state. These Buganda demands were:

1. *General Demands*
   (a) Defence: Buganda was to have her own army, but would form a military alliance with Britain for a specified period of time, subject to revision from time to time.
   (b) Foreign affairs: Buganda was to establish foreign relations by herself where possible, and otherwise in conjunction with Great Britain for a specified period of time.
   (c) Economic aid: It was to seek aid from Britain in its economic and technical development. A Five Year Development Plan was to be drawn up by Buganda following the attainment of its independence. It was to encourage free enterprise and make conditions favourable to foreign investment. The Government's policy on state ownership was that such ownership would be restricted to those essential services which could not be beneficially run by private enterprise.

2. *Relationship with Neighbouring Countries in East Africa*
   (a) Customs: Buganda would join the common customs of East Africa.
   (b) Communications (including road, rail, water, and air services): There was to be joint negotiation for the membership of Buganda on the bodies controlling those services.
   (c) Higher education: All existing institutions of learning were automatically to fall under Buganda's jurisdiction, although it was conceded that Makerere University College [now Makerere University, Kampala] was to retain its status as an interterritorial institution. It was demanded that Buganda have her full share in the management of this university college.
   (d) Judicial: Buganda was to have its own High Court and District Courts, although appeals from the High Court, it was granted, would lie to the Court of Ap-

peal for Eastern Africa and finally to the Privy
Council.

   (e) Interstate trade in East Africa: Any manufacturing
and/or secondary industries operating in Buganda
would be licensed in Buganda, and all excise duty
had to go to Buganda.

   (f) Monetary System: Buganda would remain in the
sterling area.

   (g) Immigration: This was to be controlled by the Kabaka's Government, although movement of persons
between Buganda and other neighbouring countries
in East Africa was to be free and unrestricted.

3. *International Relations*

   (a) The fundamental rights of man and the rule of law as
understood in the free world would be strictly observed.

   (b) On its attainment of independence, Buganda would
be associated with the great family of nations—the
Commonwealth; it would also seek admission to the
United Nations.

   (c) Posts and telecommunications: Being services conducted on an international level, such services were
to continue to be run as before, but the post office
was to fall under the Kabaka's Government and
therefore Buganda would make its own postage
stamps.

4. *International Rearrangement of Services*

   (a) The Lukiiko would continue to be "the legislative
and deliberative body for Buganda".

   (b) "All powers now exercised by Her Majesty's Representative shall rest in the Kabaka and his Government" (all laws and Buganda's budget), which would
be effective "after the approval of the Kabaka, who
is the Supreme Head of Buganda".

   (c) Buganda was to have an army of which the Kabaka
was to be the Commander-in-Chief.

   (d) Buganda would have its own police force for the
purpose of maintaining law and order. In this con-

nection, the present Uganda Police Force responsible for the Buganda Province was to be immediately brought under the Kabaka's jurisdiction.

(e)   Kampala, Entebbe, Masaka, Mubende, and all townships and trading centres, as well as Entebbe Airport, "without prejudice to its international status", were to be immediately brought under the jurisdiction of the Kabaka's Government.

(f)   "All Lands vested in Her Majesty under the provisions of all Buganda Agreements were to revert to the Kabaka of Buganda for the use and benefit of all".

5.   *Finance*

"As to the financing of the whole scheme as outlined above, Buganda intends to use:

(a)   The existing resources which will be greatly increased by the change over from British control

(b)   by raising local as well as overseas loans and by inviting outside capital.

"In conclusion, this Lukiiko's decision has been made imperative by Her Majesty's Government's failure to recognize the fact that any possible parliamentary democracy ought to be built on the existing institutions in Buganda, that is to say, the Kabakaship and the Lukiiko. Her Majesty's Government's oversight of the Kabaka, his Government and the Lukiiko representations to that effect can only result in hard feelings. The only possible way out of these difficulties is for Buganda to go it alone and establish its own *'Anglo-Buganda Cordial Relationship'* as outlined above."

We will analyse the essential characteristics of federal and unitary constitutions elsewhere. It is clear that Buganda's constitutional framework as outlined above could only be consistent with a unitary *sovereign Buganda state,* severed from the rest of Uganda; not even a confederal relationship with the rest of the Protectorate was considered.

The British Government had adopted a firm line, partly because of the pressure from the rest of Uganda and partly because Buganda's secession was intrinsically impracticable. The Colonial Secretary, in a reply to the Kabaka, rejected almost all the demands the Buganda Memorandum had made.[47] He re-affirmed his determination to carry out the three-point pro-gramme of the appointment of a Relationships Commission, a general election, and a Constitutional Conference for drawing up Uganda's self-government constitution.

The Colonial Secretary explained why he could not promise that Buganda's relationship with the rest of the Protectorate would be federal: "It would be wrong for me to attempt to lay down in advance either what the Relationships Commission will advise, or what the Members of the Constitutional Conference will agree as to the form of Government for Uganda after Inde-pendence."[48]

The Lukiiko had, in addition to the Memorandum, passed a resolution denouncing the Agreements and declaring Buganda's intention to secede.[49] The Governor rejected it on 4 October 1960. The Colonial Secretary now confirmed this rejection: "Her Majesty's Government would not accept any question of any part of the Protectorate seceding from Uganda, so long as Her Majesty's Government is the protecting power."

The last paragraph of the reply was a firm warning and an in-dication of the growing impatience of the British Government with Buganda's inability to see and accept realities:

> Buganda still has the opportunity to use this period of continued security [from Her Majesty's Government] to negotiate with Her Majesty's Government a satisfactory relationship with the other parts of the country, designed to preserve the Kabakaship and the Lukiiko intact and to confirm them in the exercise of their powers. But if this opportunity is deliberately thrown away—as it would be if Buganda were to seek to overthrow the Agreements in a mood of impatience at this stage—*I do not believe that there would be an-other.* I therefore call upon Your Highness to join with me and with His Excellency the Governor in an urgent effort to restore co-oper-ation and good will between us *before it is too late.** [50]

The British Government had shown remarkable patience. No

* Author's emphasis.

wonder it was being accused of being too soft with Buganda by the majority in the Protectorate. As if no word of caution deserved a second thought, the Lukiiko chose to ignore the Colonial Secretary's letter. It set up a committee, the "Buganda Independence Committee", to work out in detail the actual method of establishing Buganda as an independent state severed from the Protectorate. Much time and money were spent by the members of this Committee as they travelled abroad seeking advice and support for their cause, but to no avail.

The afternoon and evening of 31 December 1960 were historic moments in and around the precincts of the Lukiiko at Mmengo. The Lukiiko was debating secession; restless crowds thronged its gates and menacingly demanded a "Declaration of Independence".

The Protectorate waited with anxiety, and some sense of uncertainty, to see if the Lukiiko would adopt the "Declaration of Independence", and if it did, what implications this might have. Finally, after one of the most momentous and stormy debates in its history, the Lukiiko declared Buganda to be an independent sovereign state with effect from 1 January 1961. Buganda had seldom witnessed such a great emotional grip on her people.

As expected, the Governor promptly issued a declaration stating that Buganda's resolution for independence would have no effect whatever and everything would carry on just as before. He then issued a stern warning against anyone who, having realized the complete emptiness of the "Declaration of Independence", might be tempted to give it meaning by taking the law into his own hands: "The forces of law and order are such that should any misguided persons attempt to interfere with the orderly life of the people, the law will take its course and retribution will surely follow." [51]

It is reasonable to assert that, in the long history of the struggle for self-determination and sovereign power, no "Declaration of Independence" by any subject people has ever been as meaningless and ineffective as the one announced by Buganda. Nothing changed; government went on as before. The three-point programme for constitutional change was duly effected. As usual, law and order was *enforced by the Buganda Government.*

The Protectorate Government, however, still operated in Buganda.

It is significant to note that within a fortnight after the "Declaration of Independence" the Independence Committee split into factions; the most enlightened members of the Committee —three lawyers and one teacher, all University graduates—resigned and submitted their Minority Report to the Speaker for transmission to the Lukiiko. Their intellectual probity could not reconcile itself with the grotesque fiction of empty independence. They wrote in their Report:

> Unilateral declaration by the Lukiiko that Buganda was independent on 31st December, 1960, without putting her independence into effect would be a mere bluff and positively unwise and would belittle the importance of the Lukiiko in the eyes of the world and the people of Buganda. To this may be added the fact that all the laws of Uganda affecting Buganda were to be observed in spite of the independence as declared by the Lukiiko. This, in particular, makes it obvious that the present Lukiiko would have no constitutional powers.
>
> We considered in all our deliberations that unilateral declaration by the Lukiiko was not the best road to independence. That is precisely why we think that the best way would be to negotiate with the Colonial Secretary if we are to achieve the best for Buganda and her throne." *

Their Report placed emphasis on negotiations with the British Government, which, in effect, was agreeing with their view. They further suggested: "it is now the time to elect this Lukiiko directly on universal adult suffrage, as an indication that *this nation* [Buganda] is now fit for self-government. We consider this matter to be of such great urgency that it should be done now without further delay".† This was an important recommendation. The Lukiiko that had declared independence was not directly elected; it was an extremely conservative institution in all matters of government. The Lukiiko was incapable of grasping

---

* *Minority Report of the Buganda Independence Committee*, dated 10 January 1961, pp. 1–2. The co-opted Members who resigned: W. W. Kalema, Luyimbazi-Zake, and Godfrey Binaisa, later Q.C. and Attorney-General; Fred Mpanga was the only one who remained closely tied to the traditionalist group in Mmengo.

† Author's emphasis.

the realities of modern constitutional change. If anything more constructive was to be done, said the Minority Report, a new Lukiiko was an essential prerequisite. There was no guarantee, however, that a new, directly elected Lukiiko would not be similarly disposed. In fact, as later events showed, the new Lukiiko was in many respects a replica of the old one; but it was a suggestion in the right direction.

The minority recommendations would receive no serious attention from the Lukiiko; that was certain. They were made by the intellectuals who believed in government by means of political parties rather than the method that obtained in Buganda—government by feudal chiefs. We saw how the believers in political parties were liquidated, and so it is not surprising that Buganda, while observing all the laws that bound it to Uganda, still maintained its fiction of having successfully seceded; its politicians were too weak and too afraid to stage a vigorous and spontaneous opposition to this monumental political folly.

Incompatibility of Buganda Separatism and African Nationalism

In the 1920s, at the time when the seeds of Buganda separatism were being sown by such actions as her opposition to the Legislative Council, no part of the Protectorate could have opposed such moves as being contrary to national unity; the concept of nationhood did not exist; nor could any tribe, even as late as the interwar years, seriously challenge Britain's deliberate policy of sustaining Buganda as *primus inter pares* among Uganda's tribes. The formulation of what policy might be adopted in governing the country was firmly in the hands of British Protectorate officials who passed whatever legislation they needed through a Legislative Council that the Ugandan African conceived as a British monopoly. The separate development of each tribe as a district or kingdom fully and effectively kept African interest out of anything that might be happening politically on a nation-wide basis.

With the advent of Africans in the Legislative Council, especially the directly elected Africans from the elections of 1958, interest and concern for national matters began to preoccupy them. They quickly grasped the dangers of the conceived British policy to elevate Buganda beyond any reasonable proportion; consequently they began to criticise such policy. Not surprisingly, Buganda reacted by reasserting its superiority, its special position, and the charge that the other tribes were envious of her. Indeed, it is probable that the sustained criticism from the non-Baganda concerning British policy in Buganda drove the Baganda more decisively towards secession, as they now felt that the other tribes were hostile to them.

The bulk of criticism against Buganda was sensible and widespread; 1960, the year of the Buganda Memorandum, of conferences with the Colonial Secretary and the Governor, and of her "Declaration of Independence", provides representative examples of the criticisms levelled against British rule in Buganda, and against the Baganda themselves.

In a parliamentary question W. W. Nadiope from Busoga asked why the Protectorate Government should have paid for the expenses of the Kabaka and his delegation to London so that they could confer with the Colonial Secretary on Buganda's secession.[52] The Chief Secretary replied that the payment was made because "certain important aspects of constitutional development" were to be discussed.

G. B. K. Magezi, the Member for Bunyoro, tired of Buganda's claim to a "special position", reminded the Chief Secretary that under the Interpretation and General Clauses Ordinance. Buganda was as much a "local Government" as any other. This was a direct attempt to eliminate Buganda from its pedestal. Magezi then posed the question whether the Protectorate Government was equally willing to pay the expenses incurred by the Kingdom of Toro when flying its local advisers out from London; the purpose of these "advisers" was to advise Toro on the constitutional issues relative to its Agreement with the British Government.

This Council must realise that according to recent figures, this central province [Buganda] contains only one million Baganda and the rest of the population is non-Baganda [approximately 0.9 million]. . . . I believe that Buganda will not produce the answer to our problems from London, the answer is going to come from within ourselves. . . . what is required is that the Baganda themselves keep the sense of keeping Uganda as one country and trying to work with other areas.[53]

A Member for West Nile, G. Oda, protested against "favouritism" towards Buganda. A delegation from his district which visited Entebbe for discussions on constitutional issues had been required by the Protectorate Government to pay its own expenses. "Is this what we are doing here for uniformity in this country?" he asked.[54]

We have observed that Buganda's plan for an independent state claimed all the towns within its borders. The Member for Toro, J. Babiiha, posed the question:

In view of the local misunderstanding that Kampala and the national institutions therein belong to the province in which the town is situated, will Government please make a statement to the effect that Kampala is a national capital and that all provinces of the Protectorate have a claim to the national institutions in it?[55]

The Chief Secretary conceded that it was the principal town in the country and that it contained many national institutions in which the whole country had an interest.

It was demanded of the Minister of Local Government to explain to the Legislative Council what control the Uganda Government had over the finances of the Kabaka's Government.[56] This was an honest search for a method of controlling Buganda's fruitless expenditure on the Independence Committee then touring foreign countries in search of ideas and support.

Opposition to Buganda's secession was not found only in the Legislative Council; it embraced the whole country. Opposition even developed in the conferences of Katikkiros and Secretaries-General. It is relevant to quote the resolutions passed after Buganda had declared its intention to secede:

Resolution No. I:
Whereas this conference most strongly feels that Uganda should develop as a united country to independence; and whereas this is without prejudice to whatever form of Government we shall have; be it now resolved that Buganda's move to secede be condemned and that the rest of Uganda must and wishes to move

forward to independence together with Buganda, as one united country.

Resolution No. II (addressed to the Colonial Secretary):
Whereas it has come to our notice that Buganda's petition to secede has been laid before Her Majesty the Queen for consideration; and whereas it has come to our knowledge that it is your firm stand that Buganda should remain an integral part of Uganda; be it now resolved that this Conference of Katikkiros and Secretary-Generals fully and strongly endorses your stand that Buganda must remain an integral part of Uganda in view of our strong desire that Uganda moves to independence as a united country.*

It serves no useful purpose to indulge in a lengthy discourse on the proportion of blame to be assigned to Buganda for its separatism; Buganda was, naturally, like most other powerful tribes, influenced by its own history. Diligent effort is being exercised today by many Baganda and non-Baganda to bury the past dissensions and forge the bonds of single nationhood—and not without some real success.

Buganda separatism was contrary to the spirit of African unity and nationalism; Buganda's attitudes were simply tribal nationalism. These attitudes were not unknown on the African continent; they were common among the dominant tribes of Nigeria, the Yoruba, Ibos, and eventually the Hausas.[57] In Ghana, when still the Gold Coast, the forces of tradition, the Ashanteman Council, the Joint Provincial Council, and the Northern Territories Council combined in their demand for a federal constitution and an upper house.[58]

In each of these examples the traditionalists, or those who clung to tribal nationalism, were strongly opposed by the nationalists. At the All-African People's Conference held in Accra in December 1958, the following resolution was passed:

Whereas . . . some of the African traditional institutions, especially chieftaincy, do not conform to the demands of democracy

* The resolutions were drafted by G. S. K. Ibingira of the Ankole Delegation; *Minutes of the Conference of Katikkiros and Secretary-Generals Held at Fort Portal, 27th–29th October, 1960*, p. 4.

. . . actually support colonialism and constitute organs of corruption, exploitation and repression which strangle the dignity, personality and the will of the African to emancipate himself . . . Be it resolved that [they] be invited to intensify and reinforce their educational and propaganda activities with the aim of annihilating those institutions . . . and that governments of independent countries be called upon to suppress or modify these institutions.[59]

It was a strongly worded resolution. A conference of PAF-MECA held in Nairobi was attended by some leading Uganda politicians who "unreservedly" condemned the Lukiiko's secession move and called on the "Buganda government to revoke its resolution and adopt a spirit of co-operation with the rest of Uganda".[60] Opposition to Buganda separatism was not a concept evolved by "jealous" Uganda tribes: it was held in Eastern and Central Africa—in fact, continent-wide.

It was on this score, failure to keep in step with the rest of the continent, that Buganda earned itself the greatest discredit; for the domestic constitutionalists in Uganda, Buganda had emerged as the toughest single problem: on one hand was Buganda's demand to secede or to obtain full autonomy, and on the other, the unequivocal opposition to such a demand by the rest of Uganda, which insisted that Buganda be part of a unitary state after independence.

Such was the problem that confronted not only the Relationships Commission, which recommended on the form of government, but equally the two constitutional conferences which wrote Uganda's Self-Government Constitution in 1961 and her Independence Constitution in 1962.

More recent events (February–May 1966) indicate that perhaps the fears articulated by Buganda were reasonably well grounded. Practically every institution they sought to protect and preserve was destroyed by the Obote regime—the Kabakaship itself, along with the Great Lukiiko. However, to assert that this materialisation of their fears proves or justifies their previous bid to secede would be claiming that the events of 1966 were an inevitable phase of Uganda's constitutional development—which is an unacceptable thesis. The events that brought about the destruction of these two institutions of Buganda were components of Obote's manufactured "revolution" of 1966 and not a logical conclusion of our constitutional evolution.

The Demands for Federalism

To the catalogue of constitutional problems occupying the public mind we should add the idea—so tenaciously pursued yet so little understood—of "Federal Union". In the closing years of British rule the claim to federal status became such an important issue that an examination of the circumstances under which it arose may be in order. Each area developed as a separate entity without cultivating loyalty to any higher African authority; the kingdoms, most particularly Buganda, claimed to have existed as autonomous states under the British Protectorate. Consequently, and logically, they now saw no need of being brought under a strong African central authority when the British withdrew from Uganda.

It was asserted, not without controversy and confusion, that Uganda had been developed as a federal union. In their Memorandum seeking the termination of British protection the Baganda claimed this in no uncertain terms; that *after* the three western kingdoms had each concluded agreements with Britain:

> Uganda then changed its policy and began developing along federal lines. Each tribe was encouraged by British Administrative Officers as an entity in itself and the foundation of a Uganda nation was destroyed.
>
> For a period of fifty years in Uganda the British have been following the pattern of a federal form of government, that is, every tribe unto itself.[61]

Seeing that Buganda staked this claim, the Kingdom of Toro, which some witty politician referred to as "the carbon copy of Buganda", followed suit. After some hesitation Ankole and Bunyoro did the same, later followed by Busoga. But none of these claimants, except perhaps Buganda, ever defined what they meant by federal status; none made any distinction between unitary and federal forms of government. At a later date the Relationships Commission observed "some tendency for the terms to prove misleading, because many were prone to assume that they involved a clear-cut choice between something like the constitution of Great Britain and something like the constitution of the United States or Switzerland." [62]

It is convenient to discuss this issue by posing and answering a number of questions. What is federal government? Was Uganda constitutionally a federal state? What were the factors that gave rise to the desire for federalism? Why was it opposed in some areas?

A sound definition of federal government was offered by Sir Robert Garran: "A form of government in which sovereignty or political power is divided between the central and local governments so that each of them within its own sphere is independent of the other." [63]

There must be two distinct spheres of sovereign authority: one in which the Central Government alone is sovereign and empowered to act and to legislate and the other in which the local or state government itself is sovereign and competent to pass any laws or take any action it feels is necessary.

Professor Wheare, a leading authority on the subject, stated federalism to mean "the method of dividing powers so that the general and state governments are each within a sphere, co-ordinate and independent." [64]

Such are the governments of the United States, Switzerland, Australia, and Canada. It is necessary to ask, in view of this definition, if it is true that the British developed Uganda as a federal state; did all or some of its member "states", such as the Kingdom of Buganda, exercise in one sphere sovereign power and in another sphere responsibility coordinated with that of the Uganda central authority? If it did, then the claim that Uganda was federal must stand, otherwise the claim must be dismissed as being without foundation.

THE UGANDA CONSTITUTION PRIOR TO 1961

As we have observed, from the establishment of British Protection in 1893 until the Constitutional Conference of 1961, the Constitution of Uganda was never embodied in any single comprehensive document. Instead, it was embodied in Orders-in-

Council, royal instructions, and local ordinances. In the case of the kingdoms, especially Buganda, the domestic constitution, or part of it, was to some extent also embodied in the Agreements with the British Crown.

The Central Government of Uganda was formally constituted in 1920 by an Order-in-Council which established the Legislative Council, designed to legislate locally *for the whole Protectorate;* its powers—comprehensive in nature—were:

> to establish such ordinances, and to constitute such courts and officers and to make such provisions and regulations for the proceedings in such courts, and for the administration of justice, as may be necessary for the peace, order and good government.[65]

The limitations on the powers of this Council were those usually associated with a colonial legislature: the Governor's veto, his right to reserve certain bills, the ultimate power of disallowance or actual legislation by the imperial Parliament in London; the whole administration of the Protectorate was entrusted to the Governor, who was also the Commander-in-Chief. Within these limits to the exercise of imperial authority the Uganda Legislative Council was, within its territorial sphere, actually sovereign.*

There was no law that required it to exercise its authority subject to the constitutional rights of any kingdom. Consequently, there was no other authority in Uganda to claim an independent sovereign sphere of responsibility, even in a limited field; the fundamental prerequisite for federal government was therefore absent.

It is true that the Buganda Agreement of 1900 stipulated that if there were legislation contrary to the provisions of the Agreement it was to be held that such provisions constituted an exception to such legislation. We have seen that these Agreements, however elaborate, did not have the force of law; in the event of any crisis between the Protectorate Government and any native state, the British Crown could and would abrogate them with impunity. Another reason why there could be no exercise of sov-

* It is accepted in British constitutional law that within the limits imposed by the imperial Parliament, a colonial or protectorate legislature is sovereign.

ereign power for any kingdom in Uganda was the doctrine of Acts of State in British Constitutional law.[66] Since the concluding of agreements or treaties is a prerogative of the Crown and beyond challenge in the law courts, any provisions of any agreement with any native state could be legally violated by the British with impunity. For this reason the Kabaka's exile could not be successfully challenged in the courts. To recall the ruling of the Uganda Chief Justice in this case, the question of the deportation was not a justiciable issue, for the Crown was by law the judge of its own case in such a matter. The judge, in upholding the submission of the Attorney-General, said, "Whether just or unjust, politic or impolitic, beneficial or injurious," the deportation and withdrawal of recognition "was no matter on which a Court of Law could give an opinion."

Of all the Agreements with the several kingdoms, the one with Buganda was the most thorough and sacrosanct. In spite of this, and apart from the general limitations just mentioned, the Buganda Agreement, incorporating the domestic constitution of Buganda, had definite features of subordination to the British Protectorate authorities.

The powers of the local legislature of Buganda, the Great Lukiiko, appeared quite extensive: "to discuss all matters concerning the native administration of Uganda and to forward to the Kabaka resolutions which may be noted by a majority regarding measures to be adopted by the said administration." [67] Had this power been without limitation, even though it related to "native administration", it could have been argued that this was tantamount to a sovereign right; however, in the same clause this "right" was taken away:

> The Kabaka shall further consult with Her Majesty's representative in Uganda before giving effect to any such resolutions noted by the native council (the Lukiiko) and shall, in this matter explicitly follow the advice of Her Majesty's representative.[68]

This was unquestionable subordination of the Lukiiko's legislative right to that of the Protectorate Government's; there was no trace of a sovereign sphere of government for Buganda. The Agreement stipulated that the appointment of both chiefs and ministers in the Buganda Government was conditional on the approval of Her Majesty's Government.[69]

As this was a fact in Buganda kingdom, it does not need much discussion to conclude the same applied to the other kingdoms in western Uganda. Their Agreements, apart from recognizing the rulers, did not contain much more.[70] They did not spell out their domestic constitutions; on the contrary, this was done by ordinances enacted by the Legislative Council.[71]

Buganda may have claimed federal status, reinforced by the Buganda Agreement of 1955, which marked the reinstatement of the Kabaka and a redefinition of Buganda's powers, but the reforms of Charles Dundas were not backed by any sacrosanct legislative enactment; they were merely attempts to create more power for Buganda administratively. After Dundas's reforms the Protectorate Government later reversed its policy and assumed the responsibilities it had surrendered to Buganda; it was done without the need to legislate, and it was done quietly, without fuss. The 1955 Agreement was a novel development; for the first time it was stated by an Order-in-Council that certain provisions of this Agreement, when published in the *Gazette* by the Governor, would have the force of law. This was definitely an improvement on the well-established rule that such Agreements had no legal force.[72]

The comparatively extensive powers of legislation under the 1900 Agreement were repeated: the Kabaka was empowered to make laws with the advice and consent of the Lukiiko, binding upon all Africans in Buganda; this was the only provision dealing with legislative powers. As before, it was not exclusive to the Lukiiko. No law was to be enacted by the Kabaka unless the draft thereof had first been approved by the Governor.[73] Although it was stipulated that if the Agreement's provisions conflicted with Protectorate laws, such Agreement provisions would prevail, there was no substitute for the Governor's right to reject *any* legislation passed by the Lukiiko.[74]

It is true to say that the most important and most exalted institution in Buganda is the Kabakaship. If Buganda possessed any substance of federal status vested with exclusive sovereign rights in some specified spheres, the foremost among such exclusive rights would have been those of the Kabaka and the institution of monarchy; it would have been natural, it would have been proper, but this very heart of the kingdom was dependent on the will of imperial authority. The new Agreement stipulated, as did the one of 1900, that the Kabaka would be recognised as ruler of the kingdom, but this recognition of his status was dependent on his expression of loyalty to the British Crown; however, it is true that this Agreement did grant Buganda greater administrative autonomy. There was no surrender to Buganda of specific rights in respect to its relations with the Protectorate Government—it would not be independent.* Another general characteristic of federal government is some degree of financial independence; the state government must have some source of revenue that is exclusive and beyond the reach of the Central Government. This was not so in Buganda. If the Protectorate Government so chose it could cut off its grants to Buganda and bring all services to a grinding halt—compelling Buganda to submit to imperial policy. This was the subject of several complaints by Buganda against the Protectorate Government: "The Protectorate Government's action to make cuts in the Kabaka's Government grant greatly injured this kingdom." The Lukiiko pointed out that these cuts almost paralysed "The Kabaka's Government because no Government of any description can function without finance."[75]

It is clear that there was no sphere of government in which Buganda or any other kingdom or district was independent of the central authority; it is equally clear that the Protectorate Government exercised superior authority and was sovereign over the whole of Uganda. In the absence of the fumdamental prerequisite that states within a federal government each be, in certain spheres, coordinate and independent, we conclude that, in law, the British never developed Uganda as a federal union; it was unquestionably a unitary state. Evidence for this view was overwhelming in the rest of the country. As we have noticed, in

* The Buganda (Transitional Provisions) Order-in-Council, 1955, Art. 3. It is interesting to note that in the case of protected states such as those in Malaya, the native ruler was by law entitled to sovereign immunity in English courts: *Mighell v Sultan of Johare, 1894, 1 Q.B. 149, C.A.* In contrast, this had never been established as law in relation to any ruler in Uganda, not even the Kabaka of Buganda.

the African Authority Ordinance of 1919, the African Local Governments Ordinance of 1949, and the District Administrations Ordinance of 1955, which was the base for the administration of Uganda (excluding Buganda), made the authority of the chiefs and district councils completely subordinate; they had no independent authority. Since all local or "native" constitutions were enacted by laws of the central legislature, the central authority could increase, diminish, or abolish all local powers, and even their very existence.

In fact, Sir Andrew Cohen, during the tenure of his office as Governor, said publicly that Uganda was a unitary state. In a joint memorandum with the Kabaka issued in March 1953, he declared, "The Uganda Protectorate has been and will continue to be developed as a unitary state." [76]

This was not just acting on his own; he had the full backing and authorisation of the British Secretary of State to so declare.

CAUSES OF DEMANDS FOR FEDERAL UNION

Despite our conclusion that, in law, Uganda was not a federal union, the reality of there being strong tendencies towards it remained. Many of the factors that usually persuade states to form federal, as opposed to unitary, unions were present. In fact, a review of these factors helps to explain why some people held Uganda to have been, to some degree, a federal state. Why, we may ask, do states federate instead of developing some other form of union? Professor Wheare has answered this question with penetrating thoroughness and insight. There are a multitude of reasons; we may summarise the major ones as follows:

(1) a sense of military insecurity and a consequent need for common defence; a desire to be independent of foreign powers and a realisation that only through union can independence be secured;

(2) a hope of economic advantage from the union;

(3) some political association of the communities concerned prior to their federal union, either in loose confederation, as with the American states prior to 1783 and the Swiss cantons before 1846, or as part of the same empire, as with Canada, Australia, and Nigeria.[77]

All these factors were in operation in the formation of federations in America, Canada, Australia, and Switzerland, but federation may also be instigated by the imperial power, as was done in the Caribbean and Central Africa. It is obvious that they were present in regard to the kingdoms and districts of Uganda; but it is clear that these factors weighed little in the minds of the exponents of Uganda as a federal state.

The most powerful factors in Uganda were the differences among tribes: tribes had different cultures and different languages, and each, kingdom and district alike, had developed independently of the others. The division of administrative units according to tribes, with each tribe alone, or with a few minorities, being a kingdom or district by itself, accentuated this demand for independent existence, particularly in local matters.[78]

This diversity struck the Munster Commission, who recorded:

An acute conflict has arisen between national and local policies. Behind this lies the deeper antagonism between democracy and tribalism. Uganda is an artificial country with many variations of race, tribe, language, so that there is every temptation to her peoples to cultivate an exclusive tribal mentality. . . . But the sense of nationality is weakest where tribalism is strongest—most of all in Buganda, which has always had special status.[79]

Diversity of language, race, and religion alone does not necessarily lead to a federal form of government; the Union of South Africa, in which there were two distinct ruling races, the English and the Afrikaners, with different religion and language, formed a unitary state in 1910 out of the four provinces—the Orange Free State, Natal, the Cape, and Transvaal.

It is equally true that cultural differences in Switzerland, Nigeria, and Canada were directly responsible for the desire for local autonomy and for a federal, as opposed to unitary, government. In Switzerland there were German, French, Italian, and Romansch minorities and in Canada the French and English; in both cases there were different religions, Roman Catholicism and Protestantism. There was even greater diversity in Nigeria. In the same way, some people in Uganda claimed that because of the mere presence of these factors which bring about federal union, Uganda must be a federal state.

The mere presence of these factors alone does not bring about federalism. We have seen the case of South Africa, where diversity existed within a unitary rather than a federal government. Indeed, when these prerequisites for federalism exist, the people may still form a unitary state—not a federation but a confederation, a government in which the Central Government is made subject to the will of the regional governments. Such was the first constitution in the United States (1777) as embodied in the Articles of Confederation of the United States. Describing such a union, a then contemporary expert, Alexander Hamilton, stated, "In our case the concurrence of 13 distinct sovereign wills [states] is requisite, under the confederation, to the complete execution of every important measure that proceeds from the Union." [80]

In concluding this review of the factors conducive to federalism it is essential to state that the presence of proper leadership at the proper moment in history is a vital prerequisite. All other factors may be present, but if the leaders disagree and reject federal union, then it cannot work. In the United States it worked because of leaders like Washington, Hamilton, Jay, Madison, Franklin, and James Wilson; in Nigeria, because of Dr. Azikiwe, Awolowo, and the Sarduna of Sokoto. In Canada it was made possible because of John A. Macdonald and Alexander Galt. In South Africa, where factors conducive to federal union existed, leaders like Smuts, de Villiers, Merriman, and Botha did not accept it—they formed a unitary state.* No one in Uganda could claim, before the Constitutional Conference of 1961, that Uganda had, since 1900, had any recognised leaders representative of local opinion who were conscious of the need for national unity; in any event, local politicians had no political power to determine their constitution. Everything was designed according to the exclusive will of the imperial power. The British policy of indirect rule tended to create ideal conditions for federal union while, at the same time, the actual legal and constitutional set-up

---

* E. H. Walton, *The Inner History of the National Convention of South Africa*. It should be noted that the common linking factor among the South African leaders (white, not black) in considering a federated or unitary form of state was the safeguarding of the interests of the whites against the aspirations of the blacks. Thus, in this "protection" context South Africa naturally became a unitary state.

was based on unitary rule. We conclude that the mere presence of conditions conducive to federal union *does not* automatically bring about this form of government; consequently, Uganda could not have been federal simply because of the existence of some conditions conducive to federal government.

MONARCHY AS A CAUSE OF FEDERALISM

So far we have reviewed in general terms the conditions under which federal union does or does not take place. Monarchy in Uganda deserves special mention as the most powerful single factor in the demand for a federal government.

The centre of Uganda's development was the central Kingdom of Buganda. On its western border it was flanked by the smaller kingdoms of Ankole, Toro, and Bunyoro. In each of them, for generations before British rule, the king had been the highest authority. To understand the excessive tenacity to tribal rule among these kingdoms one must go back centuries to see what role the king played in his community. It would be misleading to say that it was only in relation to "primitive African tribes" that this peculiar structure of government obtained. Walter Bagehot's description of the position of a king in ancient Greece fits the rulers of any Uganda kingdom before British overrule was established:

If we carry our eyes back from historical to legendary Greece . . . We discern a government in which there is little or no scheme or system, still less any idea of responsibility to the governed, but in which the main spring of obedience on the part of the people consists in their personal feeling and reverence towards the chief. We remark, first and foremost, the King. . . . his supremacy has been inherited from his ancestors, and passes by inheritance, as a general rule to his eldest son, having been conferred upon the family as a privilege from Zeus. In war, he is the leader foremost in personal prowess, and directing all military movements; in peace, he is the general protector of the injured and oppressed; he offers up moreover those public prayers and sacrifices which are intended to obtain for the whole people the favour of the gods. An ample domain is assigned to him as an appurtenance of his lofty position, and the produce of his fields and his cattle is consecrated in part to an abundant, though rude hospitality. Moreover he receives frequent presents, to avert his enmity, to conciliate his favour, or to buy off his exactions; and when plunder is taken from the enemy, a large previous share, comprising probably the most alluring female captive, is reserved for him apart from the general distribution. Such is the position of the King in the heroic times of Greece . . . the person by whom all the executive functions, then few in number, which the society requires, are either performed or directed.[81]

Like the Stuart kings of England, the rulers of African kingdoms claimed to rule by divine right. Their position, surrounded by complementary legend, myth, and history, was that of a mystical and majestic being. Each constituted the centre of order and life in his kingdom, performing functions very much like those Bagehot attributes to the kings in Ancient Greece.[82]

The absence of a king due to death or deposition was often a prelude to disorder or chaos as rival princes contended for the throne. This was, in part, the reason why chiefs and ordinary subjects of the kingdoms were most reluctant—almost by instinct—to accept any changes in the management of their social order which might lead to the eclipse or destruction of their king or kingship. The Baganda, as often happened, voiced their highest expressions of fear over their kingship at the prospect of becoming part of a unitary state of Uganda.

This is largely the reason they made attempts to secede; their reasons were made public when they petitioned the Colonial Secretary:

Buganda is an ancient kingdom with a long history and her dynasty exceeds thirty-seven kings in an unbroken line. The history of Buganda begins with a king, and continues throughout the centuries with kingship, right up to the present day. There is not a single period in our history when the Baganda had no king ruling over them. The Baganda have a system of clans and by means of royal marriages among women of various clans, and since by custom members of the royal family belong to the clan on their mother's side, a situation has arisen in passage of time, whereby most clans have had a ruling monarch or an outstanding prince as a member of their clan. This custom has had a profound effect on Kiganda society. As a result the king in Buganda bears a personal relationship to every single Kiganda family in the kingdom. In other words it is inconceivable for a Kiganda society to exist without a king.[83]

Although the kings in the western province did not practise the same system of marrying into all the clans or requiring their princes to adopt their mothers' clans, it could be said they occupied a like position in their respective kingdoms to that of the Kabaka in Buganda. For ages it was unthinkable that the ruler of a kingdom should be subject to any other person. Even after British rule had been established, the only modification of this view was the acceptance of the Governor and the British Crown. It was possible for the kingdoms to reconcile their pride to this limitation of their rulers' power because it had an alien source. Although effectively established, the imperial power was still regarded as remote, and since it did not interfere with the daily life of the rulers and their subjects, it became tolerable and acceptable, even without consideration of its superior military strength.

When it suddenly became clear that the British were to leave and were, obviously, to be replaced by African politicians, the reaction was considerably different: there was fear that Uganda African politicians succeeding the British might exercise their new-found power in such a manner as to eclipse or even destroy the various kings. This fear became greater because most of Uganda's tribes were not monarchies, and from these tribes—as it later happened—might emerge the future leaders that would displace the British.

There was also the preservation of traditional feudal dignity to consider; the kingdoms generally believed they were more advanced than the other areas. Buganda, the "chosen tribe" under British rule, was itself a strong kingdom. It became unthinkable that a commoner from Buganda, or worse, a man from a republican tribe, might secure a position above that of the Kabaka. This feeling prompted them to challenge the Colonial Secretary's statements that the future of Uganda's kings and the kingdom governments would be determined by a conference of Elected Members of Parliament: "The right of the Legislative Council to discuss the status of a monarch who was responsible for the introduction of British Protection over the whole of Uganda is highly questionable".[84]

There was another overwhelming reason why the kingdoms opposed a unitary state: their societies were essentially feudal. In this system the chiefs played a leading role and their appointment had always depended on the favouritism of the rulers. Democratically elected kingdom assemblies are of recent origin. Those in privileged positions in the kingdom governments believed that attempts to democratise their institutions, including above all the removal of the kings from politics, must be resisted, or otherwise democracy would destroy their power and privilege; history was to prove them correct.

But the forces of progress could not be held back for long; the kingdoms, even Buganda, leading champion in this reluctance to change, had to recognise that Uganda, including themselves, had to develop as a single nation. The natural course for them to follow was the demand for a federal constitution in which they would exercise exclusive powers relating to such matters as kingship and traditional customs.

It was because of this train of thought that the rulers of all the kingdoms—Ankole, Buganda, Bunyoro, and Toro—initiated the "Kings or Rulers Conferences." For the first time in their history the Uganda kings marshalled combined action to find ways and means to safeguard their traditional rights and positions.

On 20 February 1960 they issued their historic "Rulers Proclamation"; the full text is of interest:

WE the traditional Rulers of the Ancient Kingdoms of Ankole, Buganda and Toro, who symbolise the tried customs, ideals and achievements of our people,

WHEREAS we are concerned that our peoples be free to choose their form of Government without fear or prejudice,

AND WHEREAS we are desirous that national liberty shall not be achieved at the expense of individual freedom and ideals,

WE THEREFORE have invited our Ministers to take counsel together to devise means whereby our peoples may live together in amity and contentment being secured against possible exploitation by any individual or minority group,

AND to discuss practical courses of mutual action which will advance the economic and cultural wealth of our people,

AND to discuss means to safeguard the rights of the people to choose and change their own form of government without FEAR or FAVOUR.*

It was signed by the Omugabe of Ankole, the Kabaka of Buganda, and the Omukama of Toro. Because of his long-standing quarrel with the Kabaka, the Omukama of Bunyoro did not participate. His absence, however, did not mean he disagreed with this endeavour to confirm the future position of the kingdoms after Uganda's independence.

THE CONFERENCE OF KATIKKIROS AND SECRETARIES-GENERAL

Following their issue of the "Proclamation", the rulers organised a meeting of their Katikkiros to discuss ways of implementing it. The meeting was held in Mmengo and opened by the Kabaka on 2 March 1960; he referred to the meeting as "the most historic occasion in the annals of the four ancient kingdoms and Uganda at large."

The Katikkiros soon discovered that without support from the whole country their efforts stood little chance of success. Motivated by a desire to preserve their traditional institutions, along with a determined spirit of cooperation with the other tribes of Uganda, they requested the Governor to allow them to hold a full conference with all the Secretaries-General; they put their views to the Governor eloquently:

Your Excellency,

. . . we are agreed that for the peoples in the kingdoms to live together in amity and contentment they must have friendly relationships with the rest of Uganda. And our considered opinion is that the best means to bring this about, is by the Secretary-Generals and ourselves holding a round table conference in the near future to discuss our common problems.†

* This account was made available to me by the Omuhikirwa (Prime Minister) of Toro Kingdom, Mr. Samson Rusoke.

† The letter was dated 7 April 1960 and was signed by all of them.

The Governor consented to such a meeting taking place, and it proved to be the forerunner of many like meetings. The birth of this conference was of historic significance; it was the first time leaders of local administrations—each had always regarded itself as a "state"—came together to know one another and to understand each other's problems. Unquestionably it was a creditable achievement through the initiative of the kings; no doubt their main purpose was to canvass support of federal status for their respective kingdoms, but, once initiated, the conference was not the monopoly of this pressure group; politicians soon invaded it.

A new chapter in the march towards unity, although at the eleventh hour, had been opened. This was demonstrated by the remarks of the Chairman of the conference, the Secretary-General of Bukedi District, when he addressed the Colonial Secretary, who was present in Uganda at the time:

> Sir, the 17th day of May, 1960, saw the birth of the first conference of the Prime Ministers and Secretary-Generals of Uganda. It was on that day sir, that the said leaders of Uganda, for the first time, tried jointly to solve their own problems. It was the first time that we tried to find out the community of points between us, and to avoid exaggerating our differences. We have now succeeded to establish a strong personal relationship between the needs of the various local governments, a strong feeling of oneness in spite of differences, a pride of being Ugandans, and a determination to do all we can for its progress.*

In view of the disagreements and divergencies of view which were soon to follow in the months ahead, it may be possible the Chairman claimed just a bit too much unity, certainly more than actually existed—but there can be no question that his words reflected a definite, positive trend.

The conference met from time to time, as the need arose, to usefully discuss a wide range of topics affecting local administrations. The highlight arrived when the Katikkiros began canvassing for federal status. Since a commission was shortly to be established to make recommendations on what form of

* This was contained in a Memorandum handed to the Secretary of State on 20 September 1960.

government would best suit Uganda, it was openly proposed by the Katikkiro of Buganda, at a meeting held at Makerere, that Uganda adopt a federal form of government.* The result was a severe blow to Buganda; there was no one to support it—not even Buganda's fellow kingdoms.

It was not because the concept of federal status was rejected; the disagreement with Buganda rested on the form or approach to be followed. The Buganda delegates wanted a commitment made to federalism before any other steps were taken. The others preferred, with enthusiasm and unanimity, the implementation of the major recommendations made by the Constitutional Committee. In effect, if these proposals were implemented a considerable degree of power would automatically be placed in the hands of the politicians associated with the Legislative Council.

The issue of what form the government should take continued to hold public attention until the Uganda Constitutional Conferences were held.

Opinion vacillated for and against federalism except in Buganda, where the Baganda were spearheading the drive for the establishment of federalism. At the fifth meeting of Katikkiros and Secretaries-General held at Gulu the issue was extensively debated, and a wide divergence of opinion resulted. Among the kingdoms, Buganda and Toro supported federal status. While declining to use the terms "federal" and "unitary", Ankole described a form of governmental set-up that called for a treble chamber, making it clear that such a scheme could only exist within a federal pattern. Like Ankole, Bunyoro did not use these specific terms, but, unlike any other kingdom, it advocated a strong central government.[85]

There was also a division of opinion among the districts. West Nile (with its nine tribes), Bugisu, Kigezi, Karamoja, and Lango, while conceding the necessity for constitutional safeguards for the kingdoms, vigorously argued for a strong central government based on Uganda's current constitutional structure, which was unitary Madi district was divided on the issue.

It would be wrong to say that opinion in the western king-

* The Resolution for Federalism, moved on 18 May 1960.

doms was unanimous for federalism. In Ankole, and among enlightened people in Toro, there was a strong undercurrent from the intelligentsia, who were firmly in favour of a unitary form of government; however, it would not be true to say that all the non-monarchical districts favoured unitary rule. It is on record that the districts of Madi and Acholi advocated a federal government on a provincial basis as the best means of withstanding Buganda domination.[86]

The absence of a sufficient number of influential people who understood the precise meaning of, and the distinction between, the terms federal and unitary, along with a lack of willingness to accept advice from those who knew better, resulted in the generation of much heat with too little light. Many views were fortified by arguments whose foundations were rooted in ignorance or half-knowledge of how the fears or needs of each area could best be satisfied in a united and independent Uganda.

For this reason the Governor made an effort on 16 August 1961 to advise the Conference of Katikkiros and Secretaries-General held at Jinja:

> Much has been said about whether various parts of Uganda should be in federal, semi-federal or in unitary relationship with each other. I prefer not to deal with the problem in this way but to consider the form of relationship rather than what it is called. If a cook bakes you a cake you do not worry what it is called, but what it tastes like and what it is made up of.[87]

While the commoners were busily engaged, the kingdom rulers were devising other ways of seeking support for federalism; their objective was to bring a uniformity based on their own pattern to the structure of all districts. They wanted each district to have a "constitutional head" who would be equal to them. They hoped to promote a desire for federal union and gather sufficient sympathy for it to materialise, particularly since each district would then feel on a par with the kingdoms.

On 16 November 1960 the Chairman of the Kings' Conference held in Bunyoro addressed his views to the Chairmen of all the District Councils:

> . . . it has been decided and agreed upon by the Uganda Kings'

Conference held at Masindi from 14th to 16th November, 1960, that each District be represented by one Ceremonial Head to be recognised as the Symbolic Leader of that particular District and to have a seat in the Kings and Leaders Conference of Uganda in the future Government for the Protectorate. . . .

For your information this conference is firmly of the opinion that due to the special circumstances obtaining in Uganda a federal form of Government is the only suitably applicable system for the future Uganda.[88]

THE STAND OF PARTIES ON THE FEDERATION ISSUE

We have been considering the activities of local government officials who, although they wielded powerful influence, were, strictly speaking, civil servants or traditional conservative rulers. By this time the Uganda politicians inevitably entered the controversy on what form Government should take, it is fair to say they were also divided in opinion.

In the Legislative Council the issue increasingly caught the attention of Members. C. J. Obwangor made the following remarks amid applause from most of the African representatives:

I wish on my part to express that our sole aim as far as we are concerned with our people, should be the unitary form of government in this country. A federal form of government in politics and economics, as far as the area and conditions of Uganda are concerned may be, believe me, selfishness and shortsightedness, because to deal with the practical and financial affairs of the country would be very costly. I disagree entirely with my colleague Mr. Musazi, when he mentioned in the budget debate that this country should be developed on a federal form of Government; I was horribly shocked.[89]

Even a representative from the Kingdom of Bunyoro, G. B. Magezi, stated in the Council that he would never "suffer federal government" because he felt "it would be a disadvantage to the people outside Buganda to accept a federal form of Government." [90]

In the demand for a strong central government the politicians in the Legislative Council were supported by the Protectorate

Government; in 1957 Governor Cohen made this point clear in one of his most moving speeches to the Legislative Council:

> When self-government is achieved, a strong central government will be needed so that this country may take its place in the world, so that it may provide the people with the services and the life which they need and want and so that it may lead the country in further progress and development. . . . We are the trustees for the central government of the future, which, when self-government comes, will be a government of the people of the country. . . . In all actions, and particularly in our relations with the native governments and district authorities throughout the country, we must bear in mind this responsibility of trusteeship for the central government of the future.
>
> No one can justly accuse us of being a government with overcentralised tendencies. A remarkable devolution of authority for local services is in process of taking place in the different parts of the country as a result of the reforms of last year. But if excessive demands are made, demands which appear to encroach on the rights, responsibilities, functions or revenues of the central government of the future, it is our duty as trustees for that government to resist such demands. We certainly intend to carry out that duty.[91]

Even by 1960, when two political parties had already emerged which favoured a strong central government (D.P. and U.P.C.), they could not afford to be so bold as to reject federalism out of hand without running a definite risk of losing substantial support.

If the general tenor of African Members of the Legislative Council was in favour of a strong central government, there is no doubt they and the Protectorate Government were also in favour of safeguarding the position of the kings; whenever it was found necessary to reassure people on this issue it was always done. In February 1959 the Governor made what he called "an important statement" on the position of hereditary rulers:

> When the Secretary of State was in Uganda in October, 1958, he made it clear that he, as I, believed strongly in maintaining the prestige and dignity of the rulers and that it would be a continuing anxiety of the British Government to see how their standing and prestige could be preserved in any constitutional changes. . . .

These views . . . remain unaltered. Although it is still too soon to say what the constitution of Uganda will be before or when self-government is eventually achieved, I wish to make it clear that it is the government's firm intention to seek provision in all constitutional development to secure to the hereditary rulers a position which will appropriately reflect their traditional status and prestige.[92]

OPPOSITION TO FEDERAL GOVERNMENT

We have noted some of the reasons for a federal government as articulated by the pro-kingdom advocates, but those who opposed the schemes set forth by the kingdoms did not lack genuine grounds.

It is considered that in a federal union the greater the parity of states in the union the better; it is unsuitable that such a union should be contracted when a single member state is so powerful as to dictate to the other union states. Such was the position of Prussia in the German Empire.[93] When one state is able to dictate policy, then even a union as loose as a confederation can be transformed into a unitary state.

John Stuart Mill accurately noted:

. . . there should not be any one state so much more powerful than the rest as to be capable of vying in strength with many of them combined. If there be such a one, and only one, it will insist on being master of the joint deliberations: if there be two, they will be irresistible when they agree; and whenever they differ everything will be decided by a struggle for ascendancy between the rivals.[94]

This was precisely the problem Uganda faced: not the districts against the kingdoms, but the other kingdoms and districts versus the Kingdom of Buganda. By virtue of history, geography, and economy it was feared that under a federal union Buganda might get away with too large a share—certainly larger than that of any one of them, or even greater than that of all of them put together. Because of this fear Madi and Acholi revived the idea of establishing Provincial Assemblies in the north, east, and west as the best way to combat Buganda domination.[95]

This does not mean there has to be absolute equality of states before they federate; some divergence in size between the units is almost certain to exist before federal union is even desired—this is a typical feature of modern federations. The first Dominion of Canada was formed when the maritime provinces of New Brunswick and Nova Scotia federated with the more prosperous, more populous province of Quebec, which then included Ontario. The Australian states of Western Australia, Tasmania, and South Australia, with their small, predominantly agricultural population, federated with the more populous industrialized states of New South Wales and Victoria. In all these cases it has been essential that the weak not be oppressed by the powerful; that each unit derive benefit from union.

In the countries of Asia and Africa the struggle for federalism within a single state has been motivated by traditional and conservative elements, as opposed, in general, to nationalist movements. In India, apart from its enormous size and population, it was because of the demands of Indian "princely" states that the Indian Constitution of 1935 was enacted, conferring autonomy on the various states.

In Ghana, in 1953, the Ashanteman Council, the Joint Provincial Council, and the Northern Territories Council—in short, the forces of tradition—combined to demand a federal constitution for Ghana as a direct result of their fear that the nationalists would do away with traditional institutions.[96]

It took a commission to enquire into the desirability of federalism in Ghana before it was rejected; a compromise was found in the establishment of Regional Assemblies along the same lines as those suggested for Uganda by the districts of Madi and Acholi.[97]

In Uganda, also, the issue of federalism had reached such magnitude that it required a commission of experts, the Relationships Commission, to make recommendations on the most appropriate form of government for Uganda.

6. The Munster Commission of 1961

The demands of the swiftly rising nationalist parties for immediate independence contrasted sharply with the forces of tradition demanding federal union and safeguards for their institutions; inevitably this brought a clash of interests in Uganda which could best be resolved by a detached, competent commission. There were other serious matters that required expert opinion before the Uganda Constitutional Conference could ably discuss them: the "Lost Counties" issue and various other boundary disputes, the powers to be exercised by the district councils, and the financial relationships of the various parts of Uganda with the central government.

The need for appointing a commission to recommend solutions to these problems had been admitted as early as Sir Andrew Cohen's era. It was a most welcome announcement when the *Uganda Gazette* of 15 December 1960 published the appointment of the Relationships Commission or, as it became popularly known, the Munster Commission.

Its terms of reference were:

To consider the future form of government best suited to Uganda and the question of the relationship between the central government and the other authorities in Uganda, bearing in mind,

(a) Her Majesty's Government's known resolve to lead Uganda by appropriate stages to independence and to this end to develop stable institutions of government which will properly reflect the particular circumstances and meet the needs of Uganda; and

(b) the desire of the peoples of Uganda to preserve their existing institutions and customs and the status and dignity of their rulers and leaders; and

(c) the special relationship that already exists between Her Majesty's Government and His Highness the Kabaka's Government and the Native Governments of Bunyoro, Ankole and Toro as set down in the various Agreements that have been made with the traditional rulers and peoples of Buganda, Bunyoro, Ankole and Toro, and to make recommendations.[1]

Clearly, it was a comprehensive mandate; equally clear was the dominating concern for the pacification of the traditional forces in the kingdoms, particularly Buganda.

The Commission began its work in January 1961 during a period of great political excitement in the country. Buganda had declared its "independence" only a month before, after effectively blocking the registration of voters.[2] In areas other than Buganda political campaigns were widespread in anticipation of the first country-wide general election to be held in March.

There was no district or kingdom the Commission did not visit in its search for information. True, the Kabaka's Government—in a mood of fictitious independence—declined to cooperate.[3] The Kabaka personally met the Commission and later stated that the case for his government was contained in the pamphlet *Buganda's Independence*, a copy of which was given to the Commission. In other areas the Commission received enthusiastic support from the public in the execution of its formidable task.

The various constitutional and political problems facing the country vividly struck the Commission. Before proceeding towards a detailed analysis of the Munster Report, it might be of interest to note, in general, the Commission's reaction to the necessity and effects of indirect rule.[4] While admitting that the development of native governments side by side with British administration would lead to "inevitable conflict", they exonerated

British policy as having been the only sensible approach to native institutions.

British policy always assumed the existence of infinite time for the peaceful, harmonious fusion of indigenous and British systems of government. The Commission was correct on this point when it asserted:

> The essence of the present crisis is time, Uganda's constitutional progress cannot proceed in the leisurely style of Britain's. A constitutional conference is to assemble within a few months and a realistic plan must be made now. Yet this is the most awkward juncture, when the strength of Buganda's tribal government is at its zenith, and the democratic system imported by Britain is relatively new and inexperienced.[5]

Against this background the Commission rejected a unitary form of government as an unalterable British policy for Uganda; they recorded the gravity of the situation lucidly:

> The prospect that the country might disintegrate, and suffer miseries like the Congo, had suddenly become a real source of anxiety. Against this background the hypothesis of a unitary state could no longer be taken for granted. The whole question needed to be studied afresh, and this was in substance the commission entrusted to us.[6]

In the light of the above attitude it might be useful, at this juncture, to examine the Commission's findings and recommendations under specific headings.

Buganda

It was recognised that Buganda enjoyed a special status by virtue of its Agreements with Britain; the 1955 Agreement, especially, left Buganda with considerable administrative autonomy, but the question of whether Buganda enjoyed, legally, federal status was never specifically answered. It would have been impolitic to say Buganda had no federal status, however legally sound such a statement may have been. Indeed, the Commission seemed to support Buganda's claim to federalism when they acknowledged, "Buganda is thus a state within a state, enjoying a considerable degree of independence and protected by treaty." [7] Buganda was even ranked by the commission as "a native state" when, in law, this had never been decided and when in fact it had only been the embryo of a colonial Protectorate established in 1893.*

Although the 1955 Buganda Agreement made the Kabaka—on paper at least—a constitutional monarch, in reality the commission found it beyond doubt "that great policy-making power remains in the hands of the Kabaka personally, so that he, advised by one or two dominant ministers, has the effective direction of affairs".

ON BUGANDA SECESSION

The Commission found that opposition to Buganda's secession was not from non-Baganda alone, but came also from "the more intelligent Baganda." It is striking that even in Buganda, apart from the Kabaka's Government, no witnesses testified in favour of secession. However sympathetic members of the Commission may have been towards Buganda, they felt bound to reject the idea of Buganda seceding, and their reasons were those held by every serious-minded Ugandan at the time. Having observed that "the loss of this territory by secession would remove the heart from the country", they stated:

> The plain fact is that secession would be likely to be the first move towards the break-up of Uganda, substituting a number of weak and unstable countries for one that could be strong, and stable. . . . But worse than that, there would be grave danger of civil war, as in the Congo. We do not voice this apprehension lightly.

With this distinct possibility in view the Commission proceeded to propose federal status for the Kingdom of Buganda.

CONSTITUTIONAL STATUS OF BUGANDA

Federal Relationship. Buganda's relation with Uganda was, in substance, to be federal because "for many practical purposes it is federal already."

* In para. 94, the Commission observed, "Buganda is a native state of exceptional strength and cohesion."

Division of Power. There was to be a division of powers as in a usual federal type, giving some exclusive powers to the central government and some exclusive powers to Buganda but leaving the residuary power in the hands of both with a provision that in case of conflict the central government's legislation should override Buganda legislation.[8]

For the first time the features of Uganda federalism were introduced and, as Professor Wheare has said, "both the Central and Buganda Governments were each within a sphere, to be co-ordinate and independent",[9] it was a recommendation unknown to the Uganda constitutional set-up. We can conclude that when the Commission claimed that Buganda was "for many practical purposes federal already", it was not referring to its status in strict constitutional law but rather to the devolution of administrative responsibility to Buganda for the management of many local services. To confer actual federal status it was recommended that the Governor's powers of veto over Buganda legislation (reserved under the 1955 Agreement) should automatically cease and not pass to the future central government.[10] It was no longer necessary for the Kabaka to swear an oath of allegiance to the British Crown pledging his cooperation with the Protectorate Government.[11]

Buganda's Exclusive Powers. The sphere in which Buganda was independent and alone possessed the right to legislate covered the following:

(1) the Kabakaship;

(2) the Kabaka's Government—i.e., the status and duties of his ministers and the management of the public service and local government in Buganda (subject to urban exceptions). The Buganda Appointments Board was to be affiliated with the Public Service Commission of Uganda, and its higher judicial appointments were to be made on the advice of the Uganda Judicial Service Commission;

(3) the Lukiiko, its powers and procedure; and

(4) such further traditional customary matters as Buganda might ask to have included and which might appear to concern only the tribe and not other races or the rest of the country.

It was emphasized that these would be absolute legal guarantees "unalterable to Buganda's disadvantage without Buganda's own consent".[12] They would be "markedly stronger than, for example, the guarantees provided by the Constitution of the United States, where the requisite majorities can alter the constitution against the wishes of up to one quarter of the states". The Commission emphasized that "these guarantees would be legally enforceable, with an ultimate appeal outside Uganda so as to ensure complete impartiality." In fact, it was recommended that the ultimate Court of Appeal for such constitutional matters should be the Privy Council in London.

To disarm Buganda's grave apprehension for her future, it was emphasized that "no guarantees of equal strength were given to either the Asantehene in Ghana or to the Princes in India, whose eclipse the traditionalist party are fond of citing".*

The Uganda Government's Exclusive Powers. On certain reserved subjects the Lukiiko would have no legislative power, such as constitutional matters, foreign affairs, nationality, the armed forces, the national police force, and the fields of taxation at that time belonging to the central government.[13]

Direct Elections to the Lukiiko. It was recommended that the Lukiiko be directly elected on the same electoral law as operated for the National Assembly. Although the Commission acknowledged "some danger of the Kabaka's Government exercising undue influence" in the elections, it was thought that this would not be enough "to endanger the experiment seriously".

Optional Indirect Elections to the National Assembly. The Constitution of Uganda should specify Buganda's obligation to send representatives to the National Assembly by specified alternative methods of election, direct or indirect.[14] the choice of election method being left to the Buganda Lukiiko to decide.[15] No other recommendation made by the Commission was subjected to more passionate political attack than this one for indirect elections. Under these circumstances it would be unreasonable to contend that this was too high a price to pay for the paci-

---

* Munster Report, para. 154, "Sanctions for Guarantees". It is true that in Ghana no similar entrenchment and guarantees were made. See the Ghana (Constitution) Order-in-Council, 1957, S.I. 1957 No. 277.

fication and persuasion of Buganda to accept the prospect of remaining an integral part of Uganda. As the Commission stated:

> We have to find some kind of bridge across the gulf between tribalism and democracy. Any device which will provide this is of great importance at the present point in time, whatever shortcomings it may have in the opinion of purists.[16]

It was nevertheless provided that if Buganda should refuse to send representatives to the Central Legislature, or if it should attempt to withdraw its representatives, there would be provision for direct elections to be held—as was done in 1961—against the wishes of the Lukiiko if the need arose.

On the Kabaka and Other Rulers. We have noted that the monarchy, as an institution, was to be entrenched with the firmest possible guarantees but that it also made a strong recommendation:

> Looking ahead, it seems that the best security for the Kabaka and other rulers is not to oppose the swiftly rising tide of democracy, but to accept the position of constitutional rulers with a guaranteed position in the new state. Even if they have doubts about the value of guarantees in the long run, they are much more likely to endanger their thrones if they disrupt the country's unity and delay its independence for their own sakes.[17]

This was indeed sound advice. To put it differently, as Walter Bagehot wrote on English monarchy: "Probably in most cases the greatest wisdom of a constitutional king would show itself in well considered inaction." [18] The future of the Kabaka and the other rulers lay in their acceptance of change and their assumption of a new role in their kingdoms as constitutional monarchs acting on the advice of their elected ministers. It was a sound theory to recommend, although its practicality in reality was considerably in doubt.

The Commission had gone a long way to meet Buganda; they offered it exclusive legislative powers over the institutions most dear to its mode of life. They guaranteed to Buganda the soundest constitutional safeguards then feasible. As a result of these safeguards, along with great persuasion by her well-wishers, Buganda eventually but reluctantly agreed to formally drop her secession argument. However, at the same time that these safe-guards were being prepared Buganda, through the constitutional conferences, was still attempting to press her demands for complete independence; only this time she was doing so under the guise of federalism. All the same, this recommendation of federal status was a sound and fair compromise between the concept of a unitary state at one extreme and secession at the other.

Constitutional Status of the Western Kingdoms

Comparing the western kingdoms—Ankole, Bunyoro, and Toro—with Buganda relative to the premise that Buganda was a native state, the Commission observed that these kingdoms "occupy an ambiguous position, being neither full native states nor yet ordinary local authorities." It noted, "the Agreements made with these kingdoms have not given them administrative independence of the kind given to Buganda." The rulers of these kingdoms wanted a federal government with each of their kingdoms as a member state of the union, but unlike Buganda they strongly advocated a united Uganda and were firmly opposed to secession by any part of the country.[19]

Not forgetting their claim to federal status, it was long known that these three kingdoms had never had federal status and that they could not afford to have federal status. Governor Crawford brought this home when addressing the conference of Katikkiros and Secretaries-General at Jinja:

> In view of the size of these kingdoms and in view of their greater reliance on the central government for services, money and staff it is clearly not possible to give them so great a measure of autonomy as can be given to the much richer and larger Buganda.[20]

It was not unexpected that the Commission would recommend, instead of full federal status, semi-federal status for them;* the element of federalism lay in the fact that they alone would have legislative power or "immunity from interference", as it was put, in relation to the following matters:[21]

* Toro's demands for full federal powers were noted but rejected. Munster Report, paras. 132–33.

(1) the kingship and the customary law of succession to it;
(2) the ruler's "right to give formal assent to measures passed by his Council";
(3) the ruler's "right of formal appointment of ministers, chiefs and other officials";
(4) royal ceremonial functions and traditions;
(5) local languages; and
(6) special features of local culture, such as local customary marriage laws. In respect of the foregoing each kingdom was to have the same guarantees as those accorded to Buganda.[22]

In other respects these kingdoms were to remain very much as before; i.e., they were to operate as components of local government and the powers of their Councils would be the same as those given to the other districts.

A legal fiction was proposed to pacify the kingdoms for having been denied equal status with Buganda; it was noted, "In law their legislation will be bye-laws". It was then recommended that the by-laws should be called "laws" to mark the special status of the Councils and these rulers' constitutional right to give formal assent to laws.[23]

Constitutional Status of
the Districts

Concerning the other districts—the Eastern and Northern Provinces plus Kigezi—the Commission recommended a unitary relation with the Central Government. Not only were some of these districts "of recent creation and of questionable strength",[24] but their argument was overwhelmingly against federation and in favour of a strong central government based on the form existing in Uganda at the time, 1961, but with growing local governments.

One of the most interesting developments was the demand of these districts to have constitutional or ceremonial heads; there is no doubt that this demand was adopted from the kingdoms. It was regarded not only as dignified for each district to have a constitutional head but also as a demonstration of equality with

Buganda—if not in the spirit of "what you can do I can do better", then certainly in one of "what you have I also can achieve". We noted how the rulers themselves suggested the creation of these posts in the various districts; whatever the motives might have been, the desire for district constitutional heads had become firmly established.

As early as 1940 Busoga had created its own constitutional head, the Kyabazinga; in 1960 Lango instituted the Won Nyaci; and Kigezi was unyielding in its appeal to the Governor to establish a Rutakirwa.

It was recognised that these demands were basically "symptoms of tribalism which should not be unnecessarily encouraged".[25] It was also accepted that "the future constitution must recognise African wishes and plan in African terms." It was eventually conceded that districts wanting ceremonial heads could have them.[26]

The Self-Government Constitution

Each of the component states of Uganda was given a position, as far as was possible, commensurate with its history, tradition, and wishes. Buganda became a federal state and acquired a degree of autonomy she had never enjoyed even under British rule as did the other kingdoms with their semi-federal status. Being closely attached to the centre—the districts soon learned—was the best safeguard against Buganda's demands, while, at the same time, it was also the best method of acquiring needed services.[27]

In one way it was an ingenious semi-federal constitution; in effect it was a federation between Buganda and the rest of the country, despite the semi-federal status of the other kingdoms. Viewed in this way there was no region strong enough to dominate the rest and none weak enough to be taken undue advantage of. Like so many aspects of Uganda's constitutional evolution and government, the recommended form of government, or the "future constitution", was a well-balanced compromise.

In addition to the basic structure of government there were

other matters intimately connected with the basic constitution which the Commission considered.

The contest in public opinion over the form of government had led some, particularly in the kingdoms, to believe that a second chamber would provide a suitable place in the new constitution for the rulers; in addition to the rulers, all the district constitutional heads would be members. In this way, it was felt, the rulers could keep in touch and influence political trends and thus safeguard their positions.*

The issue of whether or not a bicameral legislature was desirable for Uganda had been considered by the Constitutional Committee in 1958. If the second chamber was to be composed of traditional rulers with the power to delay or reject some acts of the lower house—as had been suggested—then, it was feared, this would lead to a "clash between the traditional rulers and the political leaders which it is vital should be avoided if—as is every one's wish—the traditional rulers are to survive as institutions".[28]

A few years later the Relationships Commission held the same objection to rulers' membership in a second chamber:

> By their presence in the second chamber and by having some measure of political power, they would aggravate the antagonism between the political parties and themselves. They would be tempted to take part in national politics, so that they might easily become involved in contests with the elected House, in which the political parties would find pretexts for attacking the position of the rulers.[29]

For this reason the proposal for the creation of a second chamber was rejected.

There was, however, a more plausible argument: the Constitutional Committee conceded that a second chamber composed of Elected or Nominated Members might serve a useful purpose in the future, especially after the Governor's reserve powers were abolished.

* Such proposals were contained in the *Memorandum of the Eishengyero Relationships Committee.*

The Relationships Commission was "more impressed" by the argument for a second chamber based on the form of the United States Senate. Still, they rejected the principle of a bicameral Parliament and recommended a unicameral system; their main reason was a need for simplicity: "We think it better that the future constitution should be clear, simple and financially economical. We conclude, therefore, that the arguments against a second chamber outweigh those in favour of it." [30]

The desire for a second chamber was not peculiar to Uganda's political and constitutional evolution; it was held in other emerging dependencies. In Nigeria, by virtue of its size, wealth, population, and structure, it was a natural development.[31] In Ghana, a country the size of Uganda, the forces of tradition combined to demand federalism and a second chamber. It is of interest to note that the scheme was rejected there on precisely the same grounds as in Uganda:

> . . . it has been observed that the establishment of a second chamber might be a cause of friction between the chiefs and the people, particularly if important legislation were delayed by the conservatism of traditional members in the upper house. The interests of the chiefs and of their people should be the same, and accordingly it is open to question whether there should be separate representation of traditional authorities.[32]

THE HEAD OF STATE

The question of who was eventually to be Uganda's Head of State had been one on which the kingdoms held strong emotional views; it was subtly tucked under the cloak of "what form of government" and the repeated demands for federal status.

Contrary to popular belief, the Baganda negotiators at the several Constitutional Conferences never formally proposed that the Kabaka should be Head of State, but his position was given such pre-eminence among their collective demands that they must have expected their listeners to assume that he should eventually become Uganda's Head of State.

They demanded that no one, not even the Prime Minister, was

to take precedence over the Kabaka in Buganda regardless of the function; the only exception to this demand that they were prepared to concede was for Her Majesty's representative, since they assumed there would be a British Governor-General. The Baganda also made certain that even the country's capital city, Kampala, in addition to Entebbe, the seat of government, was to be Buganda territory in which the Kabaka was entitled to precedence over anyone else.[33]

The rulers of the other kingdoms came out strongly against any compromise with Buganda that might give the Kabaka any grounds for eligibility as Head of State; in this argument they had sympathy and active support from some districts. They recommended to the Commission that a Council of State consisting of themselves and the constitutional heads of the districts should elect the Head of State.[34]

In newspapers and on political platforms in Buganda it was strongly demanded that the Kabaka should have the post of Head of State. Everyone knew there would be no political power attached to the position; nor would it be right to say that the rulers wanted this post because of the emoluments attached to it. It was coveted mostly because of prestige and dignity—and for this reason it was a highly emotional issue.

The Commission prudently recommended that the post should be held by an expatriate Governor-General during internal self-government "so as to allow time for the problem of a future African Head of State to be debated further in Uganda in the new atmosphere which independence will bring".[35] It is an astonishing example of the effects and influence of indirect rule that these rulers, and indeed the ruled, delighted in the prospect of their former colonial master continuing to hold the most dignified position in the state after independence in preference to one of their own Uganda citizens, regardless of his tribe.

PARLIAMENT

Views on occasion differed as to the composition and size of Parliament, but this was not one of the leading points of controversy. What the Commission recommended concerning Parliament had already been accepted by the people in general.

The National Assembly. The national legislature (at this time called the Legislative Council) was to continue under the title of the National Assembly.* Legislative power would reside in it, with the formal assent of the Head of State. After independence the National Assembly, as normally happens, would become a sovereign legislature subject to the entrenched rights of the four kingdoms and the other restrictions incorporated in the constitution.

Membership of the Assembly. No specific recommendations were made on the size of the National Assembly because it was felt that the new Assembly "should evolve out of the present Legislative Council as smoothly as possible", but it was recommended that Ministerial Members should no longer be sitting ex officio.

The Assembly was to be elected, as the Wild Committee had recommended in 1959, by universal adult franchise on a common roll subject to Buganda's opinion for indirect elections. The Commission had witnessed how effectively registration and elections had been boycotted in Buganda. With this in mind they recommended the registration of electors under compulsory powers which would impose penalties for failure to supply information to the registration officer. It observed, "if some such system had been in force, it would have been much harder for the Kabaka's Government to frustrate the registration of electors in Buganda last year." [36]

It was recommended that the life of the Assembly, like that of the British Parliament, should have a maximum span of five years subject to earlier dissolution by the Head of State acting on the advice of the Prime Minister.[37]

Parliamentary Government. If a government was defeated on a vote of confidence, the constitution should provide expressly for its resignation. Having noted that "good progress" was already being made, it was recommended that the British Conven-

* At this time the membership was 101, excluding the Speaker but including 82 Directly Elected and 9 Specially Elected Members.

tions of cabinet government should be followed so far as possible.

We will speak more on what brought about the existence of the Opposition in parliamentary democracy; we will also examine its desirability. We should note that at the time the Relationships Commission sat, the country was so evenly divided that the existence of a substantial Opposition—in the absence of a merger of political parties—was clearly inevitable.

Whatever their diversity of views, the national politicians conversant with the British type of parliamentary democracy were unanimous in the opinion that a Parliamentary Opposition should be recognised in any future constitution; it was recommended that provision be made for the post of Leader of the Opposition and for the salary attached.*

SAFEGUARDS FOR MINORITIES

We have reviewed the problems created by the existence of a settled, wealthy Asian community; considerable information was offered to the Commission suggesting how the interests of Asian minorities could best be safeguarded.

The Commission recognised the undesirability of entrenching any special provisions for Asians in the constitution, as this would have the tendency to leave them open to attack;[38] it was also recognised that it would be difficult for Asian candidates to be elected to Parliament by an African rural population.

It was recommended that the system of adding Indirectly Elected and Specially Elected Members to the Assembly (where only Members of Parliament could elect them) should continue. This would allow people with special knowledge to be elected by Parliament and, at the same time, permit the Asian and other non-African minorities to be similarly elected.

In the same vein it was felt that the method of indirect election would also provide an opportunity to elect women to Parliament, since in straight, direct elections they stood little chance of being elected by the general electorate. The Commission ac-

* Munster Report, para. 173. It is worth noting that at the time of independence the main parties, U.P.C. and D.P., had alternately constituted the Opposition.

curately noted that "political reform is proceeding very rapidly but social reform lags behind and it may be generations before women are able to take advantage of their new political opportunities." [39]

In their conclusion the Commission recommended that these additional Indirectly and/or Specially Elected Members' seats should continue for a period of at least ten years.

THE COUNCIL OF STATE

The expression "Council of State" has featured in constitutions of various British dependencies, but it has not acquired any specific constitutional connotation, since each particular case has had different functions and status ascribed to it.

In the case of Uganda the Commission recommended that we follow the counterpart scheme then existing in Kenya.[40] The Council of State was to be appointed by the Head of State on "advice"—but it was never stated on whose advice, although it was assumed to be on the advice of the Prime Minister.

Although it was not designed to be a second legislative chamber, the Council of State did, in fact, exercise considerable quasi-judicial functions. It was to examine bills before the Assembly and draw attention to any unfair discrimination based on race, tribe, or sex. Individuals and associations would have right of access to the Council in order to make complaints. The Council would have the power to delay discriminatory bills for about six months and to require a three-quarters' majority as requisite for passing any legislation held by the Council to be unfairly discriminatory.[41] In this way the Council, it was hoped, would provide a safeguard against violations of certain human rights which the Assembly could otherwise invade by a two-thirds' majority.

The Council was also required to report publicly to the Head of State and to the Assembly on the use by the government of any emergency powers. Through this provision it was assumed that the interests of Asian and other minorities would be protected.[42]

The recommendation was inherently objectionable for a number of reasons. To begin with, the Council was not to be an

elected body. Out of eleven members at least four were required
to have legal training and were to be appointed on the advice of
the Judicial Service Commission. Six other members were to be
appointed on the advice of the Prime Minister, but the Chairman was to be a judge of the High Court. There were to be at
least one European, two Asians, and one woman. Whatever
its theoretical merits, it was not sound politics, nor was it the
soundest of constitutional devices.

At some stage in its existence the Council was bound to disagree with measures passed by the National Assembly; a conflict between these two bodies would then be inevitable. The
right to delay any legislative measure is best vested in an elected
—not appointed—organ of state. In any event, its functions
would have been more safely entrusted to the High Court in the
normal processes of law. The argument that the Council was
there to prevent unfair legislation, whereas the High Court could
only interpret what was already law, is outweighed by the associated disadvantages of the scheme.

It might have been preferable to endow the High Court with
the function of considering discriminatory or unfair legislation
still being debated by Parliament. The High Court would then
have given declaratory opinion on the legality of any such legislation in relation to human rights. Even now, when no such provision exists, it is not certain whether an individual can or cannot successfully seek an injunction in the High Court to frustrate
discriminatory legislation during its passage through Parliament.

HUMAN RIGHTS

The inclusion of provisions safeguarding human rights in constitutions had become a common feature;[43] it was felt the best
safeguard for any minority group was a fundamental and common denominator for the protection of individuals whether from
majority groups or from other minority groups. For this reason a
Code of Human Rights was recommended for inclusion in the
Constitution, as had been done in Nigeria and—less elaborately
—in Malaya. We should note that the Code of Human Rights
was designed to cover the protection of personal property, personal liberty, employment, and livelihood. In an effort to disarm

the fears of wealthy Asian merchants, it included a provision that property could not be taken compulsorily without fair and adequate compensation.

CITIZENSHIP

As we saw earlier, misunderstanding and bad temper had been evoked by confusing citizenship with the common roll. It was originally felt by Africans that the participation of non-Africans in elections on a common roll meant inevitable conferment of Uganda citizenship.[44] The Constitutional Committee in 1959 urged the separation of citizenship from electoral rights: "We recommend that Her Majesty's Government should be asked to give an assurance that on the introduction of the Common Roll there will be no question of a claim to citizenship or land rights being established by those admitted to it." [45]

It was in this spirit that the Commission urged the separation of citizenship from such matters as land rights; it was a realistic recommendation. To have recommended that any Uganda citizen should be automatically entitled to land rights would have been selling Uganda to the monied Asian minority. It was recommended, in order to protect the land rights of Africans, that "the right to own land ought to be treated quite separately. It is a question of the highest social and economic importance for Uganda, and Uganda is entitled to settle it as she thinks best." [46]

The Commission must have anticipated that not all the people in the non-African communities would eventually become Uganda citizens; those who would not qualify for citizenship were not to be put to undue disadvantage. Because of this argument—as it obtains in most countries—fundamental human rights were to be for everyone, citizen and alien alike.

It was observed, "Virtually the only internal laws which should turn upon citizenship are the electoral law, the law relating to immigration and emigration, and the law as to treason".[47]

There were many other important aspects that bore the Commission's recommendations: the police, the legal system, land tenure, and financial relationships. It was suggested that these would be better discussed in relation to the actual constitutional provisions relating to them. Although they were vital issues, they never evoked much emotion or as much public controversy as the topics just reviewed (even though they were indissolubly connected); at a later stage police and finance were to assume prominence as contentious issues.

THE "LOST COUNTIES"

To conclude the various recommendations of the Commission we should consider what solutions they proposed for the issue of the "Lost Counties".

The Commission regarded the dispute as more a political than a legal one, and they preferred to recommend political as opposed to legal solutions.[48]

Regarding Bunyoro's petition to the Queen, they noted that it was

> . . . a skillfully devised attempt to go behind the settlement of 1900 and to revive Bunyoro's original title to her lost territory. . . . One issue, presumably, is whether the questions raised by the petition are political rather than legal. On this matter it would not be right for us to express a positive opinion. But we are obliged to say, after studying the petition, that we think it right to assume that Bunyoro's claims are essentially political and that we must ourselves deal with them accordingly.[49]

It was not mentioned what factor led the Commission to recommend a political solution; it has been submitted that this was probably because, legally, the British Government would have found itself in the embarrassing position of having no option but to return *all* the counties to Bunyoro. Others may argue that submission of the dispute to a judicial determination would have meant a declaration entitling Buganda to the whole of the disputed area.

The basic legal concepts are clear on the matter; sovereignty over every part of Uganda, including the disputed area, before and after the annexation of the counties by Buganda was vested solely in the British Crown. Secondly, it had been established that the 1900 Buganda Agreement was not a proper agreement in law, nor did it have any legal validity in British municipal courts—even though the Agreement was scrupulously observed by the Protectorate Government for obvious political reasons. Despite the legal attitude towards the validity of the 1900 Agreement, the Commission argued that the Agreement, which incorporated the counties into Buganda, made any transfer of territory from Buganda difficult.[50] We have concluded that the actual spoils of conquest—the disputed counties—were legally vested in the British Crown and there should have been no legal fetters on how to dispose of them after the termination of the Protectorate.

It seems reasonable to infer that the reluctance to assume absolute rights over the "Lost Counties" and consequently absolute power for their disposition, the British Protectorate, and the Commission, had to play on the "fact" that the counties had already been "surrendered" to Buganda and that there was no way of pulling them out of the Buganda Agreement of 1900.

Be this as it may, the Commission recognised the authenticity of Bunyoro's claim, if only in part. The history of the dispute was aptly summarised in one small, lucid paragraph:

> The Mahdi's revolt in the Sudan cut off the approach from the north, so that the British power arrived from the east, and penetrated the country from Buganda. Buganda naturally became Britain's ally and helper, and Buganda's enemies were at first Britain's enemies. This naturally led to fighting against Bunyoro, then ruled by her turbulent King Kabarega. Toro was one part of his former dominions which was made independent by British power. Another penalty inflicted upon him and his people was the assignment to Buganda of the "lost counties" when the territory of Buganda was settled by the 1900 Agreement between Buganda and the British Crown.[51]

While it appeared that there was a prima facie case for Bunyoro's claim, the difficulty obstructing a swift solution of the dispute was the great reluctance of the British Government to hurt the feelings of either Bunyoro or Buganda. There was indebtedness to both; to Bunyoro because it had been "a loyal and cooperative kingdom under the Protectorate" and to Buganda because "we must remember Buganda's services to the Protectorate in its early years."[52]

The dispute assumed such a threatening magnitude for

Uganda's future stability that the Commission felt compelled to recommend that a referendum be held in the counties which held a majority of Banyoro. Voting was to be county by county in order to decide if the inhabitants wished to be transferred to Bunyoro. It is interesting to note that the Commission did not want the transfer of any county to take place while still under British rule. The preparatory work for the referendum was to be done during the life of the Protectorate, but the hand-over to Bunyoro—assuming she would be successful—was to be coordinated with the demise of the Protectorate.[53]

It was a fairly equitable solution under the prevailing circumstances; Bunyoro had claimed much more territory, but it was content with the Commission's recommendation. As we will note later, Buganda rejected the proposals out of hand.

The recommendations of this Commission were to form the basic structure of Uganda's future constitution; the Report embodying these recommendations was to provide the basis for the two Constitutional Conferences in London in 1961 and 1962. Some observers have called the Report a most "unimaginative document";[54] however, taking Uganda's historical development into account and considering the strong pre-independence feelings of various political groupings, it is difficult to see how the Commission could have made better recommendations. Indeed, their Report will remain a positive document in Uganda's constitutional history.

7. The Era of Internal Self-Government

The General Elections of 1961

While the Munster Commission was gathering evidence for its report on the future form of government, political campaigns were in full swing for the general election of March 1961. It would be the first general election covering the whole country—in spite of Buganda's determination to frustrate it.

Political parties, which had established a fairly extensive grip on the country, went all-out to obtain the maximum possible support. Everyone knew that whichever party won the election, the prize would be that of forming the first African government exercising considerable responsibility under the transitional period of internal self-government. It was not an unreasonable calculation for the major parties to have assumed that the party which won the election and formed the first African government would quite likely win the pre-independence elections also and thus become the ultimate successor to the British Crown on the attainment of sovereign power.

Before considering the slogans and promises made to the electorate it is convenient to mention the various political parties that participated in the elections. They were allocated the symbols of their choice.[1]

PARTY	SYMBOL
Uganda People's Congress (U.P.C.)	— the hand
Democratic Party (D.P.)	— the hoe
Uganda National Congress (U.N.C.)	— the key
Uganda Hereditary Chieftainship Party (U.H.C.P.)	— the tree
Uganda African Union (U.A.U.)	— the motor car

It is of interest that by this time people from a variety of professions and occupations had developed a political interest to the extent of directing party policies and standing for election. A breakdown of candidates by occupation reveals the following:[2]

OCCUPATION	NUMBER OF CANDIDATES
teachers	— 67
businessmen	— 34
farmers	— 22
political party officials	— 13
lawyers	— 12
traders	— 11
clerks	— 7
co-operative union officials	— 6
others	— 26
Total	198

The vast majority of the 198 candidates were standing for the first time; 22 of them were former Members of the Legislative Council, and 26 of them had stood as candidates in the 1958 elections. By March 1961 the final list of candidates had been reduced, as a result of the parties rearranging their candidacies, to a total of 163. The breakdown was:[3]

PARTY	CANDIDATES
U.P.C.	— 61
D.P.	— 77
U.N.C.	— 20
U.H.C.P.	— 4
U.A.U.	— 1

The machinery for these elections was entrusted to the Supervisor of Elections.

PARTY CAMPAIGNS

Of considerable interest is the manner in which these parties presented their pledges to the electorate; before we analyse the "manifestos" and policies of the leading parties, it is essential to outline the fundamental forces that controlled to a large measure the results of the election.

Religion. We have reviewed the extent to which some missionaries—because of their considerable hold on the people— sought to control and influence political trends. True, they did not campaign actively for a political party in every part of the country, but it is equally true that in some districts—Kigezi, Acholi, West Nile, Madi, and the Kingdom of Ankole—the Roman Catholic priests carried out an extensive and untiring campaign for the D.P. and were largely responsible for its success in those areas. Priests put their vehicles at the disposal of D.P. supporters; they financed and planned campaign efforts in many places.

In many up-country places, especially close to polling day, priests held special masses to exhort their followers to vote D.P. Indeed, on many a Sunday hardly a village service ended without the preacher rubbing in the attributes of the D.P. and the contrasting evils of the U.P.C. to his spell-bound listeners, without actually castigating the few Catholics in the U.P.C. as being communist and unworthy of holy sacraments.

We have noted that the D.P. was overwhelmingly Roman Catholic; to increase its membership—besides wooing the reluctant and uncertain support of followers of other faiths—Roman Catholic priests made a systematic and massive effort to baptise uncommitted pagans. Such baptisms were made with exceptional haste. To anyone who witnessed them there was no doubt that the overriding intention was not to retrieve a lost soul for Christendom; it was clearly intended to swell the votes for the D.P. On certain occasions in some remote areas priests rehearsed the method of voting in their churches after services to ensure that no ballot paper would be spoilt or cast in the wrong ballot box.

In this way—although the hierarchy dissociated itself from these activities—the Roman Catholic Church played an effective part in supporting the D.P. in the elections. It seems true, in general, that Catholic priests have greater influence and control over their followers than their counterparts in the Protestant and Islamic faiths. They were accorded a higher degree of blind obedience by the majority of their supporters during the period under discussion; they could direct the faithful to vote for the D.P. in confidence of receiving maximum support.

But let it not appear as if supporters of the Catholic Church alone mobilized political support on a religious basis. It is correct to say it was they who began organized appeals for political support on a religious basis, but this appeal was so powerful that the other political parties—and adherents of other faiths—would with certainty be defeated if they did not employ the same tactics.

Consequently, in the areas we have mentioned the Protestants reacted by employing more or less the same methods as the Catholics. In remote village churches they preached the political gospel of the U.P.C.; the lower clergy were the most energetic in this exercise. They, too, carried on the extensive and swift baptism of literally hundreds of people to ensure their support for the U.P.C., but they were sternly rebuked by their archbishop for indulging in politics. The truth is, nevertheless, that at the village level control from the top was very slight and the clergy at this level carried on their political campaigns undeterred. It is a reality of history that the D.P., from its inception, reflected Catholic hegemony and that the U.P.C. eventually, although not initially, served a like role for the Protestants. During the protracted struggles for political power both sides functioned on a no-holds-barred basis—both inside and outside the realm of religion. As they saw it, they had no alternative; they felt they had to use the methods the Catholics had introduced. It would be fair to observe that Catholic priests and their supporters were far better organised and wealthier than their Protestant and Muslim counterparts. The Muslims, perhaps because they were a smaller group and more susceptible to central direction, generally tended to move together in any one direction; traditionally they sided with the Protestants. This alliance was maintained and even strengthened despite positive attempts by the D.P. to disrupt it.

But, we might ask, what argument did those who spoke on a religious platform use? It was both elementary and appealing: it was the vindication of one's faith as triumphant above all others. It was a matter of both personal and spiritual honour; it was more felt and believed than argued and reasoned. One's faith had to be the ruling faith, for it alone could do justice to all manner of people and thus govern the country well. It is a reasonable generalisation that this attitude could be applied not only to the electorate but also to a substantial number of the candidates. It should be pointed out that those who took an independent line of approach towards religious appeal were the intellectually critical and independent men found mostly in the U.P.C. leadership. They were drawn from both Protestant and Catholic groups; they were in a state of revolt against being blind followers of their respective faiths, although, being realistic, they appreciated the tremendous role religion played in the politics of the time and quite a number accepted taking advantage of it.

Tribal and Ethnic Loyalties.　　We have indicated how Uganda developed as a collection of many tribes, which for a long time lived a separate existence from one another.

Within any given district or kingdom there was little or no homogeneity; there might be a dominant tribe, but it is certain there would be other minority tribal groups in most of them. The sudden appearance of limited opportunities for standing as a candidate in a national election often caused conflict where there had been none before, or accentuated it where it did exist, as each prospective candidate took advantage of his tribal support to oust a rival who might belong to the same party.

It happened in some situations that the better candidates were dropped because they came from minority tribal groups within particular districts or kingdoms and their opponents cultivated tribal animosity against them in order to gain more support for themselves. In this way the politicians accentuated tribal or ethnic differences and undermined efforts towards building a common citizenship and a genuine concept of national unity—regardless of which party they represented.

Under these circumstances it is not surprising that political parties generally sponsored candidates in constituencies where such candidates commanded general ethnic and tribal (besides religious) affinity and support. It was sensible to do so, and it was sometimes inevitable, but it was also an admission of a fundamental shortcoming—absence of homogeneity in Uganda.

On the anchor sheets of religion and tribalism the political parties superimposed elaborate "manifestos" and to some extent pretended what they did not practice: that elections had to be fought, be won or lost, on no other basis than the lofty promises in these manifestos. Although five parties participated, only two were of significance.

THE DEMOCRATIC PARTY

We have noted that the Buganda Government resolutely opposed these elections and intimidated those who participated in them. The overwhelming authority this feudal government had over its people was well demonstrated when it decreed a boycott of registration for these elections; only 2 percent of the electorate registered, despite passage of legislation to prevent intimidation of potential voters.

Credit must largely go to Benedicto Kiwanuka and the D.P. that even 2 percent managed to register. Kiwanuka was a Muganda; with the exception of Bataringaya and Oda, the top leadership was composed of Baganda. All the Buganda leaders, with the exception of Senteza Kajubi and Bemba, were practising Catholics. Finally, to appreciate the nature of their opposition to the Buganda Government, the whole Kiganda leadership of the D.P. had a grudge of one sort or another against Mmengo and, certainly, against the Kabaka; they had either been deprived of office in the Kabaka's Government or this same Government, they alleged, frustrated their political ambitions. Kiwanuka,

Bemba, and Mugwanya belonged to this frustrated group. We have noted the rivalry and conflict of religious politics in Buganda; at the time of these elections the feudal regime in Mmengo, despite its colouring by Basude as Minister of Justice, was firmly Protestant. It believed and practised—like so many before it—the supremacy of Protestant rule. It should not be surprising that when an opportunity to challenge Mmengo arose with these elections, the Catholics—in effect, the D.P. led by Kiwanuka—took up the opportunity with great resolution and fortitude.

In normal circumstances the D.P. could have counted on obedience from its Catholic followers; statistics show that there are more Catholics in Buganda than Protestants. Kiwanuka had reason to believe that if he urged his followers in Buganda to register and vote they would respond favourably. But the intensity of loyalty to the monarchy, combined with the acute probabilities of social sanctions and hidden intimidation, prevented the majority of Catholics from responding to the overtures of the D.P.'s "promised land" and religious appeals; the D.P. had miscalculated!

It is well known that those who did register and vote in Buganda were (besides being Catholics) teachers, nuns, priests, monks, and school children or staff in Catholic hospitals and schools. This was because they—being relatively more removed from village life—were particularly susceptible to the arguments of the D.P.; they were part of a growing intelligent class to whom the realisation of social justice was more commendable than blind loyalty to feudal kingship. They felt the cause of their religion more acutely and sometimes even as a vindication of their honour.

Despite only 2 percent registration, the D.P. derived tremendous benefit from this; no other party, not even the Buganda-based parties of U.N.P. and U.N.C., could claim any substantial slice of this 2 percent. The U.P.C. was on very weak ground in Buganda.

Reasonably assured of twenty-one seats from Buganda, Benedicto Kiwanuka and his supporters gathered momentum and soon launched their campaign in the remaining areas of Uganda.

They produced a manifesto for the elections—"Forward to Freedom"; it touched on all the problems affecting and facing the country. Unlike the U.P.C., it did not advocate a socialist policy, but it is reasonable to generalise that the manifestos of both parties had many similar features. The problems of national realisation, such as Africanisation, the needs of social development in education and health, and the desire for swift economic progress were all considered; the unchanging aim of both parties was to provide some sudden and dramatic change—"a sudden break from darkness to light"—as the country emerged from colonial rule to self-rule. On the delicate and emotional issue of the form of government, federal or unitary, even the outspoken D.P. felt that at this juncture it was imprudent to be unequivocal; it contented itself with analysing the merits and demerits of each system and ended by saying the D.P. would accept whichever form the majority of the people in Uganda accepted.[4]

The fundamental factors determining the outcome of these elections have already been mentioned, but it is difficult to assess the extent to which party manifestos influenced voting. Only a small percentage would care to buy or read them, and opponents often took the opportunity to distort them. It was conventional and indeed proper, if only to impress the colonial regime, that the parties should have produced manifestos. But undoubtedly the massive support of the D.P. outside Buganda came from the Catholic Church and its followers. For these elections the D.P. was more disciplined and better organised than the U.P.C.; it was not surprising that the D.P. won.

In Buganda, purely because of technical and legal reasons, they romped home with twenty-one seats; it was a mockery of representative democracy. In the electoral district of Bugerere, P. S. Mulema (D.P.) polled seventy-two votes to win by a majority of eleven in a district whose electorate exceeded thirty thousand people; a like situation applied in most of the D.P. victories in Buganda. Be this as it may, the D.P. was able to snatch victory from the U.P.C. and form the first African government in Uganda.[5]

THE UGANDA PEOPLE'S CONGRESS

When elections finally came, the U.P.C. had been in existence for barely a year; it was a tremendous achievement that it polled the most votes outside Buganda.* It did not have sufficient time to organise itself or to evolve a rigid code of disciplined administration and conduct, and it was also relatively poor in material support.

Like the D.P., it had anchor sheets which had existed long before its formation; it had religious, tribal, and ethnic loyalties. All that was now required were prominent leaders from religions and tribal groups to come together for the prosecution of a common political objective. Their supporters would automatically follow them, or so it was assumed.

It is not extravagant to claim that, of all the parties, the U.P.C. had the most prominent and colourful personalities among its leadership. They were more experienced politicians; many of them, unlike the D.P. leadership, had participated in the Legislative Council. Eloquent men that they were, by their unceasing attacks on colonial administration they acquired respect and affection from masses of people who had never even seen them. When they mobilised their campaign efforts, it was with confidence and buoyant enthusiasm.

As the election results showed, the U.P.C. was undisputed master of three provinces; the leadership knew it even before the elections. They also knew that their support in Buganda was negligible. The question they had to answer was whether they could win with the support of only three provinces—without Buganda.

A meeting of the National Council of the U.P.C. took place at the Metropole Hotel in Kampala one and a half months before the elections to answer this question. Some held the view that

* *Report on the Uganda Legislative Council Elections*, 1961, p. 17. The votes cast were as follows:

U.P.C.	494,959
D.P.	515,718
U.N.C.	31,712
U.A.U.	1,172
U.H.C.B.	6,559
Independents	48,457

despite its popularity the U.P.C. could not win without some support in Buganda; they argued that the Governor should be persuaded to postpone elections until the impasse in Buganda had been resolved, in order to enable Buganda to participate fully in the elections.* This undoubtedly would have broken the D.P. supremacy in Buganda, and the U.P.C. would have emerged with the largest number of Elected Members.

Had this view been pursued, it is not improbable that the Governor would have acceded; the U.P.C. at this time claimed all but one of the African Members of the Legislative Council. Had they presented the proposal to the Governor in his official capacity and, in view of the fact that even the Governor knew of the U.P.C.'s majority support in the other provinces, he might well have agreed. In any event, the postponement of elections would have entailed prolongation of colonial rule—and that was unacceptable regardless of how brief a period was involved. It was not a request that would have been rejected out of hand by a Colonial Governor, but the advocates of this view were in a minority—they lost.

Confident and blinded by their popular support in three regions of the country, the majority at the U.P.C. meeting unhesitatingly settled for elections as scheduled, even if it meant that the D.P. would start with the advantage of commanding all twenty-one Buganda seats. The strength and intensity of the D.P.'s religious appeal outside Buganda was certainly underestimated. The U.P.C. then launched its own campaign.

Like the D.P., it had issued a manifesto containing its promises to the electorate. Its slogan was "Unity—Justice—Independence". All the problems facing Uganda were analysed and solutions proposed. It was a more vigorous and more socialistic programme, although in broad outline it shared similar features with the D.P. manifesto. It appealed to the country to rally behind the U.P.C. with a promise in return of acquiring immediate independence. As to the form of government, the U.P.C. contented itself with saying in diplomatic phraseology that it would

* The author proposed a campaign to postpone the elections until the Buganda issue was settled to minimise the D.P.'s strength in Buganda; only G. B. Magezi supported him. He was attacked by the then Secretary-General, J. Kakonge, and outvoted.

safeguard and honour the dignity and status of hereditary rulers while at the same time promoting a strong central government to run the country; again, it is not easy to assess the extent to which the manifesto influenced voters.

There was an infinite variety of local issues in every constituency which had great influence on an electorate largely "locally minded" and only remotely concerned with the problems of a nation-to-be. The degree of success that party manifestos had in influencing the electorate was directly proportional to the ability with which the candidates and their supporters could articulate the general principles of a manifesto in order to give it meaning in regard to the specific problems of a given constituency. In this respect the U.P.C. was more blessed; it had eloquent speakers who not only could muster the arguments of their manifesto so as to make sense but who could also distort the arguments of their opponents with similar precision.

The final result of the elections could not have been unexpected to any detached and well-informed observer, however disappointing the result may have been to the U.P.C. The breakdown was:[6]

PARTY	NUMBER ELECTED
D.P.	43
U.P.C.	35
U.N.C.	1
Independents	2

THE INFLUENCE OF PARTY SYMBOLS

In concluding our review of these elections, mention should be made of party symbols and how they were used in the election campaigns.

It is well known that a political symbol in an election has one and only one value: to identify a particular party or candidate. By itself it has no intrinsic quality that should influence the electorate to vote for or against its holder. It was interesting to witness the extent to which these party symbols were effectively given intrinsic value in order to influence voting. Examples: the hand for the U.P.C. and the hoe for the D.P.

U.P.C. candidates and supporters indulged in eloquent and lengthy expositions on the value of the hand to man. It feeds him; indeed, his entire success and livelihood depends on it. Without the hand, the hoe the D.P. was using could not have been manufactured nor could it cultivate. It was a superior symbol; it "should be voted for".

At the other extreme, the D.P. drew graphic illustrations of the tremendous potential of the hoe: upon it depended the growing of food and man's livelihood. As an agricultural country, Uganda depended on the hoe for its wealth. The U.P.C. could not claim the supremacy of the hand, since the hand alone, without the rest of the body, is a dismembered and useless part of the human frame. And so the arguments went on and on.

It is difficult to say what percentage of the electorate voted under the influence of a symbol; that quite a number did should be beyond dispute.

THE CONSTITUTION
AFTER THE 1961 GENERAL ELECTIONS

Apart from the changes in the structure and functions of the Central Government of Uganda, there were no changes of consequence in the basic constitutional set-up of the country after the 1961 general elections. Buganda was still engaged in protracted negotiations with the Governor for the conclusion of yet another Buganda Agreement, but these negotiations were not finalised until October 1961, when the first Constitutional Conference was concluded in London.

Toro, which for some time had assiduously imitated the obstinacy of Buganda, was also negotiating a new Agreement with the Governor.[7] The desire of the rulers and their people to conclude fresh Agreements that generally lacked legal validity demonstrates the great diplomatic use to which the British put these Agreements, for otherwise they would have been rejected as fraudulent, especially at this hour close to our independence.

The Agreement with Toro was a provisional one; the Omukama and his government were anxious to extract, in writing, certain undertakings in this Provisional Agreement by which they could pin down the British Government at the forthcoming

Constitutional Conference. The Agreement was primarily concerned with ensuring the safety of the throne and the establishment of a ministerial form of government. Much of what was agreed to in this document formed the substance of the provisions for this kingdom in the new Uganda Constitution.

THE CENTRAL LEGISLATURE

The recommendations of the Constitutional Committee on reforms for the Protectorate Government began taking effect, although with several modifications.

The Council of Ministers. The term "Executive Council" after a country-wide election was considered outmoded; the executive was henceforth to be called the "Council of Ministers".[8] In his Communication from the Chair, Governor Crawford explained the composition of the government and legislature to a new and very much enlarged Legislative Council.

The Council of Ministers would only be advisory to the Governor, in whom the final power of decision remained vested. The demand for a Chief Minister, which had been formally recommended by the Constitutional Committee, was rejected by the Colonial Secretary in his despatch of 14 September 1960. Having stated that this was still the official view, the Governor nevertheless held out some hope for this issue:

> . . . the Secretary of State has authorised me to say that he has been informed by me of the request made by the Leader of the Majority Party that a Chief Minister should be appointed and that while the Secretary of State is not prepared to reach a decision on this matter at this juncture, he does propose to review the question very soon.[9]

Meanwhile, the Leader of the Majority Party, the Hon. Benedicto Kiwanuka, was appointed Minister without Portfolio and Leader of the House. He was to be brought into close consultation with the Governor and Chief Secretary on matters that fell within the sphere of responsibility of the Chief Minister when the time came to create that office.

The Council was to consist of ten "unofficial" elected ministers and three ex-officio ministers: the Chief Secretary, the Minister of Finance, and the Minister of Legal Affairs. In accordance with usual practice, the last three members were the British officials who always seemed to vacate a colonial government last. Of the ten elected ministers only one was a non-African.[10]

In addition to these a cadre of junior ministers, called Parliamentary Secretaries, were appointed to the Ministries of Finance, Local Government, Commerce and Industry, Education, Health, and Agriculture and Animal Industry. Undoubtedly, although these junior ministers were only advisory to the Governor, their appointment was a decisive step towards a fully African government.

The Legislative Council. The Legislative Council underwent a corresponding change; although its name did not change, its membership had increased. The Royal Instructions of 20 February 1960 set out the new composition. It consisted, after the general election, of the following: the Governor; the Speaker; three ex-officio Ministers; Nominated Members; Representative Members; and nine Specially Elected Members.[11]

The last category was a completely new feature; it was an anticipation of what Lord Munster would soon recommend. The Specially Elected Members were elected by the Directly Elected (Representative) Members together with the ex-officio Members.* From now on the term Representative Member was to mean the Directly Elected Members. The Nominated Members, seven in number, were appointed by the Governor after consultation with the leaders of the House and the Opposition.

The Legislative Council had changed in character as well as in size. Legally, for the first time, it could be said Uganda had a representative form of government.[12] It remained so for more than a year—until the general elections that followed the first Constitutional Conference in September 1961.

There were wide-spread demands from the U.P.C.—and now the Buganda Government as well—to hold a new election in

---

* The procedure for electing "Specially Elected Members" was prescribed by the Governor and published as Legal Notice 67 of 1961, under clause 6 of the "Additional Instructions".

order to give Buganda another chance at more representative government, but this clamour was dismissed by the Governor in April:

> I have recently seen statements that fresh general elections may be held in a few months time, or later in 1961, with a view to forming another new Government. For the avoidance of any misunderstanding I should state that the holding of further elections is not contemplated this year. The new Government which has just taken office will remain in being until any new Constitution, involving a fresh general election, has been decided upon, and can be implemented.[13]

In July 1961 the Leader of the House, having exerted considerable pressure and already threatening to boycott the London Conference, was made Chief Minister.[14]

The Constitutional Conference of 1961

We now focus attention on one of the most momentous periods in Uganda's constitutional evolution: the era beginning with the Constitutional Conference of 1961, which resulted in internal self-government and eventually led us to independence. Before considering the 1961 Conference and the details of its major constitutional decisions, it is appropriate to review the political alignments of the various parties in the intervening period before the Conference since their stand on various political issues would significantly determine the ultimate character of Uganda's independence constitution.

PRELUDE TO THE CONFERENCE

If the victory of the D.P. gave impetus and greater hope to the Democrats inside and outside the government, it correspondingly served a tremendous role in drawing closer all the anti-D.P. forces, eventually consolidating them into a powerful and united Opposition.

After their recent defeat the U.P.C. calmly reviewed their relationship with Buganda. It was clear that they commanded majority support in the other three provinces; it was equally clear that they had lost the election because of their weakness in Buganda, where, of the twenty-one rural seats, they won only one, the D.P. taking the balance. It was a source of comfort to the U.P.C., as it was a basis of anxiety for the D.P., to know that the real political power in Buganda lay not with the D.P., which had secured a merely technical victory, but decisively with the traditionalists at Mmengo under the ultimate direction and control of the Kabaka; the British authorities were equally aware of these facts.

The obvious strategy for the U.P.C. was to forge an alliance with the Mmengo traditionalists; it is interesting to examine how it all began, as this was not only the outstanding achievement of nationalists pacifying sceptical traditionalists but also a basic turning point in the political and constitutional history of Uganda. It meant that in order for Buganda to defend its autonomy and prestige, it had, for the first time, to seriously consider aligning itself with the indigenous political forces in the other provinces of the country; by so doing—however slow the pace— it would gravitate towards integrating itself with the future nation-state of Uganda, which would possess a single personality by the law of nations after independence. It was a momentous departure from Buganda's traditional stand of being a state enjoying a separate existence and, after independence, endowed with unlimited sovereign power. With national unity now a distinct possibility the prospects for independence had become brighter overnight.

The Establishment of the U.P.C./Mmengo Alliance

The ultimate objective attained between the U.P.C. and Mmengo was the formation of the well-known and ill-fated alliance between the U.P.C. and the K.Y. (Kabaka Yeka). Tremendous activity and diplomatic skill was required to produce this outcome; not all the leading members of the U.P.C. were in favour of this alliance at the outset.

When I put it to Obote that if ever the U.P.C. hoped to be in government it had to establish a *modus operandi* with Mmengo, Obote shrank at the idea; in fact, he opposed it. The majority of the leadership were indifferent, and some were mildly hostile, but I was utterly convinced of the rightness of this approach; and for the first time I felt that if Obote was going to stand in the way of this alliance and consequently stop the U.P.C. from exercising power, he had to be evicted from his leadership role. The only person I mentioned this to was W. W. Nadiope, then Vice-President of the U.P.C. and probably the most powerful figure in the party. He agreed with my views at a brief meeting held at the Uganda Club; my aim had been to replace Obote with Nadiope.

I do not know whether or not Obote ever discovered my intentions during this particular period. All I know is that a few days later he changed his mind completely and agreed to accommodate Mmengo; I had no other quarrel with him, and now the way was clear for me to work and forge the necessary link.

Over a period of nearly seven months, assisted quite independently by B. K. Kirya, I set out to work on the reluctant and evasive functionaries in Mmengo to convince them of the wisdom and advantages of working with the U.P.C. I was a frequent guest of my late friend, Kabaka Mutesa II, and his quiet Katikkiro, Michael Kintu.

Gradually, but steadily, the general body of the U.P.C. leadership came to realise and accept the correctness and necessity of working with Mmengo. In late May, when the U.P.C. Elected Members met in the Legislative Council buildings to extend a mandate to Obote and myself to negotiate with Mmengo, they were formally endorsing an inevitable development.

Truth must be told: although publicly Obote was hailed for statesmanship in having established a working relationship with the obstructionist regime in Mmengo, he in fact did little to establish this relationship. Perhaps his maximum contribution, as leader of the party, was not to oppose or hamper those like myself and Kirya who were engaged in the complex task of persuading Mutesa and his government to work with the U.P.C.; he did, occasionally, meet Mutesa and talk with him in the most formal terms.

There were fundamental realities which the Mmengo regime had to take into account in making up its mind to come to terms with the U.P.C. rather than with the only other alternative, the D.P. These were the basic realities that had, unfortunately, shaped the political outlook in Uganda for a long time—religion and tribalism, along with a third and even greater factor of universal application, self-interest.

We speak first of religion. The regime in Mmengo was, by tradition, Protestant. It deliberately frustrated those Baganda Catholics who were interested in politics and public service. To this Mmengo regime it was as much a necessity to maintain the status quo as it was a resolution of the D.P. to have it reversed. The D.P. had been directly formed as a result of this frustration and as the instrument by which justice could be attained for the Catholics.

When the D.P. won the first general election in 1961 and thus formed the first African government in Uganda, it came as no surprise when the traditionalist Protestant regime in Buganda both resented and feared this last-minute political ascendency of the Catholics. The distinct possibility suddenly dawned on Mmengo that a Catholic-led government might just take over from the British at independence; worse than this was the prospect of such a government not only effecting reforms but going even further—to the extent of vengeful victimisation of the Buganda Protestant aristocracy and its leadership. There were grounds for this fear, grounds born of a long period of frustration among Catholics. To forestall what was obviously inevitable, Mmengo actively sought an alliance in the hope of strengthening its hand in dismantling the D.P. government before independence.

On the other hand the U.P.C., despite the prominence of a few leading Catholics, was basically a Protestant-led party. Several of its leaders had attended the same Protestant school—Kings College, Budo—as did many of the people in the Mmengo establishment, either as teachers or as students. In this respect they shared a common history and a similar tradition imparted by the same educational background; this made it easier to establish a *modus vivendi*.

During this period the Buganda Constitutional Committee had for a considerable time been engaged in inconclusive meetings with Governor Crawford. It was pressing for extensive constitutional powers for Buganda, which would, in fact, give her a high degree of autonomy. The U.P.C. members of the Legislative Council took every opportunity to press the Governor to conclude these talks and grant those Buganda demands that were commensurate with the dignity and status of a federal state; the Legislative Council proceedings of 1961 verify this.

At the opposite extreme, and rather untactfully, the Baganda D.P. members who were in the government resolutely opposed the idea of any concession being given to Buganda. Benedicto Kiwanuka, then Leader of the House in the Legislative Council, demanded that the Governor allow him to take part in the talks with Mmengo. It was then alleged—with damaging effect to the D.P.—that he wanted to be in the talks only in order to frustrate the Mmengo regime's demands.

It must be stated that Mutesa II was quite sceptical at the beginning about Obote's suitability as a leader. These initial fears were soon eroded by persistence and tact on the part of those in the U.P.C. who established the alliance. To condemn them for having forged the alliance, headed by Obote, is to forget that these men believed (for sure Kirya and myself) completely in the rightness of the alliance they were trying to establish.

When Obote later dissolved the alliance and began to plot political death for Buganda, we chose, rather than betray our allies and friends, to stand by them in what eventually became a very costly undertaking for some of us.

The forging of this alliance had one fundamental and far-ranging effect on the future constitution of Uganda: the U.P.C., by committing itself to supporting several of Buganda's demands for substantial federal status, was paving the way for a federal constitution in this country. Although the D.P. was in Government and strongly opposed this devolution and partial surrender of sovereignty to Buganda, it was known that these objections of the D.P. could not stand against the combined front of the U.P.C. and Mmengo, which represented the real political power in the Protectorate.

In an atmosphere characterised by tension and uncertainty the Lukiiko met in September to decide if Mmengo was to attend the forthcoming Constitutional Conference in London. The political opponents of Mmengo were not too happy when the decision was taken to attend the Conference. It meant that the anti-Mmengo delegates, including Benedicto Kiwanuka, who had recently been elected by legal technicality, would carry less weight at the Conference when the representatives of the Mmengo regime, who obviously had overwhelming support from the Buganda establishment, attended in order to speak for Buganda.

Only a week before the Conference was scheduled to open in London a meeting was held at the Bulange in Mmengo between the U.P.C., represented by Obote and myself, and the Buganda Constitutional Committee. This meeting covered all the points the Committee had recently discussed with the Governor; a joint statement was then issued—with the approbation of many —stating that "complete understanding" had been reached on all the various and outstanding arguments Buganda had used in her threat to boycott the Conference. Obote attended this meeting merely to symbolise the authority and leadership of the U.P.C.; he took very little part in establishing this understanding—which took more than six months to realise.

The Internal Self-Government Constitution of 1961

The Conference opened at Lancaster House in London on 18 September 1961 under the Chairmanship of the Rt. Hon. Ian Macleod, M.P., to frame Uganda's Internal Self-Government Constitution. It held seventeen plenary sessions and then ended on 9 October 1961. Its principal conclusions, embodied in a report, formed the basis for Uganda's Internal Self-Government Constitution.* We will single out several prominent features for discussion, along with the specific provisions designed to resolve the long-standing problems of relationships.

THE LEGISLATURE

The Conference established a legislature for Uganda which was to consist of Her Majesty and a National Assembly; the

* The Independence Constitution was based on the Internal Self-Government Constitution.

name "National Assembly" replaced that of "Legislative Council". It was to consist of eighty-two Elected Members and nine Specially Elected Members.[15] It was vested with legislative power for the whole country, but because of the federal character of the constitution certain powers were reserved for the legislature of Buganda.

The Division of Powers. We have noted that a fundamental characteristic of a federal constitution is the division of powers between the centre and the federated regions so that each is within its own sphere independent of the other. It was the granting of this status to Buganda that went a long way toward mollifying and integrating it with the rest of the Protectorate. But the determination of Buganda to be fully autonomous was certainly the most protracted and most controversial feature of the 1961 Conference in London.

Having stated that, subject to the provisions of this constitution, the Legislature of Uganda was to have the power to make laws for the peace, order, and good government of Uganda,[16] it was provided that this power did not extend to matters specified in Part I of Schedule VI to the Constitution.[17]

It was the Buganda legislature alone that was empowered to legislate in respect of that Schedule, but it was precluded from exercising any legislative right over any items in Schedule II—which were exclusive to the Uganda National Assembly.

As is often the case with federal constitutions, it was provided that when laws validly enacted by both the Buganda and Uganda legislatures were inconsistent, those of the Uganda legislature would prevail and the laws enacted by the legislature of Buganda would, to the extent of the inconsistency, be void. This was, of course, in relation to the concurrent powers both of them were to have.[18]

Qualification for Membership in the National Assembly. The provisions concerning qualification and disqualification for membership in the National Assembly under the Internal Self-Government Constitution, which departed in some measure from the standard pattern of colonial legislatures, were reproduced almost *in toto* in the Independence Constitution.[19]

The points to note here are the increased optional powers which were specifically vested in the legislature of Uganda to determine the disqualification for office of persons employed in a variety of occupations.[20] This covered such persons as holders of offices whose responsibility covered the conduct of any election to the National Assembly or who might belong to any of the armed forces of the Crown or be members of any police force.[21]

Unlike the final Independence Constitution, however, it still provided for a British subject or a British-protected person to be eligible for election.[22] This was an inevitable consequence of the fact that there was as yet no Uganda citizenship and the whole population of the Protectorate was still automatically divided into these two categories.

The validity of the election of any Elected or Indirectly Elected Member could be questioned only in the High Court, which was vested with final jurisdiction.*

Optional Indirect Elections for Buganda. Of all the controversial issues bitterly contested at the Conference, the foremost was the decision that the twenty-one Buganda representatives to the National Assembly would be elected *not directly, but "indirectly" if a directly elected Buganda Lukiiko (by resolution) opted to perform the function of electing representatives while sitting as an electoral college.*

Just as the traditional Mmengo regime demanded this condition with uncompromising tenacity, so the Democratic Party under the leadership of the Chief Minister, Benedicto Kiwanuka, opposed its inclusion in the Constitution. This provision was one of the highly regarded issues on which the U.P.C. had agreed to support Mmengo at the Conference; extracts from speeches at the Conference indicate the intensity of feeling with which it was contested.

At this Conference the Chairman proposed that Buganda be granted the option of electing directly or indirectly; he pointed out that the Munster Commission itself had recommended it. To disarm objections he also pointed out that 90 percent of the Lu-

* The Uganda Constitution (1961), S. 38. This was unanimously approved by all delegates to the Conference, U.C.C. (61), 4th meeting, p. 1.

kiiko, who would be the electors, would themselves be elected democratically on a universal adult franchise; he gave assurance that the saza chiefs would not take part in this election.[23]

The Chief Minister could not be persuaded to abandon his stand; visibly disturbed and still protesting, he said:

> In the 1955 Agreement with the Kabaka there was provision for the introduction of direct elections by 1961, if this had not taken place before then. In fact, this has now come about. It is unfortunate that in a country which the Secretary of State recognises is ready for independence it should now be proposed to introduce indirect elections for the first time. *The reasons for doing so have not been stated.*
>
> Indirect elections are inconsistent with stable government and will put an end to party politics. . . . One party might gain thirty-six seats and another twenty-five in an election. It would not be known how the twenty-one members representing Buganda would vote and it might be possible for them to side with the party which had gained twenty-five seats, so that the country would be governed by the minority party. Then the Government would be at the mercy of the Buganda representatives.*

Kiwanuka missed the point at issue; if the issue had been, as he argued, that the Buganda representatives—as a block—were not to choose their affiliation, the question whether they should be directly or indirectly elected was of no material importance. If, as he postulated, the safeguard against what he termed "instability" had to be direct elections, it then stood to reason, especially in view of the prevailing circumstances in Buganda, that these indirectly elected representatives would have succeeded with equal distinction under direct elections. What he forgot was that the differences between the types of direct and indirect elections proposed could do nothing to change the minds of those elected; the remedy lay in entirely different areas. But he went on to register his protest nonetheless:

> In the past, blood has been shed for the principle of one man one vote. In Uganda that principle has been implemented. Now it is

* Record of the 11th Meeting, U.C.C. (61), p. 2. This was exactly what happened, even with direct elections, which Buganda had effectively boycotted. Elected by a minority vote in Buganda, Kiwanuka, though defeated in the other three provinces, was able to govern the whole country. (Author's emphasis.)

proposed to disenfranchise the people of Buganda. . . . there is no legal or moral obligation on the Secretary of State to support this proposal, which is in direct conflict with the principles of democracy.

The Chairman has spoken of compromise but I would like to ask on what do we compromise now? Speaking on behalf of the progressive elements in Buganda, I say it would be a great disappointment if anything less than full democratic elections were agreed to. Speaking for the elected government of Uganda, I must say that myself and my party would not, and no African nationalist could, support the present proposals.[24]

He was supported by his array of D.P. delegates; Okeny (East Acholi) went to the extent of claiming that granting of this option to Buganda "would lead to confusion and bloodshed".

What lent additional bitterness to the controversy was the Mmengo delegation pressing, with the acquiescence of the U.P.C., the Secretary of State to accept the existing Lukiiko without its being directly elected prior to its electing Buganda's representatives to the National Assembly.

While the London Conference was in session, the Secretary-General of the U.P.C. in Kampala released the sensational statement that the twenty-one Buganda representatives—twenty were D.P.—would be ordered to withdraw from the National Assembly by direction of the Secretary of State; the existing Lukiiko Members would elect representatives of their choice. The claim that this scheme would not necessitate fresh elections in other parts of the country made it a foregone conclusion that the U.P.C. would be called upon to form a government.

Despite the assurance of the Secretary of State that it would be an elected Lukiiko which would exercise the option, feelings were rapidly running high. Wisely and significantly, the Mmengo delegation would not be drawn into these heated exchanges; their spokesman, Mr. Sempa, said, "Many provocative remarks have been made in discussion but the Buganda representatives have no wish to indulge in unfruitful controversy." [25]

As expected, it was the U.P.C. leader, Mr. Obote, who led the argument among the Uganda delegates for Mmengo's claim to these optional elections. Knowing as he did, unlike Kiwanuka, that politics is basically the art of the possible, he judiciously sensed that the Secretary of State, himself an astute politician, would lean more heavily towards the powerful combination of the Mmengo and U.P.C. delegations; Obote was a much better judge of what was likely to succeed under the circumstances. His speech on this issue is indicative:

Mr. Kiwanuka has dwelt at considerable length on the merits of direct elections. He has, however, failed to appreciate one of the most important elements of direct elections, namely, that they should be free. If they were not, the elected representatives cannot truly say that they represented the people of their country.

It is well known that no free direct elections were held in Buganda during March; only one-twentieth of the people eligible to vote were registered. The twenty-one Directly Elected Members representing Buganda in the Uganda Legislature were elected by twenty thousand people. This contrasts sharply with the case of Mr. Nadiope, of my own party, who was elected to serve in the Legislature by over twenty-one thousand people in just his own constituency. I could not agree with Mr. Kiwanuka that there should be direct elections at all costs. In the past I have tried to educate the people of Uganda to recognise the importance of the free vote. My efforts in Buganda failed, but I continued to work toward the objective of a National Assembly containing directly elected Buganda representatives in whom the Baganda would have complete confidence.

The second point I wished to make to the Conference was the importance of recognition by the Lukiiko of the Central Government. In the past, direct elections were endorsed by resolutions of the District Councils before taking place; when Ankole held out against direct elections they were not forced to have them. In contrast, elections have been forced upon Buganda, with undesirable results. The position was that most people in Buganda did not recognise the Central Government, and I doubted that this was in Uganda's best interests.

I think the proposals were formulated in the light of the prevailing situation in Buganda. It was vital that the people of Buganda should recognise the Central Government. In my view it was better that this be achieved through indirect elections than that the existing situation be allowed to continue.

The Conference continued with more exchanges; Mr. Kiwanuka at one stage threatened a "walkout":

> It would be a grave mistake to include these proposals in the Constitution in the face of wide-spread disagreement. If however, Her Majesty's Government proposed to incorporate the proposals in an Order-in-Council without reference to what has been said in the Conference, there seems to be little purpose in going on with the Conference.[26]

The Secretary of State once again gave assurance to dispel the fears expressed, and for a while the Conference managed to hold together in an uneasy peace; but it was merely postponing the inevitable. Once, Mr. Kiwanuka, followed by his supporters, rose from his seat and—after he had reaffirmed the D.P.'s distaste for indirect elections—walked out.

He had to return the following day after the Secretary of State decided to continue the work of the Conference; no concession was made to the D.P. Macleod firmly held to the proposal, and despite subsequent attacks against it during the election campaigns, it was embodied in the Constitution.[27]

What is startling, however, and where it may be said Kiwanuka had a legitimate complaint, is that the *reasons* for demanding optional elections were never given by the Buganda delegates in any session or to any Committee of the Conference. There was no doubt that this demand was motivated by an acute desire to maintain the effective loyalty of their people to their traditional legislature, the Great Lukiiko. Direct elections to the National Assembly, it was feared, would minimise the stature and significance of the Lukiiko and, in time, would have diminished or destroyed the distinctiveness and autonomous character of Buganda.

If the price to be paid for integrating Buganda with the rest of the Protectorate was the granting of an option for indirect representation in the National Legislature, it was worth paying, said Obote. When Kiwanuka threatened refusal to compromise on this issue the Secretary of State expressed the consequences of Buganda's nonparticipation in very clear terms:

Everyone must be prepared to work with a spirit of compromise so that the Conference would succeed and Uganda can then proceed to internal self-government and full independence. *This goal will not be achieved without Buganda's participation in the National Assembly* and the proposals under consideration do offer a solution, possibly the only solution, to this problem.* [28]

The politics of the issue apart, it is not correct to say that the granting of this option was undemocratic; it suffices to note that some of the leading democracies of today have houses of their national legislatures indirectly elected. We can conclude that indirect representation or indirect election is more a characteristic of federalism than of democracy.

Widening of the Franchise.   We have noted that the evolution of the franchise broadly followed the pattern of imperial constitutional evolution; the widening was directly related to political and constitutional evolution in other spheres. Under this Constitution the franchise was extended to all persons who would later become Uganda citizens under specified conditions—British-protected persons and British subjects. This novel development was the introduction of a principle strenuously fought for over a number of years—the principle of universal adult suffrage—as embodied in the Constitution.[29]

It apparently appeared strange that the qualifying age for voters became a point of controversy during the Constitutional Conference. The D.P. delegation took the view that "it would be unfair to deny the right to vote to anyone who was required to pay taxes". People in Uganda paid taxes at the age of eighteen, and the principle of "no taxation without representation" was borne in mind.[30]

The U.P.C./K.Y. front supported the almost universal voting age of twenty-one years. They pointed out, with positive effect, that even by law it was only when a person reached twenty-one years of age that he was regarded as sufficiently possessed of sound judgment to be fully liable for criminal and civil responsibility. They exposed the absurdity of the argument of "no taxation without representation" by disclosing that under the income

* Author's emphasis.

tax law even a child was liable to taxation; did it follow that he had the right to vote? It was further argued that only men paid taxes at the time; at what age were women to vote who did not pay taxes?

The other reasons why D.P. and U.P.C. took different stands were never actually revealed at formal Conference meetings, but they were strongly felt and held.

It was the feeling of the U.P.C., and not without grounds, that the D.P. had registered thousands of school children as voters, many around eighteen years of age. The qualifying voting age of twenty-one meant that the U.P.C. could successfully challenge the legality of the minors the D.P. was attempting to keep registered; they were subsequently removed from the register of voters.*

The D.P. felt required to defend its supporters under twenty-one, many of them still in school, who had registered in large numbers and helped to vote their party into power during the previous elections, but first the D.P. had to bring the official qualifying age down to eighteen. They failed to do so.

The Secretary of State favoured twenty-one, and it was to be the operative age for the pre-independence elections; the constitutional provision reflected the difficulty of trying to compromise between two completely opposing views:

> The qualifying age for the purposes of this section shall be such age (not being less than eighteen or more than twenty-one years) as the Legislature of Uganda may prescribe and until that Legislature so prescribes shall be the age of twenty-one years.[31]

Other Members and Officers of the National Assembly. It was provided in the Constitution for a Speaker to be elected from among the Elected Members of the Assembly "who do not hold the office of a Minister, the Attorney-General of Uganda or Parliamentary Secretary *or* from among persons who are not Members of the Assembly but are qualified for election as such." †

---

* Two areas where such registration took place were Kigezi and Ankole.

† The Uganda Constitution, 1961, S. 40. Some delegates, e.g., J. W. Kazzora, advocated that the Speaker should be appointed by the Governor, but this was rejected by the majority. *Record of 3rd Meeting*, U.C.C. (61), p. 3.

Because of work pressure in the Assembly the post of Deputy Speaker was created. Unlike the Speaker, he was to be elected by the Assembly from among the Assembly's own Members.[32]

The tenure of office for the Speaker and his Deputy were retained in the Independence Constitution and the practice, already established, whereby the Speaker or his Deputy had no original or casting vote was continued.[33]

The Constitution also provided for the office of Clerk, which was a constant feature of colonial legislatures and legislatures based on the Westminster model, as well as of cabinet governments within parliamentary democracies. The Clerk is intimately connected with the conduct of business in the Assembly; he draws up the Order Paper of Business for the Members and directs the administrative machinery of the Assembly under the ultimate direction of the Speaker, but unlike the Speaker he is not a Member of the Assembly. His office was constitutionally established as a public office, together with the offices of his subordinates.[34]

Procedure in the National Assembly.   With the exception of the powers of disallowance and reservation of laws, which was always reserved to the Crown until independence, the provisions for the "business procedures" in the National Assembly were reproduced in the Independence Constitution.

We have noted how colonial legislatures in British dependencies have always been given power to determine their procedures.[35] It has been the practice that such procedure is determined by the Assembly itself, in the form of Standing Orders. Since these are matters more of form than of substance, it is not intended to discuss them in detail, but we should note the limitations the Constitution imposed upon the Assembly's power to regulate its own procedure:

(1) It was specifically enacted that "the power of the Legislature of Uganda to make laws shall be exercised by Bills passed by the National Assembly and assented to by Her Majesty or by the Governor on behalf of Her Majesty".[36]

(2) Any question proposed in the National Assembly was to be determined by a majority of the votes of the Members

present and voting, save as otherwise provided for by the Constitution.[37]

Limitations on the Legislative Supremacy of the National Assembly. We will discuss the doctrines of parliamentary and constitutional supremacy in relation to Uganda's sovereign Parliament later, but we should note here the extent to which the legislature of Uganda was still subject to imperial authority in the exercise of its legislative powers. Even under a constitution conferring extensive responsibility for internal self-government (a general provision of imperial constitutional doctrine) the limitations were still considerable.

The Governor's power to withhold assent to proposed legislation and his right to "reserve" a bill for the signification of Her Majesty's pleasure were retained; other subsisting provisions were repeated in conventional form.[38] The Governor was required to reserve, for the signification of Her Majesty, any bill brought before him that appeared to him:

(1)   to be inconsistent with any obligation imposed on Her Majesty by any treaty, convention, or agreement with any country or similar international organisation outside Uganda or any agreement between Her Majesty and the ruler of a Uganda kingdom;[39]

(2)   to be likely to prejudice the royal prerogative. No bill could under any circumstances become law unless the Governor had given it his assent.[40]

There was, in addition, the power of the Crown to disallow certain types of legislation through the Secretary of State, even if such legislation had received the Governor's assent.

Most important, perhaps, was the imperial Parliament's inherent right to legislate directly in relation to Uganda.* Such power, or the power exercised through Orders-in-Council, could in law have been used to increase or curtail whatever legislative supremacy had been conferred on the Uganda legislature. In any event, the Uganda Constitution derived its legal validity from an Order-in-Council, which the British Crown had the

---

* E.g., by virtue of the Colonial Laws Validity Act, 1865, 28 and 29 Vict. C. 63.

legal power to revoke or modify at will.* In practice, however, these powers were invoked only once,† as the general feeling was that an African government was assuming extensive, unlimited powers—for internal affairs—in preparation for independence.

Summoning, Prorogation, and Dissolution. The power to summon the National Assembly for the performance of its duties was vested in the Governor; he was to announce on what date and at what time it was required to assemble.[41] Prorogation, the act of terminating any session of the National Assembly, was also vested in the Governor and was to be acted out at his discretion.

Dissolution,[42] the act of bringing to an end the existence of the National Assembly so that a new Assembly could be elected, was also vested in the Governor acting in accordance with the advice of the Prime Minister. There were important exceptions when the Governor had to act totally at his own discretion:

(1) when the Prime Minister advised a dissolution and the Governor was convinced that government could be carried on without a dissolution or that dissolution would not be in the best interests of Uganda;

(2) if the Assembly passed a resolution of no confidence in the Uganda Government but the Prime Minister refused to resign within three days after the passing of such a resolution;

(3) if the office of the Prime Minister was vacant and the Governor considered that no other Member could command the confidence of the Majority.

Unless sooner dissolved, the National Assembly was to continue for five years from the date of its first sitting and then stand dissolved.

Constituencies and the Electoral Boundary Commission. The existing constituencies were demarcated by the Constitutional Committee in 1959 and were then endorsed by the Relationships

* By the exercise of the Royal Prerogative by the Crown, under the Foreign Jurisdiction Act, 1890.

† Exercised to give the Governor power for issuing the "Writ for the General Election of April 1962" without the advice of the Prime Minister: "The Uganda (Constitution) (Amendment) Order in Council", 1962, S.I. 1962, No. 625, "Legal Notice No. 89 of 1962".

Commission two years later. But constitutional provision still had to be made for the review of these demarcations in the event that the need for such action arose. The Protectorate was to be divided into single-member constituencies in such a manner as the Electoral Boundary Commission might prescribe.[43]

The general principle enunciated required all constituencies to have nearly equal population, but exceptions were permitted for smaller or greater population quotas in order to accommodate the realities of communications, geographical features, density of population, and the existing boundaries of kingdoms, districts, and other administrative areas.[44]

For the purpose of carrying out periodic reviews and the delimitation of constituencies an Electoral Boundary Commission was to be set up consisting of a chairman and not less than two other members appointed by the Governor *after consultation* with the Prime Minister and the Leader of the Opposition.[45]

It was vital to insulate this Commission from the influence of party politics; it was provided: "In the exercise of its functions under this constitution the Electoral Boundary Commission shall not be subject to the direction or control of any other person or authority".[46]

The removal of any member of the Commission was ultimately the responsibility of the Governor; he was not bound by the requirement of consultations with the Prime Minister and Leader of the Opposition in this instance.[47]

Recognition of a Parliamentary Opposition. Before we conclude this review of the National Assembly, it is worth noting the constitutional recognition of Parliamentary Opposition.[48] A general feature of *non-representative* colonial legislatures was that the Representative Members—irrespective of their political philosophies—banded together in "opposition" to the Colonial Civil Service politicians in the local legislative council.

With the advent of representative government it seemed natural that, following parliamentary procedure, recognition should be accorded to every group of Elected Members, even if they were not the majority group.

The suggestion that the Leader of the Opposition be recognised was unanimously adopted despite the disagreements between the D.P. and the U.P.C. on other issues. It was unanimous because of the basic fairness of the principle, but also—in view of the prevailing political uncertainties—it was conceivable that the Opposition and Government parties might either change sides or remain as they were; it suited everyone's interest to stick to the rules of fair play.

The Leader of the Opposition was recognised and defined as "the Member in the National Assembly who, in the opinion of the Governor, acting on his discretion, is the person commanding support of the largest number of Members of the Assembly in opposition to the Government." [49]

In summary, we can characterise the legislature under the Constitution of 1961 as having been a unicameral Parliament based on the principles of parliamentary government and opposition and vested with considerable powers, as a representative body, to enact laws for the good government of the Protectorate but still subject to specific limitations in the interests of imperial authority.

THE EXECUTIVE

The composition of the executive branch of government followed the well-known stereotype of British dependencies approaching independence. The executive authority of Uganda was vested in Her Majesty; in practice this meant that the Crown's representative would be the Governor—who was now required to exercise his authority on the advice of the Cabinet.[50]

The executive authority of the Uganda Government was, as expected, very comprehensive: it was to "extend to the maintenance and execution of the Constitution of Uganda and to all matters with respect to which the Legislature of Uganda has power to make laws".[51] Even the executive authority of Buganda was to be exercised so as not to impede or prejudice the exercise of the executive authority of Uganda.

The Governor and His Special Responsibilities. Although there was now an African elected government, it was the practice under British rule, a practice accepted by the delegates at the Conference, that the Governor should remain a feature of Uganda's constitutional set-up. As never before—to the unanimous satisfaction of the Uganda people—he would now merely serve as the titular Head of State; he was now required to act "in accordance with the advice of the Cabinet or a Minister acting under the general authority of the Cabinet." [52]

The limitations of the legislative supremacy in, and of, the Uganda National Assembly were not unique; there were also limitations on the extent to which the Cabinet could exercise executive authority without restriction. The Governor retained limited but important powers which he could exercise at his own discretion without the authority or direction of the Cabinet. In some matters he could even override the unanimous wishes of the Cabinet:

(1) external affairs;
(2) defence, including the armed forces;
(3) internal security;
(4) operational control of the police forces; and
(5) the execution of obligations of Her Majesty or the Government of Uganda in respect of a kingdom under any Agreement.[53]

Another matter of interest, which was crucial at the time, was the discretionary power given to the Governor in relation to the pre-independence elections. Elections had been pressed by the U.P.C./Mmengo delegations to give the people a chance to select a government not only before independence but also before internal self-government. This was particularly acute because of the twenty-one *politically unrepresentative* Members for Buganda in the Legislative Council. As the U.P.C. leader stated, "The U.P.C. considers that a general election should be held before internal self-government in order to rectify the situation in which the U.P.C. received a majority of votes but did not secure a majority of representatives in the Legislative Council".[54]

He was supported by the U.P.C. legal adviser, Mr. Ibingira, who counselled:

It has been suggested that the present Buganda representatives in the Legislative Council have been legally elected; this is so but it would be wrong to suggest that a person elected by perhaps only twelve people could be regarded as in any way representative. It is important that the government should command the support of the whole country in the period of internal self-government when it assumes more powers and responsibilities.[55]

Mr. Sempa, the Mmengo spokesman, cut in with a convincing argument: "I understand the purpose of internal self-government is to enable the government to gain experience before full independence. It would be a pity if the present government were enabled to carry on until shortly before independence and then were to be replaced by an inexperienced government".[56]

Contrasting this view, as expected, was the resistance from the Chief Minister and his D.P. delegation, who demanded self-government before any elections: "I see no reason why there should be a general election before Uganda becomes internally self-governing, although I agree that there should be a general election before final independence".[57]

The issue of when to hold the next general election suddenly became one of great controversy, basically because, apart from the arguments already noted, it was a matter of sound political strategy. The U.P.C./Mmengo group felt that if Kiwanuka was to be given the extensive powers the Constitution was proposing for internal self-government, he might use these powers to unfair advantage in order to cling to power. But as it was, he was only a nominal executive and so it was better that elections be held while he was still in the same position.

On the other hand, it was popularly held by the D.P. that, with increased authority during internal self-government, they stood a much better chance of beating the menacing opposition of the U.P.C./K.Y. alliance before the new constitution became operational.

To have entrusted the fixing of the date for these elections or giving the responsibility of choosing who was to supervise them to the D.P. government would have been a direct warrant to political uncertainty and possible chaos. It was provided that the responsibility of appointing officers to conduct the coming general election and deciding other related matters was to be entrusted to the Governor at his discretion.[58]

The Governor was also entrusted with the important responsibility of appointing—at his discretion—the Prime Minister, who would be a Member of the National Assembly, assumed by the Governor to command the support of the majority of the Members in the National Assembly.[59]

Deputy Governor. The creation of the post of Deputy Governor within the constitutional hierarchy was a feature of recent origin in British African colonial affairs. It was usually occupied by a former Colonial Chief Secretary, whose role was then assumed by either a Chief Minister or the Prime Minister; therefore the whole scheme was attacked by Uganda delegates as being superfluous and a waste of money. There were solid grounds for their argument. To create a new post for a non-Ugandan, who as Deputy Governor would have very little to do in a constitutional sense, was the wrong thing to do at a time when executive responsibility was passing to elected, indigenous representatives—and, at the same time, the British Governor had correspondingly less work. Nevertheless, the Colonial Secretary had his way and the post, which had actually existed previously, was reestablished in the Constitution of Uganda.[60] The primary function of the Deputy Governor was to act whenever the Governor was unable to do so.[61]

The Cabinet. It was now stipulated that there should be a Cabinet of Ministers consisting of the Prime Minister and other Ministers,[62] the Ministers to be appointed by the Governor on the recommendation of the Prime Minister.

Briefly, the application of the principle of collective responsibility at this particular time meant that the Cabinet was to be collectively responsible to the National Assembly for any advice given to the Governor.* The long-sought goal of an executive body consisting of elected representatives of the people was thus attained, although it was still subject—in several important matters—to imperial authority.

* The Uganda Constitution, 1961, S. 57 (2). It was further provided by S. 64 (2) that there were to be "junior ministers", called Parliamentary Secretaries, to be appointed in the same way as Ministers.

RELATIONS BETWEEN LOCAL ADMINISTRATIONS AND THE CENTRAL GOVERNMENT

We now examine how the intractable problem of distribution of powers between the central authority and the local governments was dealt with under this new constitution. It was not surprising that the negotiations on this topic at the Conference were the longest and, in the view of many delegates, the most crucial.

Buganda's Semi-Federal Status. We noted the concession granted to the Kingdom of Buganda in respect to certain legislative powers which the Lukiiko was to exercise independently of the Uganda Parliament. The Buganda Constitution, incorporated in the Agreement concluded with the British Crown at the end of the Constitutional Conference in 1961, was now also embodied in the Uganda Constitution as a specific schedule, so its legal validity was beyond question. Previously these Agreements with native rulers were of doubtful legal validity. Matters on which the Buganda Lukiiko were given exclusive right to legislate included those which caused Buganda's greatest concern and fear; these fears had driven Buganda on the road towards separatism and secession.

They included the Kabakaship and the various powers, obligations, and duties of the Kabaka. No longer was the Protectorate Government or its eventual successor at independence to have constitutional power to determine the royal incumbent or the fate of the Buganda throne. To this were added exclusive legislative rights regarding the status of the Kabaka's ministers and their powers, obligations, and duties—other than those conferred by or under laws enacted by the National Assembly of Uganda.[63]

The Government in Buganda, being intensely traditional, insisted on having, and did receive, exclusive powers to legislate for its own public service and on all matters relating to her traditional and customary institutions. The exclusive control of her public service was a large concession;[64] it ensured the ruling hierarchy in Mmengo that it could, by careful manipulation of the public service and without the prospect of interference from the central government, maintain a civil service loyal to its objectives in both word and deed. This was particularly important since, unlike political party governments, it did not depend primarily on political party organisation but rather on the activities of its hierarchy of chiefs who were part of the public service.

As a gesture to the grandeur of her status Buganda was also given exclusive rights to legislate regarding Buganda public holidays and festivals. Another important concession was the power to enact exclusive legislation regarding "such taxation and matters relating thereto as may be agreed between the Kabaka's Government and the Government of Uganda".[65]

Executive Powers in Buganda. It was then stipulated that the executive authority of Buganda was to extend to the maintenance and execution of the Constitution of Buganda and to all matters for which the Lukiiko of Buganda had power to make laws. It is interesting to note the limitation of this power, which, within its sphere—assuming that Uganda was a truly federal union—should have been exclusive. Power was extensively limited when the Constitution stipulated that such executive power of the Buganda Government was to be "so exercised as not to impede or prejudice the exercise of the executive authority of Uganda".[66]

On the basis of this proviso it seems proper to contend that it was actually a feature of unitary government and, being so, detracted from the ostensibly federal character accorded to Buganda. At best, it properly placed Buganda in the realm of semi-federalism.

Beyond this exclusive constitutional executive authority, other executive responsibilities could be exercised by the Government by delegation from the Governor on certain matters that constitutionally belonged to the Uganda Government but were to be preformed within Buganda if the Kabaka's Government consented to such action.[67]

The High Court of Buganda. The Buganda delegation to the Constitutional Conference pressed for a High Court of Buganda that would be completely separate from the High Court of Uganda. They demanded a separate Judicial Service Commission whose duty would be the appointment of Buganda's judges;

they demanded that this Commission be appointed by the Kabaka himself.

The existence of two separate High Courts with equal powers in a country of six and a half million people—who had been well served by a single High Court during the previous sixty years—was not a welcome idea to many of the conference delegates. They held, but did not publicly announce, grave doubts about Buganda having an independent court. It was feared the court might be used, if the central government lost all control, as an instrument of coercion against ordinary citizens to extract obedience to the traditional government in Mmengo. If it were put to this use, not only would the fundamental liberties of the ordinary people be in jeopardy, but it would be difficult to effect any progressive reforms in Buganda through the process of political party organisations and public criticism of Government measures. Whether or not these fears were justified or associated with reality is not material, since the central problem remains: these fears were felt, and by a large number of people.

Accordingly, Chief Minister Kiwanuka—in his usual forthright manner—opposed the idea of creating a second High Court.[68] The idea would have been unpalatable even to the U.P.C. but for the ingenious compromise devised by Macleod, which gave the central government effective control over the Buganda High Court: Buganda was to have a High Court of its own, provided that such a court did not have jurisdiction over the following:

(1) issues arising from constitutional provisions on fundamental human rights;

(2) questions relating to membership in the National Assembly;

(3) questions whether a person was qualified to sit or vote in the National Assembly; and

(4) constitutional issues, including interpretation of the Uganda Constitution.[69]

All these matters were reserved for the High Court of Uganda. The greatest concession to those opposed to a Buganda High Court was that the judges of the Uganda High Court would also be the judges of the Buganda High Court; consequently, all issues relating to their tenure of office were entrusted to the Uganda, not Buganda, Judicial Service Commission. The fear of a High Court Judiciary controlled by Mmengo was removed.

In addition, the Chief Justice who would be Chief Justice for both the Uganda and Buganda High Courts was empowered to assign work to these courts—including the power to transfer cases from one court to the other.

The existence of a Buganda High Court stands out as one of the great constitutional fictions in Uganda's constitutional development; it was designed to satisfy Buganda's pride, while essentially remaining a central, Ugandan institution. Justice in Buganda was to be administered in the name of the Kabaka; allied to the administration of justice was the power given to the Kabaka of commutation and remission of sentences of prisoners serving in prisons administered by his government.[70]

Constitutional Interpretation and Right of Privy Council Appeal. The constitutional provisions for every district and kingdom were a result of hard negotiations, especially those for Buganda, which emerged with more concessions than any other area. It was natural that every delegate felt that what had been agreed to at the Conference, now embodied in the Constitution, had to be jealously and carefully guarded. For this reason, as usually happens in common-law countries, the interpretation of the Constitution was reserved exclusively for the Uganda High Court.[71]

Perhaps what most arrested the anxiety of many people was the provision allowing "appeal as of right, direct to Her Majesty in Council" from any final decision of the High Court of Uganda:

(1) on any question concerning the interpretation of the Constitution; or

(2) on any question referred to the High Court involving justiciable disputes between the United Kingdom Government or Protectorate Government on the one hand and the governments of any of the Uganda kingdoms on the other.[72]

This provision was in conformity with the Munster Commission recommendations; the Privy Council, being a court thousands of miles away, was regarded as the ultimate and most impartial judicial tribunal. Being so remote, it would be a court uninformed of the realities prevailing in Uganda at the time of any justiciable issue; that its very remoteness, rather than being a source of strength, might be a source of weakness, was never given serious consideration. It was, so it seems, preferred to a local court in much the same way as a British Governor-General was—at first—preferred to a Ugandan.

We have considered matters provided for in the Buganda Agreement that were also included in the Buganda Constitution in addition to being scheduled in the Internal Self-Government Constitution. In addition to these matters, Buganda received other substantial concessions as embodied in the 1961 Agreement which were eventually included in the Independence Constitution.

Following are comments on several of these concessions included in the Buganda Agreement.[73]

The Kabaka's Police Force. The issue of who would be responsible for public safety and public order in the country during internal self-government was a matter of keen concern for most delegates.

It was suspected, in private, by parties and groups in opposition to the D.P. Government that if constitutional power for internal security was entirely left to this government it might be tempted to use such powers "unfairly" against overwhelming political opposition to maintain itself in authority. Even the U.P.C., which originally wanted the transfer of this responsibility to the D.P. Government, revised its opinion and firmly supported the Buganda delegation in its contention that this responsibility should be left with the Governor.*

It was provided that the Governor would be responsible for defence, including the armed forces, internal security, and operational control of the police forces; "at his discretion" he could delegate this responsibility to a minister.[74] The Chief Minister's demand that he himself be given these powers reinforced the

* The U.P.C. opinion was given by Obote. See U.C.C. (61), record of 14th Meeting, p. 4.

fears of his opponents, and as a result, Macleod rejected the demand.*

Allied to these decisions concerning internal security was the concession granted to Buganda for establishing a police force of its own. This was the logical consequence of the provision requiring the Kabaka's Government to take all reasonable steps in maintaining public order and safety in Buganda.[75] This power was limited in scope; the Inspector-General of the Uganda Police was empowered to give directives regarding the operational control of any police force in Uganda, including Buganda's. Although the Kabaka's police force would be commanded by its own officers, it was expressly stated that they were subject to the authority of the Inspector-General of the Uganda Police.[76]

Services to Be Administered by the Kabaka's Government. Devolution of administrative responsibility from the central to the district and kingdom governments, particularly to Buganda, was a feature of Uganda's constitutional set-up. This feature was partially responsible for the mistaken argument that Uganda was a federal union.

The administrative services given to Buganda under the 1955 Agreement were retained, and several more were added under the Agreement of 1961. These services were divided into two categories: grant-aided (those the Uganda Government funded) and non-grant-aided services.

The grant-aided services covered education, medical, agricultural, and veterinary services; water supplies, prison services, and the Kabaka's police service were also included, along with certain road and urban services.[77]

The non-grant-aided services covered markets, ferries, development of African trade, development of cooperatives, housing, town planning, and forestry.†

The administration of these services was subject to stipulated conditions and to the laws passed by the Uganda legislature in relation to their administration.

* Kiwanuka's demands to control internal security are found in U.C.C. (61), pp. 5, 6 of the 14th meeting record.
† Contained in The Buganda Agreement, 1961, Pt. II. These were reproduced in toto in the First Schedule to the Uganda Constitution at independence.

Grants and Revenues.   Parallel to the Report of the Relationships Commission was the Hicks Report dealing with the fiscal
relations between the various local governments and the central
government. It formed the basis for all financial relations between Buganda and the central government.

The revenue of the Kabaka's Government was to be derived
from: (1) a graduated tax up to a maximum of Shs. 600/– per
annum per person; (2) rates on land and property, other than
agricultural land in rural areas, under Uganda law; (3) rents; (4)
market dues; (5) fees and fines; (6) interest on investments; (7)
royalties; (8) contributions and endowments; and (9) reimbursements in aid.[78]

This revenue scheme could be varied by agreement between
the Uganda Government and the Kabaka's Government. In addition, grants were made to the Kabaka's Government for running the services already mentioned, but such grants were made
only on condition that the Kabaka's Government administer the
services to which these grants related in a proper and efficient
manner.[79] Officers of the Uganda Government were empowered
to inspect these services in order to assist and advise officers of
the Kabaka's Government on how they should be run.[80]

Buganda came off more handsomely than any other kingdom
or district. More powers than it had ever been legally entitled to
exercise were now, by force of the Constitution, accorded to it.
This new position was an excellent substitute for secession or
greater autonomy. In the majority of these granted powers the
Uganda Government held fairly effective checks and, in constitutional nomenclature, the relation between the Buganda and
Uganda Governments was more semi-federal than federal; in
some important aspects it was actually unitary.

The Kingdoms of Ankole, Bunyoro, and Toro.   The battle-
ground for the federal-status argument of the other kingdoms—
Ankole, Bunyoro, and Toro—now shifted from Uganda to the
Victorian splendour of Lancaster House in London.

It was no secret that Buganda was getting a larger measure of
federalism than she had ever enjoyed. Because of their desire not
to be surpassed by Buganda and, no doubt, because of the uncertainty surrounding the disposition of the African government
at independence, which in all probability would consist largely

of non-monarchal Ugandans, these kingdoms pressed for a larger measure of federal status during internal self-government. They were encouraged in their demands by the activities of the major political party leaders.

Aware of their slipping grip on Buganda, the D.P. Government pressed extravagant demands for these kingdoms to be on a par with Buganda, even when it would be economically disastrous for them. The D.P.'s idea was to undermine the support for U.P.C. in these kingdoms by taking the simple but very effective position that the U.P.C. was selling them out to Buganda.

To safeguard support in these kingdoms, after promoting a certain measure of federalism for Buganda, the U.P.C. deemed it politic also to promote the principle of federalism for these kingdoms. The U.P.C. delegation submitted a memorandum to the Conference: "It is because of these kingdoms' Agreements (with Britain) and because intrinsically the spirit of kingdom institutions does not merely depend on territorial size or economic prosperity that there must be basic and similar constitutional arrangements for *all* the Uganda kingdoms".*

Having rejected the designation of "semi-federal" recommended by the Munster Commission, the Memorandum recounted the case for federalism:

It is a fact of political life that the psychology and feeling of a country matters to no mean degree. It is understandable that the term "semi-federal" is undignified and indicates a status lost between the worlds of federalism and unitary rule. More important is the cohesion and traditional outlook of these kingdoms that is so deeply rooted they consider themselves as "independent" entities. These kingdoms were to be federal to the extent that they would have exclusive legislative competence regarding their kingships and traditional institutions. We argued the prefix "semi" should be dropped to make way for *federal* status and this should be manifested not merely in name but—*to some degree*—in substance.

It is a reality of constitutional law a country can have a strong, unifying central government and, at the same time, have its com-

* The document, U.C.C. (61), p. 17, was entitled "The Status of the Kingdoms of Toro, Ankole, Bunyoro and Other Districts Like Busoga", drafted by the author for the U.P.C. delegation to the Conference.

ponent parts (or some of them) *federally* related to the centre. It could not be argued that granting federal status to these kingdoms and Busoga would inevitably weaken the central legislature. The crux of the matter rests with the form of the division of powers between the centre and the component units. . . .

Once a federal status replaces a semi-federal one for these kingdoms and Busoga we feel that the dignity and status of the kingdom rulers would be *appropriately* realised; the chiefs and people of these kingdoms would feel satisfied and the power and unifying force of the central government would in no way be materially affected.[81]

It was a document of considerable diplomatic skill; all that was really proposed was the substitution of "federal" for "semi-federal" while, in fact, the division of powers proposed was a classic illustration of semi-federalism.[82]

The D.P. Government, despite its public clamour on behalf of these kingdoms, did not submit a Memorandum supporting their stance; but Kiwanuka did express some scepticism towards the U.P.C. proposals for federalism:

. . . although not wishing to quarrel with the idea of federal status for the kingdoms . . . the effect of granting such a status would be far reaching. It would be difficult to discourage other districts from wanting a similar status and they would all have a logical case for claiming the same powers as it is proposed to accord to Buganda.[83]

The D.P delegation was content to have Kiwanuka submit the only Memorandum on the stipulation that required rulers in the western kingdoms to receive ceremonial standing (the title "His Highness" along with gun salutes) equal to that enjoyed by the Kabaka of Buganda.

In a country administered under indirect rule, where the concept of unity was only beginning, it would have been a reckless disregard of realities not to relax the anxieties of these kingdoms by providing some measure, however limited, of federalism. Although this status was not granted immediately, it was not opposed by the Colonial Secretary; it was embodied in the new Agreements concluded with each kingdom.[84]

Apart from safeguarding the thrones and related traditional matters of these kingdoms, it was expressly stated that the scope of their Councils' powers would be the same as those enjoyed by the districts.[85] There was no power to make concurrent legislation, as the Secretary of State rejected this view; it was going to be a unitary government for them.[86] The only federal principle allowed was in relation to the position of each individual ruler in his respective kingdom, where the kingdoms had exclusive powers. During the internal self-government period the Governor was left with absolute discretion to disallow any legislation or Act that might contravene any provision of the Agreements with these kingdoms.[87]

Because it was not possible to conclude these Agreements at the Conference (they were finalised just before independence), the only concessions not already noted related to the administration of justice. The Constitution provided for the High Court of Uganda to administer justice in the name of each ruler when sitting in the kingdoms of Ankole, Bunyoro, or Toro.[88] This concession was made to curb the protest reaction from the kingdoms when Buganda was granted her own High Court and they were not.

Local Administrations in the Districts and Western Kingdoms. The administrative set-up in the western kingdoms would be like those in the districts. There were several features peculiar to districts, which were concessions to their own specific desires and demands. They, too, had been clamouring for the right to have their own equivalent of a king, now called a "Constitutional Head." [89] It was provided that the Council of any district could create the post of Constitutional Head if a resolution for its creation was approved by a two-thirds majority of its members, but before the resolution could take effect the Governor's consent was required.[90]

To satisfy the growing love for pomp it was agreed that the Constitutional Head of a district would take precedence over all other persons in the district except Her Majesty or Her Majesty's representative.

Functions of the Local Administrations. We have traced the development of District Councils (now called "Administrations") under indirect rule; what is essential to note is the increase in their responsibilities. As independence drew near it was suddenly decided to give them even more powers in an effort to diminish the power of the District Commissioner; as Munster also recommended, the post of Provincial Commissioner was abolished.

The Administrations were empowered to administer the following:[91]

(1) Education Services—(a) primary schools, (b) junior secondary schools, (c) farm schools (up to the first eight years), (d) rural trade schools (up to the first eight years), and (e) homecraft centres (up to the first eight years).

(2) Medical and Health Services—(a) dispensaries, health centres, sub-dispensaries and aid posts, (b) maternity and child welfare services, (c) school health services, (d) control of communicable diseases, including leprosy and tuberculosis, subject to the overall responsibility of the Uganda Minister of Health, (e) rural ambulance services, and (f) the provision of environmental hygiene and health education services.

(3) Water Supplies—the construction and maintenance of rural water supplies subject to international obligations and to the approval and supervision of the Uganda Government.

(4) Roads—maintenance and construction of roads, other than roads maintained by the Uganda Ministry of Works.

(5) Prisons—in addition to general mandatory powers, the prison administrators were given permissive functions, covering an extensive range of subjects, if they felt competent to perform them.[92] They were entrusted with the general duty "to assist in the maintenance of order and good government within the area of its authority." [93] The provisions of the 1955 Ordinance, which entrusted local governments with the responsibility of maintaining law and order, were repeated.[94] With the consent of the Uganda Government they were empowered to set up police forces for the execution of this responsibility, subject to the approval of the Uganda Government; these Administrations were empowered to make laws in respect of

(a) any matter for which they are required or permitted to make laws, (b) personal and customary laws, (c) public security, and (d) functions they are required or permitted to carry out.

Scope of the Administrations' Legislation. At one time neither the local African courts nor the District Councils had responsibility or power over non-Africans within their jurisdiction. With the advent of representative institutions and self-government this situation had to change; it should have changed long before. Now the laws passed by Administrations would affect everyone, and non-Africans were exempt only when these laws dealt with local African customary, traditional, or cultural matters.[95]

To mark the importance of the Administrations' new status it was provided that their enactments would be called "laws" instead of "by-laws"; they were, like by-laws, still subject to the legislation of the Uganda Parliament.[96]

The powers of the Chief were redefined; he had been an indispensable feature of government under indirect rule and still was during internal self-government. There would be no appreciable detraction from his status within the new social order.

The advent of directly elected Councils partially overshadowed his position politically, as the focus now shifted from the Chief to the Councils—which were now the new bosses of the Chiefs.[97]

Revenues of the Administrations. Increased responsibilities and the approach of independence demanded that the revenues of these Administrations should be more precisely marked and not left to the discretion of the Governor, as they had been in the past.

It was provided that the revenues of any Administration, other than grants from the Government, were—so far as the Administration was authorised to collect them—to consist of: (a) graduated tax up to a maximum of Shs. 600/– per annum per tax-payer, (b) rates, (c) rents and other revenue collected by land boards, (d) market dues, (e) fees and fines, (f) interest on investments, (g) royalties, (h) donations, contributions, and endowments, (i) reimbursements, and (j) such other revenue as the Uganda Government would approve.[98]

Provision was also made for the Uganda Government to give each Administration specific types of grants.[99]

The Council for each district or kingdom, which was to shoulder these obligations, was required by the Constitution to be at least nine-tenths elected according to the electoral law for the National Assembly, subject to several stipulated modifications.[100]

To confirm their dignity each Administration was endowed with the same immunities and privileges as were accorded to Members of the National Assembly when taking part in the proceedings of the Assembly.[101] The Councils, which were constitutionally created on 1 March 1962, were not only enhanced in status but also became more representative and were now responsible to an electorate. They were very different from their predecessors, who were responsible only to District Commissioners and other Protectorate authorities when under indirect imperial rule.

"The Strength of the Bargain".   It would not be an overstatement to say that the result of this new distribution of powers and responsibilities between the various parts of Uganda and the central government offered, prima facie at least, a comfortable solution to the long-standing problem of relations between the various parts of the Protectorate. Indirect rule ensured greater development to local governments; indeed, to a large degree the history of Uganda is a history of local governments. Once these problems were satisfactorily resolved, the way was clear for smooth internal self-government and eventual independence.

8. Uganda Becomes an Independent State

The 1962 Elections

Internal self-government came—amid great excitement and high expectation—to the Uganda Protectorate on 1 March 1962, when the Internal Self-Government Constitution came into effect. Pomp and splendour characterised the ceremonies, which were highlighted by the swearing-in *anew* of the D.P. Government within the precincts of our Parliamentary buildings.

Kiwanuka became our first Prime Minister, and his Council of Ministers became the first Cabinet.* To the U.P.C. Opposition and their Mmengo allies the new era marked fresh resolution to oust Kiwanuka from authority, just as he himself was now more and more determined to remain in power.

The successful conclusion of the 1961 Constitutional Confer-

* Members of the first Cabinet in the Internal Self-Government were: Prime Minister, the Hon. B. K. M. Kiwanuka; Minister of State, the Hon. S. Bemba; Minister of Finance, the Hon. L. K. M. Sebalu; Minister of Economic Development, the Hon. A. A. Latim; Minister of Legal Affairs and Attorney-General, the Hon. P. J. Wilkinson, Q.C.; Minister of Health, the Hon. Z. R. Babukika; Minister of Home Affairs, the Hon. G. O. B. Oda; Minister of Social Development, the Hon. E. E. K. Mukira; Minister of Works, the Hon. N. E. Opio; Minister of Land and Water Resources, the Hon. M. Mugwanya; Minister of Agriculture and Animal Industry, the Hon. B. J. Mukasa; Minister of Local Government, the Hon. O. J. K. Nabeta; Minister of Education, the Hon. J. C. Kiwanuka; Minister of Commerce and Industry, the Hon. C. K. Patel. Quoted from *Proceedings of the National Assembly*, 1962, Pt. IV (1).

ence allowed no time for letting matters rest. The date for independence, announced at the final plenary session of the Conference, was set at 9 October 1962. Even before the delegates returned to Uganda, the U.P.C. and Mmengo leaders, who had participated in the Conference, were busy planning their strategy for the general elections scheduled for the following April and for the Buganda Lukiiko elections due to be held even earlier.

The Birth of Kabaka Yekka and the 1962 Lukiiko Elections

The prospect of full-scale elections to the Lukiiko was received by the traditional regime in Mmengo with all the hopes and fears of a people taking their first leap toward the unknown. It would be the first acceptable general election ever held in their kingdom; an election organised and run on laws which they had not enacted and under a situation in which they and the D.P. were—prima facie at least—on an equal footing.*

The leaders in Mmengo had to think quickly how to organise the masses and win an election, all within four months. There were numerous parties in Buganda at the time, including some that had turned pro-Mmengo, but most of them had only nominal existence, and despite the various vicissitudes the D.P. was subject to, it was—as was commonly known—the strongest party in Buganda.†

The prospect of Mmengo joining the U.P.C. and lending all its considerable weight so that the political contest in Buganda would primarily be between the U.P.C. and the D.P. was considered but rejected for many reasons—some of which were tactically sound.

Apart from a few vociferous supporters in isolated places, the

* The Legislative Council (Elections) Ordinance, 1957, was modified by the Buganda (Electoral Provisions) Order, 1962, to govern the conduct of the Lukiiko elections. See Peagram, *Uganda National Assembly Elections*, 1962, p. 4.

† Contrary to the many allegations against K.Y. of malpractices, the Supervisor of Elections exonerated them in his report: "Although this was the first large-scale direct election to be held in Buganda, the arrangements were highly satisfactory and reports of irregularities were few. No election petitions were lodged." *Ibid.*

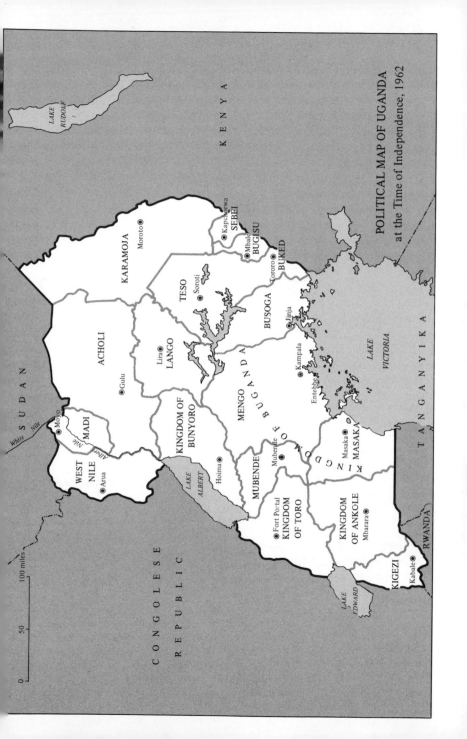

POLITICAL MAP OF UGANDA
at the Time of Independence, 1962

U.P.C. had no real support among the masses in Buganda. To have embarked on popularising the U.P.C. with any reasonable effectiveness in a matter of only a few months would have been a risk of considerable magnitude.

In any event, the Mmengo regime embarked on a systematic course of liquidating the various political parties. Through its tightly knit pyramid of chiefs Mmengo had effectively turned the bulk of the population against political parties; the leaders in Mmengo could not, therefore, turn the new leaf of advancing political parties without risking loss of support or opening themselves up to effective attack for being too changeable.

There was another vital reason why the Mmengo regime could not easily settle for supporting or forming a political party; the fear of religious appeal the D.P. would exert on the Catholic masses. Political support was still, in large measure, based on religion and tribalism, and the Catholics constituted the largest religious group in Buganda. Unless there was something to deflect a substantial number of Catholics from supporting the D.P.—for the sake of religion—the prospects for the return of the traditional government to power were doubtful.

The brains of Mmengo did not have to overtax themselves to find out what sort of organisation they needed and by what name it was to be called. The term "Kabaka" had been the fulcrum of the kingdom's existence; Buganda's desire to secede was largely inspired by anxiety for the Kabakaship. It is an institution commanding great emotional attachment among the Buganda. It was not altogether surprising, then, that shortly after the Constitutional Conference the Mmengo regime announced the formation of the Kabaka Yekka (K.Y.)—"The King Alone" —as the vehicle by which they were going to contest the Lukiiko elections. K.Y. was never intended to be permanent—it was an emergency ad hoc measure—but the result of their efforts was masterly and truly astonishing. The Mmengo regime did not need any "manifesto" outlining their programme of development if elected; it sufficed to rephrase Jesus's famous dictum: "He who is not for me is against me." Whoever was not a member of Kabaka Yekka was automatically anti-Kabaka and assumed to be living a treasonable existence. In essence, the Lukiiko elections would be a referendum on the continued existence of Buganda as a kingdom.

K.Y. was the only organisation that all monarchists could comfortably join. Allegations were levelled against Kiwanuka and many of his leading Baganda supporters, claiming that they were plotting to overthrow the monarchy and establish a republic in its place. The leaders of K.Y. consistently denied that it was a political party; they insisted that it was a "movement". This was in line with their tactic of discrediting all political parties, although they had ample evidence to justify their new alliance with the U.P.C. Kiwanuka's opponents had ample political means to attack him effectively. He was often unguarded and untactful in his public speeches on Buganda issues, even when he had justifiable cause; he should have made his arguments in more astute language.*

Despite the fact that Kiwanuka was head of the entire Protectorate, the force Kabaka Yekka brought to bear when the chiefs were organised in the open campaign for K.Y. was visibly overpowering. There were bitter D.P. protests that the chiefs were arbitrarily arresting their leaders and supporters in the villages. Kiwanuka must have felt great frustration—considering that he had all the Protectorate's forces at his command—when he could not, under the Constitution, intervene effectively to redress alleged injustices or regain the political initiative.

* It should also be noted that during this period the relations between the Kabaka and his Government and the Catholic hierarchy were very strained. In a long letter to his Catholic followers, the Archbishop of Rubaga wrote rather critically of the Kabaka's involvement in politics on the basis that the Kabaka was a constitutional monarch and therefore supposed to be above politics. The Archbishop then left to attend a conference in Canada; on learning of the letter and its expressed disapproval of the Kabaka's activities, the Kabaka ordered the arrest of Monsignor Joseph Ssebayigga, who was the Archbishop's assistant. On 24 November, a D.P. Member of the National Assembly (Mr. Mbazira) tabled a motion for the Assembly's adjournment as a means of demonstrating the Assembly's disapproval of the arrest. Mbazira said: "This is what is raising a certain uncertainty in us, when we realise at this moment of time, that this sort of thing can happen. It could have happened fifty or sixty years ago, but not now. Mr. Speaker, I raise my voice not because a Catholic priest is concerned, nor because I myself am a Catholic. No, I say this that what has been done runs counter to the Charter of Human Rights, the Charter which has been embodied in our new Constitution and indeed in the new Constitution of Buganda." Quoted from *Proceedings of the Legislative Council*, 1961, Pt. 1, p. 1963.

The great blow came when, in accordance with the Buganda Constitution, the Kabaka appointed an Electoral Boundary Commissioner to demarcate the sixty-eight Lukiiko Constituencies.* The Commissioner, the D.P. alleged, ensured that D.P. constituencies would be as few as possible. This was no great problem; with an electorate largely influenced by religion, it was easy to demarcate constituencies on a religious basis. It was certainly a demoralising situation for the D.P.†

The U.P.C., more experienced in campaigns and public speaking, rendered invaluable assistance to K.Y. in directing this campaign. It was an election of great excitement; it was a momentous event, indeed, when the overwhelming mass of Baganda, who had held out for so long, now threw themselves heart and soul into Parliamentary elections.‡

K.Y. was not without its detractors; the D.P. rightly branded it a tribal organisation. They claimed it was not working for the interests of the country's unity. *Munno*, the Catholic newspaper, more than any organ of public expression maintained political attacks against K.Y. Some leaders of the Protestants branded K.Y. a pagan organisation, probably because the appeal of the Kabaka's name had drawn the bulk of the people away from political parties that were based on religion.§ As expected, the Catholic fathers gave every assistance to the D.P., but they were resisting the inevitable.

The day after polling was completed news came from every corner of Buganda announcing K.Y. victories; amid all the unparalleled excitement and joy for the U.P.C./K.Y. supporters, great sorrow and shock dominated the D.P.

The K.Y. romped home with sixty-five seats, while the D.P. won only three, and they were from the "Lost Counties". This

* In accordance with Ss. 22, 23 of the Buganda Constitution, 1961.

† Indeed, when the 68 Lukiiko constituencies were published *Munno* commented that the boundaries were demarcated with a view to giving disproportionate share to the Protestants and inadequate numbers to Catholics and Moslems.

‡ In many constituencies, polling was more than 90 percent of the registered voters; see Uganda National Assembly Elections 1962, p. 4, para. 15 (iv). Many deposits were forfeited: *ibid.,* Appendix H.

§ Correspondence in the Protestant newspaper, *New Day,* between Rev. Welbourn and U.P.C. leaders during this period of the campaign.

period was one of the happiest during the relation between the
U.P.C. and the Mmengo regime. There was no conflict over ide-
ology, for the K.Y., in the absence of a policy of its own, was, for
the time being at least, willing to accept that of the U.P.C. The
overriding consideration was to defeat the D.P., and on this
score no allies in the prosecution of a common cause could have
been more unanimous or more committed than these two. The
basis for the harmony in this alliance could not have been a lasting one once the basic objective was realised.

It was a foregone conclusion that the twenty-one Buganda
representatives in the Uganda National Assembly would be
elected by the Lukiiko, acting as an electoral college; not a single D.P. would be among them.* It was a great loss to the D.P.,
which, in the last general election, had won twenty seats. The
U.P.C., on the other hand, assured of twenty-one Members in
the National Assembly, moved with great confidence and resolution toward the general elections to be held in the three other
regions of Uganda during April.

THE GENERAL ELECTIONS OF 1962

The results of the Lukiiko elections decisively set the pattern
and influenced the tactics of political campaigns outside Buganda. Kiwanuka, still Prime Minister, knew full well that the
return of his D.P. to power would depend entirely on his getting
a majority from the three regions of Buganda. This period remains memorable for the extremes to which he had to go in
order to maintain his position.

The politics of Uganda, as they were in the 1961 general election, were based largely on religion and tribalism. The D.P.
sought to destroy the U.P.C. by a skilful appeal to the non-Baganda masses on these twin sentiments.

Kiwanuka, his co-leaders, and the D.P. organisers all went
outside Buganda to impress upon the masses and their leaders
that Obote and his U.P.C. colleagues had enslaved or sold the
rest of the country to Buganda. It was stressed in every corner of
the country that this was the price the U.P.C. paid for the alliance. In the kingdoms of Ankole, Bunyoro, and Toro Kiwanuka

---

* This was a pledge of the K.Y. leaders during the campaign.

exerted supreme effort to discredit the U.P.C. in the eyes of the rulers by playing on their egos, stating that the U.P.C. had promised to make the Kabaka Head of State at independence. He made further dramatic gestures to secure federal status for these kingdoms and, at the same time, undermined—or at least attempted to undermine—the U.P.C. by claiming that it was against this concession of federalism for any kingdom other than Buganda.

He issued a public statement in Fort Portal that the general elections, which had been scheduled for April, would not take place unless the other kingdoms were given federal status.* Meanwhile, in a sudden and spectacular move, he flew all the rulers of the western kingdoms, along with the Kyabazinga of Busoga, to London to press this demand before the Colonial Secretary.

Sensing the shifting political fortunes in Uganda, the Colonial Secretary wisely refused to commit himself. He told the rulers that the type of government their kingdoms were to have would be decided by a pre-independence conference to be held after the April general election. The rulers then flew back to Uganda —empty-handed. Convinced that only the D.P. could support their case for federalism after these elections, and frustrated by the slight felt after their fruitless trip to London, the rulers of the western kingdoms lent their sympathy to Kiwanuka and his D.P. It was, indeed, thorough work on the part of Kiwanuka and the D.P.

The D.P.'s appeal to religion was now also intensified, especially in Toro, where potential Catholic support existed.

The U.P.C. reacted with vigorous and eloquent defence, pointing out that their alliance with Buganda offered the only way to voluntary and peaceful unity of the Uganda peoples. They questioned their tribesmen (non-Baganda) about the wisdom of believing what Kiwanuka had promised them when he had so decisively been rejected by his own tribe in the Lukiiko

---

* An Order-in-Council was issued from London in order to surmount Kiwanuka's move to postpone elections by refusing to advise the Governor to issue the Writ for holding them. The Order empowered the Governor to issue the Writ without having to consult the Cabinet: S.I. 1962, No. 625, The Uganda (Constitution) (Amendment) Order-in-Council, 1962, S. 2 (2).

elections. The U.P.C. alleged, and not without foundation, that the D.P. stood for perpetuating divisions in the country as instanced by the spreading of their dislike for Buganda to other parts of the country. It can fairly be said that the U.P.C. at this period was the most apparent symbol for unity in the country.

To retrieve their position in the western kingdoms the U.P.C. eloquently denied that they had ever opposed federalism for these kingdoms. To demonstrate this they made a motion, from the Opposition, in the following terms: "That this Assembly do request the Secretary of State for the Colonies to open negotiations with the Kingdoms of Ankole, Bunyoro and Toro and the District of Busoga with a view to granting them *appropriate* forms of federal status."

Having recalled the U.P.C. efforts at the 1961 Constitutional Conference on this matter, the mover, in the course of a lengthy appeal, said:

> Mr. Speaker, I do not want to appear to be campaigning. I will not therefore try to demand fantastic powers for these kingdoms with federal status. When one considers these areas are in fact districts and the largest of them has barely half a million people and the income which they derive in the respective areas, if compared with the Kingdom of Buganda, is very small, then as realists we must come to the conclusion that the federal powers which should be granted to these kingdoms should match their economic ability to meet the responsibilities of federal status. . . .
>
> I am asking for a principle to be conceded and that once it is conceded we should negotiate for federal status, then the kingdoms should be prepared to negotiate as to what powers they are capable of handling, but within the framework of federal government.*

Kiwanuka, having claimed that the U.P.C. had never advocated federal status for these kingdoms, and stating that the U.P.C.'s efforts were too late, accepted the motion; it was then passed by the Assembly.

Even without the U.P.C.'s efforts the die was already cast in the western kingdoms: Out of twelve seats the U.P.C. won only two of Ankole's six, and lost all of Toro and Bunyoro. In Bun-

---

* Moved by the author, G. Ibingira. *Proceedings of the National Assembly*, Pt. IV, p. 3431.

yoro the D.P. effectively circulated the propaganda that one of the bargains the U.P.C. had made with Buganda was for the "Lost Counties" never to be returned to Bunyoro.

If political fortune had smiled on Kiwanuka and his followers during the heyday of technical victories in 1961, it now irretrievably frowned upon them. Outside Buganda and in the Municipality of Kampala the U.P.C. won an unquestionable victory.* These elections were basically the same as those of 1961; appeals were made on the same basis as in 1961. It would be correct to say that outside Buganda the central issue in these elections was whether to support a party that was for or against Buganda in general and the Kabaka in particular. This political strategy was selected by Kiwanuka and his D.P. followers; the U.P.C. had no option but to defend itself on the same issue and, where appropriate, to launch counteroffensives.

With the twenty-one Indirectly Elected Members from Buganda (elected by the Lukiiko) and the thirty-seven Directly Elected Members of the U.P.C., A. Milton Obote, President of the U.P.C. and former Leader of the Opposition, was called upon by Governor Coutts to form the Government which would soon carry Uganda to independence.

The Independence Constitution

The Conference to draw up the Independence Constitution was opened by the Secretary of State at Marlborough House on 12 June 1962. It was divided into three main committees:

* Candidates had been nominated in the following order; from *Uganda National Assembly Elections*, 1962, pp. 5, 6.

Democratic Party	—	59
Uganda People's Congress	—	58
Uganda National Congress	—	6
Uganda African Union	—	1
Bataka Party of Busoga	—	5
Independents	—	10

The results of the 59 constituencies (candidates for 2 constituencies in Toro agreed not to stand as a gesture to their ruler's demand for federalism) were as follows:

D.P.	22	(474,256)
U.P.C.	37	(537,598)

The 2 seats in Toro were eventually won by D.P.

(1)   The Committee on Finance was to work out the financial relations between the Central Government and the regions. Amos Sempa was the Uganda Government's chief spokesman.

(2)   The Citizenship Committee was entrusted with drawing up conditions and requirements for being or becoming a Uganda citizen. Godfrey Banaisa, Attorney-General, was the Uganda Government's chief spokesman.

(3)   The Constitutional Committee dealt with the balance of the Constitution and, as Minister of Justice, I led the Uganda Government team.

The Conference lasted nearly a month. But it remains a fact that Obote, as leader of the Uganda Government delegation, spent most of this time not at the Conference thrashing out arguments and bargaining with delegates but in his hotel suite. The minutes of this Conference would reveal that he never participated in the Conference for more than five working sessions. One evening when I went to his suite to solicit his attendance at the following morning's session, he told me he could not attend because he needed time to think over problems alone. Yet he was seldom alone, and what he thought out was of no value unless put before the delegates to assist the Conference.

Nevertheless, he was present at both the plenary opening of the Conference and at its ending. When the Conference opened he had this to say for the Government he led: "My delegation is of the clear opinion that discussions should be confined to the reserved powers left last year to the Governor. This, in the view of my delegation, includes even the Agreements between Her Majesty's Government and the kingdoms in Uganda." [1]

Even at a date so close to independence Obote had to admit to the delegates that Uganda's greatest problem, the excessive demands from various tribes, which was not conducive to unity, still existed:

Let me agree that although I have spoken of Uganda as a single entity, it is divided in several ways. Such divisions as exist may come out during the Conference but despite any division or difference of opinion, Uganda has a single purpose, a single goal and a single mission in this Conference, namely, the achievement of Independence.

The Independence Constitution was based on its predecessor for internal self-government. We will not comment on non-controversial issues but it is essential that we consider matters that were subject to varying degrees of controversy and whose alteration in the future was to cause even greater disagreement.

PARLIAMENT

The Uganda Government, having accepted the Queen as head of their sovereign state, left the composition of Parliament as it had been previously; the National Assembly also retained its previous numerical strength.[2]

Provisions concerning the structure of Parliament,[3] such as the Speaker and his Deputy and the Clerk of the Assembly, remained unaltered.

Qualifications for Membership. These were (a) being a Uganda citizen who had attained the age of twenty-one and (b) ability to speak and, unless incapacitated by blindness or other physical cause, to read the official language well enough to take an active part in the proceedings of the Assembly. In view of the arguments of a later date concerning a one-party state, it should be noted that no membership in any political party was made a condition for election to the National Assembly. The list of disqualifications was almost a reproduction of the previous one.[4]

Qualifications of Voters. A person who: (a) had attained the age of twenty-one years, (b) was a citizen of Uganda, and (c) had been resident in Uganda for the six months immediately preceding the date he applied for registration as a voter was, unless otherwise disqualified as a voter under any law, entitled to register for the elections and to vote.[5]

The Electoral Commission. As for the Electoral Commission, the Governor-General was to appoint its members but no longer *after consultation* with the Prime Minister and the Leader of the Opposition, but rather *on the advice* of the Prime Minister, who was now charged with *consulting* the Leader of the Opposition *before* tendering his advice to the Governor.[6] The independence of the Commission in the execution of its duties was maintained.

Legislative Powers of Parliament. We noted previously the limitations on the Uganda Legislature from the time it was called the Legislative Council until the internal self-government era. Those limitations were part of the imperial constitutional doctrine, imposed, as we observed, for the safety of colonial rule.

Even at independence the Uganda Legislature did not assume the unlimited legislative power that some might have liked. We discuss these limitations on the independence Parliament after a brief review of its vested powers of legislation.

It was given power to make laws for the peace, order, and good government of Uganda (other than the federal states) with respect to any matter;[7] this was a direct unitary power in relation to the various districts.

We noted before that its powers were limited in respect of Buganda; those which it could exercise were continued to the exclusion of the legislature of Buganda on matters specified in Schedule 7 of Part II of the Constitution.[8] In matters not specified in the exclusive legislative list of each, concurrent legislative competence was conferred on both legislatures,[9] with the proviso characteristic of federal constitutions that, in case of conflicting legislation by both, Parliament would prevail.[10]

In relation to the other federal states Parliament was given power to legislate to the exclusion of any existing state legislation and to make laws for the peace, order, and good government of any federal state (other than the Kingdom of Buganda) with regard to any matters not specified in Schedule 8 of the Constitution, which listed the exclusive legislative rights of the various states.[11]

We should note that, unlike Buganda, the other kingdoms and Busoga were denied concurrent legislative power and, therefore, the important features of a coordinate relationship. They were, for all practical purposes, given a semi-unitary relation with the centre, as Schedule 8 covered only a limited number of areas in which they could exercise full authority.

Such were the powers of the Uganda Parliament in the Independence Constitution; they were apparently extensive. We now review the limitations on this Parliament, which, in the course of time, could easily constitute a source of irritation to its members as not being conducive to rapid progress.

Doctrine of Constitutional Supremacy. Because it operates under no written constitution, the English Parliament—in strict constitutional law—enjoys absolute supremacy or sovereignty.[12] Having observed its history and operation, A. V. Dicey said that within the realm of physical possibility it could do or undo anything simply because there are no written checks or limitations in the Constitution. It can control the powers of the executive, change the form of government, override the decisions of the courts, or change the succession to the throne if it so wishes. The ultimate limitation upon its power is that of the political sovereign—the electorate.

When a written constitution sets out the various organs of Government and marks out the limits of their respective powers, it invariably imposes limitations upon the powers of the legislature which involve either a denial of some legislative power or require that the exercise of such powers be conditional on specified prerequisites. To this extent the Constitution, not Parliament, is supreme; *Parliament derives its powers from the Constitution.*

The doctrine of constitutional supremacy developed when the United States established the first modern written constitution. In 1803, in *Marbury v. Madison*, the Supreme Court of the United States enunciated this doctrine in the following terms:

> That the people have an original right to establish, for their future government, such principles, as, in their opinion shall most conduce to their own happiness is the basis on which the whole American fabric has been erected. The exercise of this original right is a very great exertion; nor can it, nor ought it, to be frequently repeated. The principles, therefore, so established, are deemed fundamental. And as the authority from which they proceed is supreme, and can seldom act, they are designed to be permanent.
>
> This original and supreme will organises the government, and assigns to different departments their respective powers. It may either stop here, or establish certain limits not to be transcended by those departments.
>
> The Government of the United States is of the latter description.

The powers of the Legislature are defined and limited; and that those limits may not be mistaken, or forgotten, the constitution is written. To what purpose are powers limited, and to what purpose is that limitation committed to writing, if these limits may, at any time be passed by those intended to be restrained? The distinction between a government with limited and unlimited powers is abolished, if those limits do not confine the persons on whom they are imposed, and if acts prohibited and acts allowed, are of equal obligation. It is a proposition too plain to be contested, that the constitution controls any Legislative act repugnant to it, or, that the Legislature may alter the constitution.

Between these alternatives there is no middle ground. The Constitution is either a superior paramount law, unchangeable by ordinary means, or it is on a level with ordinary legislative acts, and, like other acts, is alterable when the legislature shall please to alter it.

If the former part of the alternative be true, then a legislative act contrary to the constitution is not law: if the latter part be true, then written constitutions are absurd attempts, on the part of the people, to limit a power by its own nature illimitable.

Certainly all those who have framed written constitutions contemplate them as forming the fundamental and paramount law of the nation, and consequently, the theory of every such government must be, that an act of the legislature, repugnant to the constitution is void.

This theory is essentially attached to a written constitution, and is, consequently, to be considered by this court, as one of the fundamental principles of our society.[13]

This doctrine has since been applied in all common-law countries with written constitutions, and also the continental European countries.

In Uganda there are as yet no decided cases to this effect, but the first provision of the Constitution stated this doctrine in no uncertain terms:

This constitution is the supreme law of Uganda and, subject to the provisions of Sections 5 and 6 of this Constitution, if any other law is inconsistent with this Constitution, this Constitution shall prevail and the other law shall, to the extent of the inconsistency, be void.[14]

What, then, were the limitations under the Uganda Constitution concerning the supremacy of Parliament?

Limitations on the Supremacy of Parliament. We had occasion to note in relation to Buganda that Parliament had no legislative powers concerning Part I of Schedule 7 to the Constitution.[15] In relation to the other federal states it was also denied legislative authority over the matters covered in Schedule 8 to the Constitution.[16] In respect of Buganda, a law enacted by Parliament could not come into effect unless the Lukiiko of Buganda had, by resolution, signified its consent to that specific Act of Parliament having effect. Such matters were:

(a) Any provision for altering or replacing of the Buganda Courts Ordinance.

Beyond the element of pride, it is not clear why the Buganda delegates pressed for the entrenchment of this Ordinance. Buganda customary courts were in great need of reform, similar to the reforms being effected in the other kingdoms and districts.[17]

The principal court of Buganda was, by this Ordinance, endowed with vast powers over both civil and criminal matters, but it was ill equipped to exercise them effectively. Few, if any, of its judges were well trained, no advocates appeared before it to represent litigants, nor was there any specific law of evidence and procedure to guide the courts other than—in practice—what the judge himself deemed proper.

This is why critics of the Mmengo Government alleged that the motive for retaining the Ordinance was to sustain customary courts as possible instruments of coercion to reinforce the ruling regime. This may not be true, and in the absence of its being true, the reason for reserving these courts to Buganda must have been her love for the *status quo*.

(b) Any provision for altering or replacing the Public Lands Ordinance 1962, so far as that Ordinance had effect in relation to the Kingdom of Buganda, or for altering or replacing any other law with respect to the tenure of land vested in the Land Board of the Kingdom of Buganda.

(c) Any provision for altering or replacing the system of mailo land* tenure in the Kingdom of Buganda as in force immediately before 9 October 1962.[18]

These two land provisions were a subject of lengthy argument by the Buganda delegates at the Conference. For a regime that was essentially feudalist and certainly capitalistic, it was imperative to have denied Parliament unfettered control of Buganda land tenure. The policy of the U.P.C., now in coalition with K.Y., was known to be socialist and comparatively radical. It would have been imprudent for the Mmengo regime to entrust their land to such allies.

In their Memorandum the Buganda delegates demanded: "Land tenure in Buganda is clearly one of the matters in which Buganda should have exclusive power to make laws. It is significant that the proviso to Article I of the Agreement provides that the revocation of previous Agreements shall not affect the title to mailo land. In this connection it should therefore be made clear that any laws of Uganda concerned with registration of lands shall not affect the substantive law of land tenure in Buganda."[19]

(d) Finally, for Buganda, any provision with respect to local government in the Kingdom of Buganda, other than local government in Kampala or any town to which Section 126 of this Constitution applies.[20]

The Mmengo regime was anxious to maintain its hold on the hierarchy of chiefs who ran local governments and, since the direct right of the Uganda Parliament to legislate in respect of local government might have diminished the loyalty the chiefs owed to Mmengo, it had to be resisted.

Even at the Independence Conference Buganda still demanded excessive powers. We have noted that Parliament and the legislature of Buganda had concurrent law-making powers; in cases of conflict the laws of the Uganda Parliament would prevail, but this was against Buganda's wish. They put their case: "Provided that where a Buganda law is especially or pri-

---

* Mailo is a system of land tenure that operates in some parts of Uganda and is somewhat like the English freehold system.

marily concerned with domestic matters of Buganda, that law shall prevail in Buganda *notwithstanding its inconsistency* with a law passed by the Legislature of Uganda".* [21]

In addition to these limitations, Parliament's legislative supremacy was also conditioned by the constitutional provisions relating to constitutional amendments and procedures for amendments.

There were, as can be seen, intricate and detailed provisions stipulating the conditions under which Parliament could alter the Constitution affecting federal states, even if such amendments were *national* in character and consequence. For example, Parliament could not legislate abolition of the option of indirect elections for Buganda's twenty-one representatives to the National Assembly;[22] it could not alter the content of Buganda's Executive Authority;[23] it could not vary provisions relating to the police forces of Buganda and Uganda;[24] it was denied power to make alterations in the sources of Buganda's financial provisions[25] and it could not change the privileges of the Kabaka[26] *unless* the Legislative Assembly of the Kingdom of Buganda, by resolution of not less than two-thirds of all its Members, signified its consent that any Act of Parliament touching on these matters should have effect in Buganda.[27]

There were similar provisions for the relations with the other federal states.[28] No amendment to the Charter of Human Rights could take effect in any federal state unless it had been ratified in each state by a two-thirds majority of all Members of its Assembly.[29] Parliament was denied the legal right of altering the constitutions of the federal states scheduled to the Uganda Constitution.[30] Finally, a bill for an Act of Parliament altering any other provision of the Constitution could not pass into law unless it had been supported on second and third readings by votes of not less than two-thirds of all the Members of the National Assembly.

These limitations on Parliament's sovereignty, otherwise known as "the methods of constitutional amendment", could, at some moment, prove very crucial. The Uganda Constitution was a great compromise; it was an astutely balanced document. It

* Author's emphasis.

had to be as a natural consequence of indirect rule if Uganda ever hoped to emerge at independence on 9 October 1962 with each district and kingdom *voluntarily participating*. By the date of independence—fortunately—there was a high degree of voluntary participation.

The questions that were now to assume great prominence were: How far could such a Constitution, imposing such limitations on the sovereignty of Parliament, serve Uganda as the best means of unifying the country and promoting rapid economic progress? Was it, by its very nature of compromise, conducive to fragmentation? Would any attempt to increase the power of the Central Government in order to make it more unifying defeat its very ends by sowing the seeds of rebellion as each component area of Uganda—especially the kingdoms—felt cheated of what they had originally bargained for and won?

All these questions were posed and answered by Obote in action. When leaving, after nearly seventy years, the British had no other interest than leaving behind a Constitution that took note of all the main aspects of Uganda's diverse peoples; they were excellent umpires. Every delegate had his full say and was given unbiased attention. The end product—this Constitution—notwithstanding its checks and limitations, was by far the best possible for holding the country together voluntarily.

When Obote later wanted to establish totalitarian rule—by concentrating all the power of Government in his hands—he had to use the gun while, at the same time, claiming he was abolishing this federal Constitution because it was divisive. He argued that his highly unitary constitution would create unity, but it is now well known that his enforced unitary and authoritarian constitution—instead of unifying the nation—divided it even more.

THE EXECUTIVE

The Governor-General. It was decided in the Uganda National Assembly, before the Conference, that the Queen of England should continue as the Head of State in an independent Uganda. The issue of who was to be Head of State for this young nation—a nation full of love of pomp and tradition—was a highly sensitive and political one.

Munster wisely recommended initially having a British Head of State after independence. The U.P.C./K.Y. Government accepted this, but this did not solve the burning problem of deciding who would be the first African Head of State. As everyone at the Conference in London knew, to have discussed this sensitive issue would have been licence to pandemonium within the Conference and probably would have resulted in delayed independence because of the wrangling over which Ugandan was best suited for the post of Head of State after independence.

Perhaps because this possibility of conflict was common knowledge, the D.P. now sought to review the entire method for selecting the Head of State—despite the fact that they had debated it at great length in Parliament.

The Leader of the Opposition opened the controversy:

> I agree that Uganda should seek membership in the Commonwealth, but the Government's decision that Her Majesty the Queen should be Head of State was not debated in the National Assembly, nor have the kingdoms and districts been consulted. I think that the people of Uganda should decide who would be Head of State and the question should be referred back either to the National Assembly or to the country as a whole.

Ibingira replied for the Government of Uganda:

> The Uganda Government decided to propose that Her Majesty should continue to be Head of State and should be represented by a Governor-General, and this decision has been conveyed to the National Assembly in a Communication from the Chair. It was debated and passed by the Assembly without a division. The Government wants a constitutional rather than an executive Head of State. . . . deferment of the decision would be difficult especially if a referendum had to be held throughout Uganda.[31]

Dissatisfied with this explanation, one Ankole delegate, J. Kazzora, developed the argument to an even more controversial pitch:

> This is one of the most difficult issues before the Conference. I think it would be impossible for Uganda to have an absentee mon-

arch because there are already four rulers in Uganda, who are supreme in their respective kingdoms. I am prepared to support the proposal that a Governor-General representing Her Majesty the Queen should be Head of State for a *limited period,* but I think the Constitution should provide for the appointment or election of the future Head of State; I suggest the four rulers should be Head of State in turn for a period of two years.[32]

At this juncture the Chairman, Lord Lansdowne, reminded the Committee that if this point was not decided at the Conference, independence could be delayed. After further clarifications by the Uganda Government, the Leader of the Opposition agreed (under protest) to have a Governor-General as proposed by the Government.

The executive authority of Uganda, as before, was to be vested in Her Majesty, who would be represented by the Governor-General.[33] The provisions for establishing the Cabinet, for the appointment of the Prime Minister and his ministers and for the functions of the Governor-General were materially the same as they were during internal self-government.[34]

Collective Responsibility. The Constitution required that "the Cabinet shall be collectively responsible to Parliament." Since the Cabinet is the driving force of any government, we should review the meaning of "collective responsibility".[35]

The expression was defined by Lord Salisbury in 1878:

For all that passes in Cabinet every member of it who does not resign is absolutely and irretrievably responsible and has no right afterwards to say that he agreed in one case to a compromise, while in another he was persuaded by his colleagues. . . . It is only on the principle that absolute responsibility is undertaken by every member of the Cabinet, who, after a decision is arrived at, remains a member of it, that the joint responsibility of Ministers to Parliament can be upheld and one of the most essential principles of parliamentary responsibility established.[36]

Indigenous participation in government was unduly delayed under colonial rule; the first Uganda African Cabinet to exercise collective responsibility came as late as March 1961, at the inception of internal self-government. The Government then in power was replaced by a different one in May 1962, which was also exercising true executive authority for the first time.

One of the greatest mistakes committed by both Uganda politicians and the "Protecting Power" was that a party, whose leaders were never tested in the exercise of executive responsibility, should have been given such vast and awesome powers as were enjoyed in this independent African government. So long as a politician has no real or specific responsibility to execute—and thus be judged for—he can say the sweetest or most convincing words and he will not be easily contradicted, no matter how ill suited he may actually be; such was, I feel, the case with A. Milton Obote.

If Obote had exercised power under the Internal Self-Government Constitution, while the British retained the ultimate say, his vicious nature would probably have shown itself, and his colleagues who later combatted his excesses would have done so at an earlier time with far better chances of success and certainly with far less suffering in the country as a whole.

All the same, it was to this untried Cabinet that responsibility was entrusted, to be exercised collectively and extending to "the maintenance and execution of this Constitution" (other than Schedules 1 to 5 of the Constitution) and to all matters for which Parliament had, for the time being, power to make laws.[37]

One of the striking features of the Independence Constitution, which detracted from its character of federalism, was the limitations on the executive powers of the kingdoms. The executive authority of each federal state was to be exercised so as (a) not to impede or prejudice the exercise of the executive authority of Uganda, and (b) to ensure compliance with any Act of Parliament applying to that state.

This provision, conditioning the executive actions of all the components of the country to the authority of the Central Government, was a restatement of what was practised during the era of Protectorate rule, when obedience of the chiefs and their people to the imperial authority had to be ensured. It was a welcome relic for the independence Government. By its very nature executive power must be related to those powers which Parliament exercises and, similarly, to their limitations. This provision could be used to override these limitations on executive powers only in exceptional circumstances.

Delegated Responsibility. For the Government of any state aspiring to modernity the sheer complexity of what has to be done by the Government—even in a young country like Uganda—demands, for the sake of efficiency, that legislative and executive responsibilities be delegated by the Central Government to the governments of the districts and kingdoms where and when appropriate.

It was passed into law that the Governor-General could entrust, either conditionally or unconditionally, to any officer or to any authority of a federal state, functions relative to any matter which the executive authority of Uganda required to be performed within that state. Parliament could also make provision for conferring powers or imposing duties, or authorising the conferring of powers or the imposition of duties, upon any officer or authority of a federal state.

In addition, the Uganda Government was empowered to enter into arrangements with the Government of any federal state for the administration of certain services within that state when these services were within the executive authority of the Uganda Government. The Uganda Government, as a safeguard, was given power to terminate such arrangements after a legally constituted Commission of Enquiry found that such transferred services were not being conducted in an efficient manner or were not being conducted in the manner prescribed by law.

In regard to legislative powers, it was also stipulated that Parliament could confer upon the legislature of any federal state authority to make laws for that state with respect to any matter other than a matter specified in Part II of Schedule 7 or in Schedule 8 of the Constitution; any such authority could be general or conferred for such a period or subject to such restrictions as Parliament might specify. They could be revoked by Parliament at any time.

Subsequent experience tended to show a varying degree of success in the exercise of delegated responsibility by the kingdom and district administrations. It turned out later that some of these powers were not properly exercised by certain authorities, especially in the kingdoms, but these were unavoidable pitfalls if experience was to be acquired.

Obote was to intervene and destroy this scheme within a few years of its inception.

THE CHARTER OF HUMAN RIGHTS

The Munster Commission recommended detailed provisions for the protection of fundamental human rights. The origin of these rights was not only the imperative need to stress a minimum set of standards in organized society after the Second World War. On the contrary, common law, which applies in England and was exported in large measure to the British dependencies—although it does not categorise these rights in a formal code—does contain and recognise them. The right to life, to personal liberty, the protection from deprivation of property, freedom of conscience and expression, and the right of assembly and association have not been absent from British dependencies; they were, however, limited by statutory laws in order to preserve effective imperial rule.

The brutalities of Hitler towards his nationals and the peoples of conquered territories led directly to the inclusion in the Charter of the United Nations of a declaration to encourage respect for human rights and fundamental freedoms; it led to the drafting and adoption of the Declaration of Human Rights. The U.N. Charter itself, in an effort to protect the rights of subject peoples, required colonial masters to submit reports to the United Nations.

The recognition of human rights enjoyed universal application. In British dependencies, especially those demarcated arbitrarily and containing diverse tribes with different cultures, various religious groups, and several minorities, it became imperative before independence that a code of human rights should be incorporated into the Constitution for safeguarding the rights of such a varied people. It began in Malaya and was repeated in great detail in Nigeria; in Uganda it was almost a reproduction of the Nigerian code. There was no controversy at the Constitutional Conference concerning its inclusion in the Constitution. In this way a sound safeguard was afforded (among others) to the immigrant communities of Asians, to members of minority tribal groups, and to believers of various faiths.

Of all the provisions in the Uganda Constitution that pose serious challenge to the governments of the future and to the people of this country, the preservation of these basic human rights ranks among the foremost. Let us consider two examples, freedom of expression and property rights.

Freedom of Expression. Every person has the right to freely express his views on any matter; "to receive and impart ideas and information without interference, and freedom from interference with his correspondence".[38] To understand the difficulties such a provision imparts we should note the qualifications the Constitution imposes on this right. It is stipulated that a law should not be held as contravening freedom of expression if it is *"reasonably required"* under the following circumstances:

(1) in the interests of defence, public safety, public order, public morality, or public health; or

(2) for the purpose of protecting the reputations, rights and freedoms of other persons or the private lives of persons concerned in legal proceedings, preventing the disclosure of information received in confidence, maintaining the authority and independence of the courts, or regulating telephony, telegraphy, posts, wireless broadcasting, television, public exhibitions, or public entertainments; or

(3) if it imposes restrictions upon public officers, but only so far as that provision or, as the case may be, the thing done under the authority thereof is shown not to be reasonably justifiable in a democratic society.[39]

The words "reasonably required" can present considerable embarrassment or difficulty—depending on what approach the High Court adopts in construing them.

First, who determines what is "reasonably required" in order to curtail this freedom of speech? Does the Uganda Parliament have the exclusive right for determining this? It is unlikely, for in Uganda—as in many other countries—the right to interpret the constitution is vested, not in Parliament, but in the High Court of the land.

Does this mean the High Court—alone vested with the power

to interpret the Constitution—will accept as conclusive proof any evidence from the Government that the measure taken was "reasonably required"? This, also, cannot be assumed; if it were so, the Constitution would have expressly stated that such evidence by the Government was to be conclusive.

We can conclude that the matter must rest with the High Court, judging from the evidence before it. It may be of some interest to examine what attitudes the courts of other common-law states have taken in interpreting their constitutions.

Broadly, there are two approaches. The first is according to ordinary rules of statutory construction. Speaking on the interpretation of the division of powers in the Commonwealth of Australia Constitution, the Australian Chief Justice stated his view in the following terms:

> It is not sufficiently recognised that the Court's sole function is to interpret a constitutional description of power or restraint upon a power and say whether a given measure falls on one side of a line consequently drawn or on the other, and that it has nothing whatever to do with the merits or demerits of the measure. . . . It may be that the Court is thought to be excessively legalistic. I should be sorry to think that it is anything else. There is no other safe guide to judicial decisions in great conflicts than a strict and complete legalism.[40]

Secondly, there is a view that constitutions deserve more beneficial interpretation than the normal rules of statutory construction might allow. In this way the federal Supreme Court of the United States has followed a direct policy—"forming attitude"; as de Winton said, "The judiciary must keep the charter of government current with the times and not allow it to become archaic or out of tune with the needs of the day." [41]

It is in the court decisions of younger countries that we can seek guidance more relevant to Uganda. The problems that face the older countries—their social and economic set-up and, consequently, the values they reflect—may in some respects be profoundly different from those of developing nations that attained freedom after the Second World War. For this reason the federal Supreme Court of India followed the United States approach with even greater boldness; when determining the meaning of "reasonableness" the Court said:

> In evaluating such elusive factors and forming their own conception of what is reasonable in all the circumstances of a given case it is inevitable that the social philosophy and the scale of values of the judges participating in the decision should play an important part, and the limits of their interference with legislative judgement in such cases can only be dictated by their sense of responsibility and self-restraint, and the sobering reflection that the Constitution is meant not only for people of their own way of thinking but for all, and that the majority of the Elected Representatives of the people have in authorising the imposition of the restrictions considered them reasonable.[42]

In other words, in determining what is "reasonable" the courts must take full cognisance of the social environment, the problems it creates, and the expressed views of Elected Members of Parliament. This was the hope of the Uganda delegates to the Constitutional Conference in accepting the entrenchment of fundamental human rights in the Uganda Constitution.

It is common knowledge that in young countries—almost without exception—the most urgent and most difficult problem is the problem of unity in all its aspects: in political and social philosophy, in economic development, and in sharing the benefits as well as the burdens of independent nationhood. It is axiomatic that the limitations on free speech in such countries— where it may be more easily used to disrupt much-needed unity and stable government—might be greater than in more highly developed countries.

In Nigeria the then federal Supreme Court already held that the freedom of expression *cannot* be used to undermine the stability of a constitutional government.* We must wait, in view of this consideration, to see what approach the Uganda High Court will take when called upon to determine like issues.

* The case of *DPP v Obi,* in the A.N.L.R., 1961, Pt. II, p. 186, is of significance not only for Nigeria, but for all developing countries. The facts were these: The defendant distributed a pamphlet containing seditious comments in the following terms: "Down with the enemies of the people, the exploiters of the weak and oppressors of the poor! etc." The pamphlet was directed against the Nigerian Federal Government.

The expression "reasonably justifiable in a democratic society" was an awkward one to use in the Constitution. We discussed the problems surrounding "reasonable", but what is a "democratic society"? Today the term "democracy" has been stretched so far and claimed by such vastly diverse and often conflicting social systems that, at best, it is only a relative standard. The Soviet Union claims to be a socialist democracy, and the United States asserts it is the bulwark of Western democracy. Practices regarded as undemocratic in the former may be acclaimed as the hallmark of democracy in the latter. What standards, then, shall the young countries use to define what is justifiable in a democratic society? Surely, the irrefutable answer must be *by evolving their own in terms of what is best for their own societies,* but not forgetting that the responsibility for construing the limits on such human rights is best left to courts of law.

Moments of frustration may arise when a court declares an opinion unacceptable to the executive. When the Ghana Supreme Court acquitted the accused in respect of an alleged conspiracy to overthrow the state and to murder President Nkrumah, he reacted by swiftly dismissing the Chief Justice and reconstituting the court.[43] The executive and the judiciary had taken different views; the former exerted itself by destroying the independence of the latter.

In Uganda, the Constitution laid down elaborate provisions ensuring the independence of the judiciary. Obote was later to surpass Nkrumah—not by dismissing the High Court judges, who had not yet delivered an unpalatable opinion—but *by abolishing the Constitution which ensured their independence.*

Protection of Property Rights. In a developing society that is basically poor and in which comparatively enormous wealth is

---

The defendant was charged with sedition; the Nigerian Penal Code (S. 50) is similar to the Uganda provisions on sedition.

The Supreme Court held that (a) the words "hatred" and "contempt" (in the statutory definition of sedition) mean not merely the absence of affection and regard, but disloyalty, enmity, hostility; and (b) the word "disaffection" connotes enmity and hostility, estranged allegiance, disloyalty, hostility to constituted authority or to a particular form of political government.

acquired and hoarded by an immigrant minority community, it is of the utmost importance to include constitutional safeguards for property owned individually or collectively. Conditions are outlined in the Constitution under which one may be lawfully deprived of his property. One of them requires provision to be made *"for the prompt payment of adequate compensation"*.[44]

Depending on the economic philosophy of the government of the day, it may be necessary for economic reconstruction to nationalise certain properties belonging either to Uganda citizens or foreign nationals. The courts, as a result, may be required to determine the meaning of "adequate" and "prompt" in relation to compensation. What has been the view in other states?

As to what is "adequate compensation", the American principle states that just compensation means "the fair and perfect equivalent in money of the property taken from the owner as to put him in as good a position pecuniarily as he would have occupied if his property had not been taken";[45] in other words, full market value or the price paid by a willing buyer to a willing seller. In India, where a similar construction has been applied, a state law makes compensation the market value on a date considerably antecedent to the date the acquisition was held to be valid.[46]

The interpretation of the word "prompt" is likely to present considerable difficulty. When Egypt nationalised the Suez Canal, legal controversy raged throughout the world press and learned juristic journals about whether compensation by the law of nations should not have been immediate, in point of time, after the Act of Nationalisation. Egypt, while accepting the view that compensation had to be paid, argued that because of the magnitude of the amount to be paid and because of the limitations on her economic capacity to pay, compensation could not be made immediately as demanded by France and Britain; she argued that "prompt" should be given a more liberal interpretation when related to compensation. This has set the pattern for developing countries vis-à-vis the older nations on the subject of compensation for the nationalisation of foreign properties.

But there is no doubt that the fundamental right of property ownership will assume increasing prominence as Uganda moves toward more rapid economic development. Land ownership is likely to be a subject of controversy in the years to come, particularly as the concept of legal freehold and leasehold titles clashes with the various tribal systems, in which most of the land was by custom vested in the tribe. Undoubtedly, the High Court will need great wisdom to guide it through such a series of potentially clashing interests.

Emergency Powers. Of all proceedings of the Constitutional Committee of the Independence Conference, the debate on emergency powers was one of the most sensitive. Before recapitulating the constitutional provisions, it is useful to briefly outline the background of the debate.

Before the Conference began, an English lawyer, Dingle Foot, M.P., Q.C., who was the Kabaka's personal counsel on the Committee, had just been *thrown out* of Nigeria after a state of emergency was declared in the western region and an administrator appointed to replace the regional government just suspended.

The Buganda delegation saw—as a distinct possibility, despite federal status—a situation arising in which their fate would be the same as that of the western region of Nigeria. Certainly Mr. Dingle Foot did not spare himself in drawing their attention to this possibility and in framing arguments against constitutional provisions that might be designed to achieve it.

For this reason the Katikkiro of Buganda, nominally the leader of its delegation, made one of his few contributions to the Conference by registering his protest against such a possibility and demanding assurances that the exercise of emergency powers would not entail the suspension of Buganda's Constitution. His Memorandum to the Constitutional Committee stated:

> It is of the utmost importance to secure that emergency powers should only be used for the legitimate purposes of national defence and public safety. They must not be employed as a political device to destroy the provisions of the federal constitution. . . .
>
> If the Central Government can assume unlimited emergency powers the autonomy of the kingdoms within their own spheres can never be secured. There is always the possibility that such powers might be used not merely to ensure public tranquility but to supersede the governments of the kingdoms. An Emergency

Regulation might, for example, be passed forbidding a kingdom government from exercising its functions and appointing an administrator in its place. Events in another part of Africa have shown that this is not a mere flight of fancy.[47]

His Memorandum then proposed a constitutional provision:

Emergency Powers shall not include any power, directly or indirectly, to suspend, in whole or in part, the Governments of Uganda, Buganda, or of any kingdom or to suspend the Constitution of Uganda (including the Constitution of Buganda) and any law purporting to give such a power shall be void.

It is interesting that, for the first time, Buganda was not arguing a case for itself alone but also for the other kingdoms—a shrewd tactic to enlist their sympathy. There is no doubt that these kingdoms shared Buganda's views.

The conspicuous length of time the possible derogation of fundamental human rights under emergency was debated was testimony to the underlying fears of some delegations, especially from the kingdoms, concerning their prospects for the future.[48] It is more appropriate to examine the end product of these debates, which was then embodied in the Uganda Constitution.

The Governor-General was, by proclamation published in the *Gazette*, empowered to declare that a state of public emergency existed.[49] Elaborate provisions were enacted—a result of the prolonged debates—to limit the duration of such proclamations.[50]

For the protection of persons detained under emergency laws detailed provisions were enacted entitling them to legal assistance before a tribunal, which had to be established to review their cases at periodic intervals; the recommendations of such a tribunal to the Minister responsible did not bind him.* It was also mandatory for the government to report to Parliament the number of persons detained and any cases in which it acted contrary to the recommendations of the tribunal. Every known precaution to safeguard the liberties of the detained—even in emergency—was taken. Finally, to the approbation of the federalists,

---

* The Emergency Powers Act 1963 superseded the Order-in-Council of 1939 under which the Governor could declare a state of emergency.

it was decided not to empower the Central Government or Parliament to suspend or supersede federal state constitutions during the exercise of emergency powers—a provision Obote was to abrogate.

We cannot conclude without examining the potency of emergency powers. It is accepted that occasions may arise when, to safeguard the safety of the state or its peace, order, and good government, emergency powers must be invoked. This may be to combat a natural disaster consequent upon an "Act of God", such as a flood or a devastating earthquake. It might be necessary if Uganda were at war or involved with internal disorders, but the most controversial use of emergency powers in young countries relates to their use as a means to meet a situation arising solely from internal political conflict, which may involve the Government's imprisoning or detaining its political opponents—real or imagined—and the general suspension of fundamental human rights. A decision to use emergency powers to this end is of the utmost gravity, and its justification can only be assessed on the basis of prevailing circumstances for any given situation.

I was to suffer detention, along with my friends, for nearly five years under an interminable State of Emergency declared by Obote in 1966. Thousands of other people in Uganda were to suffer the same fate during this period; it was a flagrant misuse of an otherwise necessary provision in any prudently drafted constitution.

Citizenship and the Immigrant Minorities. The proceedings of the Committee on Citizenship were characterised at the outset by sharp disagreement between the Uganda and British Governments. The anxiety of the British Government to safeguard the interests of immigrant communities in Uganda, which in their view, for all practical purposes, meant the Asians, was acute. Since it had failed to guarantee to the Asians an effective role in governing the country, the only recourse left to the British Government was to ensure that these minorities enjoyed all the rights of citizenship. On the other hand, the Uganda Government—while not rejecting the claim to citizenship for such people—argued that it was wrong for every Asian to be entitled to citizenship as of right without first taking into consideration his individual loyalty to Uganda as his adopted country. The Opposition, represented on the Committee by an Asian, was unmistakably inclined towards the British Government's view.*

Citizenship, we should mention, is the legal relation between the citizen and the state. This legal relation involves rights and corresponding duties on the part of both—on the part of the citizen no less than on the part of the state.[51] It is for each state "to determine for itself, and according to its own constitution and laws what classes of persons shall be entitled to citizenship",[52] but because Uganda was still a dependent territory, the views of the British Government were instrumental in bringing about the final citizenship provisions of the Uganda Constitution.

Acquisition of Citizenship. It was obvious that the several provisions for the acquisition of Uganda citizenship were primarily designed to cater to the Asians. Two principal methods of acquisition were introduced—automatic citizenship by birth and citizenship by registration.[53]

(1) AUTOMATIC CITIZENSHIP BY BIRTH—a person automatically became a citizen by the Constitution if certain specified conditions pertaining to his birth were met:

> (a) Every person who, having been born in Uganda, is on 8 October 1962 a citizen of the United Kingdom and Colonies or a British Protected Person, provided that either of his parents was born in Uganda.[54]

All indigenous African Ugandans qualified under this provision; previous to independence they were merely "British Protected Persons". The number of Asians who qualified under this provision is not precisely known, but considering that some Asians have lived in Uganda for at least a generation, it can be assumed that many young Asians of school age are citizens by virtue of this provision.

> (b) Every person born outside Uganda who was on 8 October 1962 a citizen of the United Kingdom and Colonies or a British Protected Person will, if his father becomes (or would

* Mr. Diabhai Patel, M.P.

have become but for his death) a citizen of Uganda in accordance with the provisions referred to in (a), become a citizen of Uganda on 9 October 1962.[55]

(2) CITIZENSHIP BY REGISTRATION—it was under this provision that the bulk of Uganda's Asians were, as of right, entitled to register for citizenship. Any person who was born in Uganda but whose parents were born in a foreign country was also entitled to apply for registration as a citizen in the same manner. A variety of provisions were enacted entitling married women to citizenship under certain conditions.[56] This was done primarily to cover cases of Asian women married from abroad or in other African states such as Kenya and Tanganyika (now Tanzania), although it was framed for general application. Parents or guardians were empowered to make application under these provisions for persons under twenty-one years of age.[57]

There are, however, two important qualifications to this entitlement of citizenship; although a person "*shall be entitled,* upon making application, to be registered as a citizen of Uganda", this application must be made

(a) "before the specified date", and "in such manner as may be prescribed by Parliament";
(b) "the specified date" is interpreted to mean 9 October 1964— precisely two years after Independence.[58]

In the normal exercise of its powers Parliament has gone even further to extend the "specified date" under circumstances that might warrant such extension. The provisions relating to time in the Citizenship Ordinance provided: "The power of the Minister, and any officer of the Government authorised in that behalf by the Minister, under this section may be exercised before or after the relevant date declared by Section 8 of the Constitution to be the 'specified date'." [59]

The second qualification or limitation "in such manner as may be prescribed by Parliament" has far-reaching possibilities; a sovereign legislature should be vested with powers to prescribe the modes in which citizenship can be obtained. Until this time the conditions under which a British subject (the category of the majority of Asians) or Commonwealth citizen could register were:

(c) that he was ordinarily resident in Uganda and had been so resident for a period of five years;

(d) that he had an adequate knowledge of a prescribed vernacular language or of English (this provision was enacted to test the sense of "belonging" among the several immigrant communities in Uganda; the majority in the legislature held the view that if an Asian wanted to become a citizen after a lifetime in Uganda he should be able to speak at least some vernacular language as testimony of his interest in the country);

(e) that he was of good character; and

(f) that he would be a suitable citizen of Uganda.[60]

Similar provisions were enacted for Africans from other African countries despite the fact they did not belong to the Commonwealth. It seemed fitting to do this not only because of the ideals of African unity, but because, as a practical reality, there were literally thousands of such Africans from the border countries of Rwanda, Zaire, and the Sudan who had settled in Uganda and were doing useful work for the general development of the country.

Loss of Citizenship. The principal cause of loss of citizenship was acquisition of dual nationality or citizenship.[61] It is vital that the citizen of any state, especially a young state with all the associated problems of new nationhood, should have undivided loyalty. A person who is a citizen of two states simultaneously, and thus of divided loyalty, can only serve to weaken a young country. It was then enacted that even a person who was a Uganda citizen by birth was to lose his citizenship if, not being a minor, he did not renounce foreign citizenship after 9 October 1964.[62] Provision was also made that a citizen by registration would lose Uganda citizenship if he did not renounce another citizenship or attained any other citizenship after registration.[63]

Parliament empowered the Minister to deprive of his citizenship (by order) any person not a citizen by birth if he was voluntarily claiming and exercising any right available to him by law in another country when such a right was accorded exclusively to citizens of the other country.[64]

The Significance of Citizenship. Bearing in mind the history of Uganda's development, especially the fact that vast wealth was in the hands of an immigrant Asian community, and the realities of the severe problems facing any developing country, it should not be surprising that a developing country would extend preferential treatment to its indigenous citizens in almost every sphere of development. The question of citizenship raises vital issues in the Uganda of today and will do so to an even greater extent, perhaps, tomorrow.

When the "specified date" of 9 October 1964 arrived, only a small proportion of the Asian community were registered citizens of Uganda. For those who had not become citizens the constitutional right of citizenship by registration lapsed. A number of questions then arose. What is their status? What are their rights and duties in the country? And where will their loyalty lie? If their loyalty is to a foreign state, won't the masses of indigenous people seriously begin to question the basis and the justification for the Asian community's economic dominance?

Since practically all such Asians were British subjects or British citizens of other Commonwealth countries, such as India or Pakistan, or even Tanzania or Kenya, before the specified date, under the Constitution they would continue to be Commonwealth citizens.[65] However, it was still open for them to apply for registration as citizens under the Uganda Citizenship Ordinance of 1962, which laid down the same conditions as for those applying before the specified date.[66] The important difference was that before this date they were entitled, as of right, to be registered on application; after the specified date this right no longer existed and the Minister now had greater latitude in rejecting their citizenship applications. The Charter of Human Rights incorporated in the Uganda Constitution guaranteed certain rights to everyone—citizen and non-citizen—and the rights a Uganda citizen enjoys over the Commonwealth citizen are limited in scope, limited to such things as the parliamentary franchise and candidature. But there is no legal provision barring Parliament from enacting legislation on any matter that might discriminate in favour of Uganda citizens.

The provisions on human rights do not confer absolute rights; on the contrary, these rights can be curtailed under specified conditions. It is especially relevant in this connection to note the constitutional safeguards against discrimination of all kinds.[67] Although it was enacted that "no law shall make any provision that is discriminatory either of itself or in its effect", important exceptions were attached. A law could be discriminatory but still valid if it touched *inter alia:* (a) the appropriation of public revenues or other public funds; (b) persons who were not citizens of Uganda; and (c) the imposition of restrictions on the acquisition or use by any person of land or other property in Uganda.

Any legislation, although racially discriminatory, was valid even if it imposed disability or restriction or accorded privilege or advantage, provided that "having regard to its nature and to special circumstances pertaining to those persons or to persons of any other such description, [it] is reasonably justifiable in a democratic society".[68]

These various provisions have a profound potential for an African government that might wish to launch drastic programmes for the alleviation of poverty among its masses, even if doing so discriminates against a minority group that controls the country's wealth.

The last years of Obote's dictatorship, however, witnessed public scandals relating to citizenship applications by thousands of Asians. Asians who had obtained citizenship by registration had their citizenship revoked by the Ministry of Internal Affairs and were required to make fresh applications. It was no secret that there was considerable corruption. Wealthy Asians were made to pay thousands of shillings to appropriate authorities to get citizenship certificates. Such certificates might later be cancelled and the officials require fresh applications on the grounds that the originals were not properly issued. But this was merely a device in many cases to make Asians pay further bribes for the issue of fresh certificates.

This is a matter that requires the most serious and urgent attention. The citizenship of Uganda should be sacrosanct and give pride and security to its holder, no matter what his colour. To revoke citizenship at will by the exercise of executive power robs it of the value it deserves. Government has the right to deny granting citizenship to anyone who applies; but once it grants such citizenship, it has a duty to protect it and to uphold the rights it confers on its holder, and ought to revoke it, as in most mature and stable nations, only in exceptional cases and on clearly defined grounds.

The "Lost Counties"

Shortly after independence the Buganda Government began transferring thousands of Baganda ex-servicemen from other parts of Buganda to the two "Lost Counties" for resettlement with a view—among other things—of helping to diminish or reverse the uncontested numerical superiority of the Banyoro already living there. Until the time of the referendum the two counties still formed—under the Constitution—part of Buganda. On this basis the Buganda Government could claim the right to move its subjects within her jurisdiction as she saw fit.

The issue of deciding whether these fresh arrivals in the two counties could vote or not was settled by a court declaration, which went right up to the Privy Council. The decision of the Uganda High Court that they could *not* vote was upheld in London, but by the time the Privy Council decision came the referendum had already been held. It showed that an overwhelming majority of the inhabitants of the two counties wanted to return to Bunyoro. On 1 January 1965 the transfer to Bunyoro was legally effected, thereby ending one of the greatest political and constitutional problems in Uganda's history.

The events during the period preceding the referendum were an indicator, one of several, of Obote's dishonesty and treachery toward his colleagues. To me, as Minister of Justice, and Godfrey Binaisa, as Attorney-General, it was clear beyond doubt that the Baganda ex-servicemen were not entitled to vote in the referendum. In the law office, and politically, we thought it best to have the Central Government stand clear from the very beginning by discouraging Buganda from whipping up emotions and spending money on the transporting and settling of these prospective voters in such a fruitless venture. Minutes to this effect were written, and we were supported by the Minister of Regional Administrations, Cuthbert Obwangor.

Not only did Obote encourage Buganda's hopes by his inaction, but he gave us a directive never to say or discuss anything concerning the "Lost Counties" issue; the Mmengo Government then launched itself heart and soul into this exercise of resettlement. Obote then told the Omukama of Bunyoro that he had nothing to fear, as he was going to have the counties returned to Bunyoro, but during this same period he also went secretly to Mutesa and gave him our Minutes, suggesting that he would ensure that the counties remained in Buganda if only those who professed friendship with Mutesa—Binaisa and myself—would not urge him to do the contrary. Each side in the dispute was keenly hopeful of winning, as each side now had Obote's promised support. We were presented to Mutesa in a bad light, and for a while Obote was jubilant; time and reality, however, caught up with him. The referendum Mutesa had been secretly assured was never going to materialise did take place. Obote's cousin and colleague, Adoko Nekyon, ridiculed Mmengo in Parliament for having invested its effort and money in a venture of no return; the "Lost Counties" finally changed hands.

Another inescapable lesson flows from the history of this dispute. It is outstanding testimony to the separate existence under which the various tribes of Uganda lived *before and after* British rule was established. It is disturbing that within the borders of a small sovereign state like Uganda there should exist bitter boundary and territorial disputes that assume the character of conflicts between distinct sovereign states. It is a great challenge to the leaders of this country; these problems can only be resolved by positively fostering national consciousness as a concept superior to tribal loyalty. But this can never be done through a leadership based on tribal hegemony.

Relations between Regional Administrations and the Central Government

The powers conferred and duties imposed by the Internal Self-Government Constitution on the kingdoms and districts were not reduced in the Independence Constitution. The final conference in London was to witness protracted demands from various delegations for increased powers under the Independence Constitution. We shall review how these demands were met under the Independence Constitution.

BUGANDA

Buganda's demands to have exclusive legislative powers over its mailo land tenure and the Buganda Courts Ordinance have already been observed.[69] It was demanded that "the Kabaka's Government should be consulted before any Bill relating to fugitive offenders, immigration, emigration, passports, visas, quarantine, defence, and internal security are placed before the National Assembly." This was rejected, since under the operative provisions these matters were already, and quite appropriately, the responsibility of the Central Government.[70] There were other areas where the Buganda delegation pressed for greater powers.

The High Court of Buganda. We have discussed the manner in which the High Court of Buganda was established in 1961. Now Buganda desired that the power of appointment and removal of judges be vested not in the Uganda Judicial Service Commission but in the Kabaka and his ministers:

> The proposal is that a Chief Justice and two Judges of the High Court of Buganda should be appointed by the Kabaka on the recommendation of the Council of Ministers. . . . Their independence is to be safeguarded by the provision that a judge of the High Court cannot be removed from office unless a resolution for his removal is passed by the Lukiiko and also at a joint sitting of the judges of the High Courts of Uganda and Buganda. The Lukiiko will not debate the question of the removal unless a resolution is passed in the first place by a joint session of the two High Courts as above provided.[71]

The probable dangers inherent in conceding such a demand have already been indicated; accordingly, it was rejected and the status quo of the Buganda High Court was reinstated in the Independence Constitution.[72] The Kabaka's powers of commutation and remission of sentences for prisoners in Buganda was retained.[73]

The Kabaka's Police Force. With the imminent departure of the British at independence, Buganda, still unsure about the prospects of good neighbourliness from their countrymen in the other tribes of Uganda, tenaciously demanded more power to establish, maintain, and control its own police force.[74] While conceding that the Uganda Inspector-General of Police should have ultimate control over the Buganda police force, they contended that after a short transitional period Buganda should replace the Uganda police already established in the kingdom with their own people except in the capital city of Kampala.

The Munster Commission warned against the dangers of allowing each kingdom or district to build its own police force, as it was possible that small tribal armies might be built under such a cover. Certainly the Uganda Government delegates accepted Munster's warning.[75]

After lengthy exchanges in the Constitutional Committee of the Conference it was agreed that there should be a Kabaka's police force. The appointment and disciplining of officers in the specified cadres of this force was to be done by the Buganda Public Service Commission, although there was a proviso that this was to be done *after consultation* with the Uganda Public Service Commission and the Uganda Inspector-General of Police.[76]

Operational control of the Buganda police was vested in the Uganda Inspector-General of Police. Dissatisfaction with the Uganda Government's refusal to transfer its police posts to Buganda was a matter generating continuous disagreement until the Uganda Government submitted the issue to the Uganda High Court for a declaration fixing the exact constitutional powers of each government over Buganda's police.

Financial Relations. The Uganda Government's chief spokesman on the Fiscal Committee at the Constitutional Conference was the Minister of Finance, The Hon. A. K. Sempa, who at one time was a prime mover of K.Y. He was now confronted with the difficult task of persuading his former political colleagues to abandon some of their more extravagant claims for Buganda's share in the distribution of finances.

After only two working weeks the Committee unexpectedly

completed its task. The Independence Constitution required the Government of Uganda to make financial payments to the Kabaka's Government in accordance with the agreement set out in Schedule 9 of the Uganda Constitution.[77]

This negotiated agreement between the two governments was not expressed in the phraseology a legal draftsman might have appreciated because Buganda felt she had struck a good bargain and she was now suspicious that specialized legal drafting might lead to the loss of some already existing advantage, so she insisted that the original text of the Schedule be in "ordinary language" when it was incorporated into the Uganda Constitution. And so it was.

This did not ward off future disagreement. The Uganda Government filed suit in the Uganda High Court seeking the proper interpretation of this Schedule because of its fear that Buganda claimed more revenue under it than it was entitled to. The Uganda Government interpretation was upheld.

THE KINGDOMS OF ANKOLE, BUNYORO, AND TORO AND THE TERRITORY OF BUSOGA

As the process of constitution-making entered its final phase just before independence, the western kingdoms, emulating Buganda, intensified their struggle to exact more powers.

The attitudes of these kingdoms during the Conference detracted from its progress.[78] They wished to conclude Agreements with the British Government regardless of how short-lived they would be.

In a meeting in the Carlton Towers Hotel in London, Governor Coutts pointed out to all rulers the futility of concluding new Agreements. After advising them that it was preferable to concentrate only on constitutional provisions concerning their kingdoms, he suggested that if they insisted they would end up with Agreements modeled on the Ankole draft Agreement previously accepted by Ankole and the Uganda Government.

The Omukama of Toro, supporting the attitude of his delegation, confirmed that he would prefer to have Toro's Agreement successfully concluded even if it meant postponing the date of independence. Toro threatened to boycott the Conference, and not until they realized that threats would not deter the Conference did they come to terms with the Uganda Government.

A series of meetings was held between the delegates of the western kingdoms and Busoga and the British and Uganda Governments.[79] These kingdom delegates were directed to get as much power as possible for the states. Busoga had always been a district, but she fought for and attained the federal status of the kingdoms; now she demanded a name change from "district" to "territory".

It is difficult to comprehend just what enhanced status the term territory might bring; in any event, in seeking the unusual, Busoga in fact chose what was common to all the states—territory.

The Agreements concluded in London between the kingdoms and the British Government were all of the same pattern.[80] They were all to terminate at independence. Their constitutions were part of the Agreements designed to subsist as provisions of the Uganda Independence Constitution. These constitutions were divided into two parts.

Part One concerned the office of the ruler and all the trappings that go with it—titles, dignities, succession, and regency in the event of specified circumstances. If the validity of the nomination of a successor to the throne were to be in doubt, the ultimate authority to decide was the Uganda High Court. The Court could not choose the successor; it could only declare whether his nomination was proper. The responsibility for choosing the successor, if the ruler did not, was vested in a stipulated number of dignitaries in each kingdom.*

Parliament was to have no power over these matters, and they could be altered only by the legislature of the federal state by a two-thirds majority vote of all its members.[81] To make the situation clear, a distinct schedule was provided expressly stating that only the federal states had power to legislate in relation to such matters.[82]

Part Two dealt with the set-up and character of these federal

* See paras. 1–4 of Schedules 2–4 of the Uganda Independence Constitution. The provision for Busoga was quite different, as provided in Schedule 5, paras. 1–2.

governments. Councils of Ministers were established and the method of appointment and tenure of office stipulated, along with other related matters.[83] Legislatures were defined for these federal states and their membership prescribed. The qualifications for membership in such legislatures were established, as well as the qualifications for voters.

The posts of Speaker and Deputy Speaker were created; Public Service Commissions were constituted and charged with appointing and disciplining officers of the state governments.[84] The institution and nomenclature of chieftainship, as a function of local governments, was recognized and maintained.[85] All these federal states gained comprehensive constitutions, regardless of the vast limitations on their powers.

THE EXTENT OF LEGISLATIVE POWERS OF THE FEDERAL STATES

It should be understood that "federal states" excludes Buganda but includes the western kingdoms and Busoga; the limitations on the legislatures of these states have been noted. Matters in which they were given exclusive legislative right are, for all practical purposes, negligible and do not directly affect the ordinary citizen in his daily life. They were denied even concurrent legislative power, since legislation for any other matter was vested in Parliament "to the exclusion of the legislature of the state".

A law from the legislature of a federal state other than the Kingdom of Buganda does not apply to any person who is not an African "any provision of the law or custom applicable to members of any African tribe with respect to inheritance, marriage, divorce, religion or the personal obligations attaching to a member of an African tribe as such".[86]

Because of the limitations on these legislatures it became necessary for Parliament to enact a law, as agreed at the Independence Conference, enabling federal states to enact legislation on a greater variety of topics and to fill the gaps in their respective constitutions which the Independence Constitution left blank.

The Administrations (Western Kingdoms and Busoga) Act

was enacted by Parliament in March 1963. The expressions of hostility against the original version of the Act—expressed by the kingdoms and in Parliament—were some of the strongest yet experienced during the post-independence period.

The bill for this Act, as originally published, vested extensive authority in the Uganda Government over the federal states. Virtually nothing could be done without the consent or agreement of the Uganda Minister of Regional Administration.

One might say the Uganda Government was demanding a bit too much control over the federal states, but many of the demands from these states were excessive. They wanted Parliament to grant them so much power that it could only mean Parliament granting what it did not possess under the Constitution, except, perhaps, by delegated legislation, which was purely a discretionary power.[87]

Excessive controversy over the bill persuaded the Uganda Government to withdraw it, but before its reintroduction several meetings were held to establish some basis for agreement.

Of all these federal states only one—Ankole—was then held by the Opposition party (D.P.). Busoga, Bunyoro, and Toro were all U.P.C.-led. Was it not odd that the regional governments should oppose the Uganda Government when they were all of the same party? To them it was natural: the traditional feeling that central governments were too remote, even at this late stage, had not vanished. Because of the U.P.C.'s lack of discipline and effective organisation it had no machinery for ensuring that what the centre demanded was actually conceded by the regions. The spirit of regionalism and decentralisation was still very prevalent.

A new draft bill was introduced by the Uganda Government with most of the "objectionable" clauses removed, but even then some Opposition members were not satisfied. While criticising the measure empowering the Uganda Government to establish local councils in certain circumstances, a Member from Ankole* claimed:

* Mr. B. Byanyima, one of the very few in the Uganda Parliament who had the courage to defy Obote's dictatorship after 1966.

. . . another example of central government attempt at depriving these regions of their traditional, rightful powers is found in Section 32 of this Bill. . . . I feel that these regions, especially the kingdoms, should be left to establish local government councils at their will. . . . it is in keeping with their federal status.[88]

Despite such objections, the bill in its final form was similar to the Local Administrations Act already in operation for governing the district administrations. This was in conformity with the decisions of the London Conference and the Munster Report. Some important aspects of the Local Administrations Act to regulate federal state governments include:

Powers to Make Laws.   Apart from the legislative right the Constitution conferred upon the kingdoms, the legislature of a federal state was empowered to make laws in respect of:

(1)   any matters for which it was required or permitted to make laws;
(2)   public security; and
(3)   functions it was required or permitted to carry out.[89]

This power was qualified: before a bill on these matters became law it had to be approved by the Uganda Minister of Regional Administrations.[90] The exponents of federalism attacked this provision as detracting from the spirit of a federal constitution. They advocated the removal of the Minister's control. There is no doubt that the letter and the spirit of the Constitution empowered the Uganda Government to control the delegated authority it conferred upon the kingdoms when it did not choose to legislate directly.[91]

Administrative Subdivisions.   Provision was made for the establishment, alteration, division, or amalgamation of counties and other administrative subdivisions provided it was carried out in accordance with the Uganda Constitution. State governments were empowered to establish local government councils in counties and other administrative subdivisions. The Minister of Regional Administration was also empowered to *require* each state government to establish a local government council if and when he deemed it necessary.[92]

Powers and Duties of Chiefs.   The powers of chiefs were maintenance of law and order, apprehension of criminals, execution of orders from their superiors, and collection of taxes.[93]

The anomaly of the chief remaining a servant of two masters —the Central Government and the local government—was criticised by the Wallis Report. The law put it in the following terms:

> In the exercise of his powers under the provisions of this section a chief shall be subject to the directions of the Government of Uganda or its agent and the government employing him:
> Provided that in the event of any conflict arising directions issued by the Government of Uganda or its agent shall prevail.[94]

In other words, a chief's responsibility is concurrently to two governments, but there is a proviso for resolving any conflict of loyalties. Prima facie it appears to be a most unsatisfactory arrangement, but it was enacted on the presumption that state and Uganda Government directives would be complementary and not conflicting. In practice, conflict does not usually arise on matters of policy but may arise when two orders are received. Which order is to be executed first?

Financial Provisions. Under the Constitution, payments of any annual sums of money by the Uganda Government to these federal states are to be strictly subject to the will of Parliament.[95] It is mandatory for the Uganda Government to pay annual contributions to state governments towards the cost of services administered by that state, but this compulsion was limited by two important provisions.

Services referred to in the Constitution are within the executive authority of the Uganda Government. It has the power to delegate their administration to a federal state government, and it also has the power to withdraw such services from the administration of a state if it has "reason" to do so. To do so, however, requires the recommendation of a commission appointed under the Commissions of Inquiry Ordinance.[96]

Money paid to a federal state for the administration of such services is payable "subject to such terms and conditions as may be prescribed by Parliament." [97] Whatever money is paid is charged to the consolidated fund.

The Constitution guaranteed the federal states that any money accruing to them from any tax before independence would not be taken away by Parliament except with the state's consent, unless alternative arrangements were made by the Uganda Government that did not put the state to disadvantage.[98]

Parliament then provided the following sources of revenue for the federal states: (a) a graduated tax up to a maximum of six hundred shillings, (b) rates, (c) rents and other revenue collected by land boards, (d) market dues, (e) fees and fines, (f) interest on investments, (g) royalties, (h) donations, contributions, and endowments, (i) reimbursements, and (j) such other revenue as might be agreed upon between the government and the Uganda Government Minister responsible.[99]

It was also made possible for the Uganda Government to pay the government of any state money for: (a) grants to cover the cost or part of the cost of additional expenditure for the expansion of grant-aided services, (b) deficiency grants to assist a government to maintain or expand its services, and (c) grants for specific purposes.[100]

With this Act the constitutions of the federal states became complete. It must now be amply clear these federal states differed from districts only in a few small particulars.

This Act did a great deal to bring these two types of administrations—federal and district—under one common denominator and, therefore, to foster much-needed uniformity.

In the final analysis the federal status of these states does not lie in their exclusive legislative authority over Schedule 8 of the Constitution, but rather in the methods by which their rights were entrenched; in particular, the limitations imposed upon Parliament which precluded it from altering their constitutions.[101] The character and strength of their federalism was "restrictive" on the Uganda Legislature, rather than "granting" express exerciseable powers. This was an appropriate formula. By denying federal states exclusive legislative powers over a vast variety of topics, the risk of conflict between state and central legislatures was minimised, although the traditional federal pattern for the division of powers was adopted.

The Districts. There were no material alterations in the constitutions of the districts. Councils for each district would continue to perform any functions conferred upon them by any law.[102] Each council could, by resolution, provide for its own membership; they were required to have at least nine-tenths of their members elected in accordance with the constitution.[103]

Each District Council could, again by resolution, establish the office of Constitutional Head for that district, appoint the person to fill that office, fix tenure, and establish any associated ceremonial functions. The resolution establishing the office of Constitutional Head passed only when supported by a two-thirds' majority of all council members.

The detailed constitutional arrangements for districts remained as they were under the Local Administrations Act of 1962.

While districts were not particularly keen on federalism, it does not mean they had no demands to make. Kigezi District submitted a Memorandum to the Conference demanding federal status on the ground that it would be awkward for Kigezi to remain unitarily linked to the centre when the remainder of the western region—where it administratively belonged—was accorded federal or semi-federal status.[104]

The Bugisu delegate also demanded federal status: "It is the wish of the Bagisu to associate themselves with the other people of Uganda in a federal status, a constitutional form best suited for the preservation and furtherance of their customs and characteristics." [105]

What was common to all was the desire to have Constitutional Heads. The demands for federalism, coming as they did at the last moment, had no strong force behind them. None of these district advocates of federalism ever gave a precise definition of the distribution of powers between their "states-to-be" and the Uganda Government.

The possibility that federalism was never properly understood was fortified by the lack of any articulated definition of the term.

Summary and Conclusion

We have established that Uganda was assembled into a coherent, political whole from a collection of tribes with different social systems, languages, and ethnic characteristics. During its consolidation the British acted according to the fairly well-known constitutional doctrine of imperial rule which they had evolved over a long period of time.

Largely because of their policy of indirect rule, part of the doctrine of imperial rule, the British perpetuated the feeling of a separate existence for and in each tribe; they procrastinated the participation of Africans in Uganda-wide institutions like the Legislative Council and the national civil service, where a feeling of "wider belonging" could have been cultivated.

As a result, varying degrees of separatist tendencies grew in each tribe, attaining their supreme expression in Buganda's bid for unilateral independence and, to a lesser extent, in the demands for federalism from the other kingdoms and the districts.

Certain external influences after the Second World War brought about a new set of values for the world community of nations along with an irresistible desire for freedom among subject peoples throughout Asia and Africa. Because of the determination of a small but increasing indigenous class of politicians, pressure for political and constitutional advance was launched against imperial rule. This pressure led to constitutional commissions, conferences and finally—independence.

Perhaps the politicians' appeal to religious, tribal, and ethnic loyalties for support best demonstrates that religion and tribalism were maintained as the twin problems of national unity and national consciousness. Without indulging in the unfulfilled "ifs" of our history, I could forcefully contend that had there been no religious, tribal, or regional cleavages, Uganda would have evolved a monolithic political party and, consequently, a completely different Independence Constitution.

Another important factor that tended to detract from our sense of national homogeneity was the presence of an immensely rich, socially self-contained immigrant Asian community, who to a large extent still controlled the trade of this country.

As Ugandans, we could conclude that imperial rule had positive as well as negative aspects; positive in the sense that imperial rule was responsible for the creation and evolution of Uganda as we know it today. Whether the development of Uganda by the British was motivated by a desire to better the conditions of its inhabitants or was merely a by-product of trade-colonialism is a moral question and beyond the scope of this effort.

When colonial powers claim to have made contributions towards the development of dependent territories and when dependent territories in turn claim that nothing of value has accrued from imperial rule, the standards of judgement concerning the "rightness" for each argument are often merely subjective.

The major negative aspect of imperial rule must be clear to all by now: the failure—through deliberate and consistent methods—to unite the diverse tribes and religions of this country or to harness the peoples' outlook into a sense of common nationhood and community belonging. This defect continues to rank as the most formidable problem the leaders of independent Uganda face. To speak of poverty, ignorance, and disease as the greatest problems confronting this country is to state the obvious, particularly since these are the same problems faced by all nations of the world.

National disunity is the overriding problem peculiar to young countries, and without providing an adequate solution to it any talk of eliminating poverty, ignorance, and disease must be relegated to the academic realm; to be effective it must presuppose an undivided concentration that can only be borne by a united people.

We have reviewed the evolution of the Uganda Independence Constitution and we have examined the major forces that gave it content and substance.

The first obligation any ruling party or government has towards the nation it leads is the establishment of national harmony, not by destroying tribes or clans and not by abolishing religions, but rather by making every effort to congeal these diverse social elements into a common, constructive national endeavour. Equally important is the elimination of the fear of rejection often suffered by people of traditionally "inferior" tribes or disfavoured religious groups.

Through example rather than rhetoric, political leaders must demonstrate their personal and uncompromising stand against sectional interests as the basis for any privileged political, economic, or social status.

The primary objective should be one of sustaining every man's knowledge that he personally is significant within the vast general framework of nation-building. In the early days of nationhood, when scepticism is often the order of the day, this same man may have no focus beyond clan, tribe, or religion; the obligation upon the leaders is to widen and vary this focus into a sense of community so that the individual man—spiritually, intellectually, and physically—can experience the challenging and satisfying sense of belonging to a developing nation where he is important as a builder of that nation.

Once this sense of belonging is established among the people, any potentially weak young state will automatically increase its sense of unity and soon crystallise into a strong and unified *nation*. For the leaders of Uganda to escape or avoid this fundamental responsibility is to let Uganda drift towards manifest injustice and greater internal division and, ultimately, possible chaos.

9. Afterword

On 22 February 1966 Prime Minister Obote arrested five of his ministers, including myself,* who were in the middle of a Cabinet meeting considering the terms of reference for a commission of enquiry to censure him not only for allegedly having looted gold, coffee, and ivory from Zaire, but also for making secret preparations to abrogate the Uganda Constitution.

After these arrests, Obote proceeded illegally to suspend the Constitution of Uganda and to assume absolute power in administering the country. He soon dismissed the constitutional President of Uganda, the late Sir Edward Mutesa II, who was also the Kabaka of Buganda, and the Vice-President, Sir W. W. K. Nadiope, who was also the Kyabazinga of Busoga. In May of the same year he launched an armed attack on the Kabaka's palace, the Lubiri, at Mmengo, and as a result hundreds of innocent and defenceless people lost their lives in Buganda.† The ancient Kingdom of Buganda was abolished, and soon afterwards the kingdoms of Ankole, Bunyoro, and Toro.

To justify his drastic moves Obote advanced a variety of reasons, some of which he was later to revise or contradict. His first explanation was that the five Ministers were conspiring to over-

* The others arrested were: B. K. Kirya, Dr. B. S. Lumu, M. M. Ngobi, and G. B. Magezi.
† See President Amin's confirmation in *The Uganda Argus* of 10 June 1972.

throw the Constitution, the same reason he gave for dismissing Mutesa II from the Presidency. But a year later, when he felt sufficiently strong to boast, he made a public statement at Mbale that he had made Mutesa II President of Uganda in order to trap and eventually destroy him. This was an admission of a preconceived plan that he had now accomplished by deceit.

His other reason, which came well after he had abrogated the Uganda Constitution, was that the Independence Constitution was not conducive to unity. Consequently, he introduced a series of constitutions whose outstanding characteristic was the concentration of power in the Presidency, which he had assumed. Parliament, after the disgraceful arrest of the five Ministers, was so filled with fear that it soon became a willing rubber stamp for every wild measure Obote proposed. Those who remained courageous, like the Opposition, were too few to matter.

While he condemned the Independence Constitution as "divisive and feudalistic", he slowly but surely eroded the fundamental liberties guaranteed by that Constitution; personal liberty all but ceased to exist. He directed and controlled every government activity, be it central or local.

It is obviously outside the scope of this book to discuss the causes of the Obote revolution of 1966. Although I was deeply involved in the major events that ultimately culminated in his abrogation of the Uganda Constitution, it would be unfitting to state conclusions here without going into all the facts, both known and unknown to the public of Uganda, which would substantiate such conclusions. We need note here only that the constitutional evolution discussed in this book was brought to an abrupt halt by the revolution of 1966. Although the Uganda Army did not overthrow Obote until 1971, in actual fact it had been deeply involved in Uganda politics since 1966, for Obote used the armed forces to overthrow the established order of constitutional government and they were the means by which he maintained his increasingly unpopular regime.

On 25 January 1971 the Uganda Army ended Obote's rule by a military coup. General Idi Amin Dada, Commander of the Uganda Army, was handed power by the military to run the country and later assumed the Presidency and formed a largely civilian Government. If we cannot go into the causes of the Obote revolution of 1966, it would be even more improper and superficial to attempt discussion of the 1971 revolution. However, we can list most of the reasons given by the Army for having ousted Obote:

It has been necessary to take action to save a bad situation from getting worse. We give here below examples of matters that have left the people angry, worried, and very unhappy:

—The unwarranted detention without trial and for long periods of a large number of people, many of whom are totally innocent of any charges.

—The continuation of a state of emergency over the whole country for an indefinite period, which is meaningless to everybody.

—The lack of freedom in the airing of different views on political and social matters.

—The frequent loss of life and property arising from almost daily cases of armed robbery without any strong measures being taken to stop them. The people feel totally insecure, and yet robbery increases every day.

—The proposals for National Service, which will take every able-bodied person from his home to work in a camp for two years, could only lead to more robbery and general crime when homes are abandoned.

—Widespread corruption in high places, especially among ministers and top civil servants, has left the people with very little confidence, if any, in the Government. Most ministers own fleets of cars or buses, many big houses, and sometimes even aeroplanes.

—The failure by the political authorities to organise any elections for the last eight years whereby the people's free will could be expressed. It should be noted that the last elections within the ruling party were dominated by big fellows with lots of money, which they used to bribe their way into "winning" the elections. This bribery, together with threats against the people, entirely falsified the results of the so-called elections. Proposed new methods of election requiring a candidate to stand in four constituencies will only favour the rich and the well known.

—Economic policies have left many people unemployed and even more insecure and lacking in the basic needs of life like food, clothing, medicine, and shelter.

—High taxes have left the common man of this country poorer than ever before. Here are some of the taxes which the common man has to bear: development tax, graduated tax, sales tax, and social security fund tax. The big men can always escape these taxes or pass them on to the common man.

—The prices which the common man gets for his crops like cotton and coffee have not gone up, and sometimes they have gone down, whereas the cost of food, education, and so on have always gone up.

—The tendency to isolate the country from East African unity—e.g., by sending away workers from Kenya and Tanzania, by preventing the use of Uganda money in Kenya and Tanzania, by discouraging imports from Kenya and Tanzania, by stopping the use in Uganda of Kenyan or Tanzanian money.

—The creation of a wealthy class of leaders who are always talking of socialism while they grow richer and the common man poorer.

—In addition, the Defence Council, of which the President is Chairman, has not met since July 1969, and this has made administration in the Armed Forces very difficult. As a result, Armed Forces personnel lack accommodation, vehicles, and equipment. Also general recruitment submitted to the Chairman of the Defence Council a long time ago has not been put into effect.

—The Cabinet Office, by training large numbers of people (largely from Akokoro County in Lango District, where Obote and Akena Adoko, the Chief General Service Officer, come from) in armed warfare, has been turned into a second army; Uganda therefore has had two armies, one in the Cabinet, the other regular.

—Obote, on the advice of Akena Adoko, has sought to divide the Uganda Armed Forces and the rest of Uganda by picking out his own tribesmen and putting them in key positions in the Army and everywhere. Examples: the Chief General Service Officer, the Export and Import Corporation, Uganda Meat Packers, the Public Service Commission, Nyanza Textiles, and a Russian Textile Factory to be situated in Lango.

—From the time Obote took over power in 1962 his greatest and most loyal supporter has been the Army. The Army has always tried to be an example to the whole of Africa by not taking over the Government, and we have always followed that principle. It is therefore now a shock to us to see that Obote wants to divide and downgrade the Army by turning the Cabinet Office into another

Army. In doing this Obote and Akena Adoko have bribed and used some senior officers, who have turned against their fellow soldiers.

—We all want only unity in Uganda and we do not want bloodshed. Everybody in Uganda knows that. The matters mentioned above appear to us to lead to bloodshed only. For the reasons given above, we men of the Uganda Armed Forces have this day decided to take over power from Obote and hand it to our fellow soldier, Major-General Idi Amin Dada, and we hereby entrust him to lead this our beloved country of Uganda to peace and goodwill among all.

In less than nine years since Independence, Uganda has undergone two changes of government and Constitution by force. The abrogation of the 1962 Independence Constitution may well have put an end to parliamentary government based on a viable political system. The intervention of the armed forces in national government is likely to be a feature of Uganda's public life for a long time to come. Even when power is handed over to an elected civilian government, which General Amin Dada promises, the military may always feel they can intervene and re-establish their rule; particularly if any government exhibits the shortcomings that were cited against Obote.

A challenge to future leaders of Uganda, therefore, is likely to be how to evolve a new form of constitutional government that will take into account the most viable parts of our Independence Constitution together with the reality of a military presence in public life. It is not an easy task; but to ignore it would be to do so at the eventual expense of Uganda.

Whatever form of constitution is eventually adopted for Uganda, it must guarantee dispensation of social justice irrespective of clan, tribe, or religion. A highly centralized government could be as disruptive of Uganda's national unity as a federal one, if the leaders were to seek to establish tribal or religious hegemony in a country with so much cultural diversity. The best chance for stable national unity is a Constitution and government which genuinely and fairly seek to embrace all. To compromise this fundamental postulate through deceit or by default would be to guarantee future discontent and consequent instability. This is the greatest challenge to all Ugandans, in public or private life.

Reference Notes

Chapter 2

1. Lugard, in *The Dual Mandate in British Tropical Africa*, p. 16.
2. Ingham, *The Making of Modern Uganda*, pp. 44, 42.
3. A full account of the establishment of British rule is to be found in *ibid.*, pp. 41–132.
4. J. W. Nyakatura has written an interesting book concerning the complete dynasty of Bunyoro Kings, *Abakama ba Bunyoro-Kitara* [The kings of Bunyoro-Kitara], Canada, 1947.
5. Lukyn-Williams, "Nuwa Mbaguta; Nganzi of Ankole", *Uganda Journal*, Vol. 2 (1934–35).
6. Ingham, *The Making of Modern Uganda*, p. 65.
7. *Ibid.*, p. 74.
8. A. B. Adimola, "The Lamogi Rebellion of 1911–12," *Uganda Journal*, Vol. 12 (1948).
9. H. B. Thomas, "Capax Imperial: The Story of Semei Kakunguru" *Uganda Journal*, Vol. 19 (1955).
10. K. Ingham, "British Administration in Lango District 1907–1935", *Uganda Journal*, Vol. 19 (1955).
11. Ingham, *The Making of Modern Uganda*, p. 122.
12. The Uganda Agreement, 1900, *Laws of Uganda* (1951), Vol. VI, p. 12.
13. The Toro Agreement, 1900, *Laws of Uganda* (1951), Vol. VI, p. 66.
14. The Ankole Agreement, 1901, *Laws of Uganda* (1951), Vol. VI, p. 2.
15. Reported (1926), A.C. pp. 522–23.
16. (1956) Q.B. at p. 15. Also because of S.4, Foreign Jurisdiction Act, 1890.

17. Civil case No. 50 of 1954, reported in 7.U.L.R.
18. Per Sir Kenneth O'Connar P., E.A.L.R., Pt. I (1960), p. 52, in *Daudi Ndiberema and Others v The Enganzi of Ankole and Others.*
19. (1907) I.U.L.R. 22.
20. (1908) I.U.L.R. 41.
21. Quoted in Low and Pratt, *Buganda and British Overrule*, p. 191.
22. See a statement of the Principle in Wade and Phillips, *Constitutional Law*, Ch. 20; also Brierly, *The Law of Nations*, pp. 243–52.
23. Oppenheim, *International Law*, p. 829, shows the effect of treaties on contracting parties.
24. *Ibid.,* p. 796.
25. (1924) A.C. at p. 814.
26. Stuart, *Uganda, Land of Promise*, pp. 8, 27.
27. Lugard, *The Rise of Our East African Empire*, Vol. II, p. 580.
28. Lugard, *The Dual Mandate*, p. 38.
29. *Ibid.,* p. 17.
30. *Ibid.,* p. 18.
31. Lugard, *The Rise of Our East African Empire*, Vol. I, p. 649.
32. Lugard, *The Dual Mandate*, p. 211.
33. See also Low and Pratt, *Buganda and British Overrule*, p. 164.
34. Ingham, *The Making of Modern Uganda.*
35. Elias, *The Nature of African Customary Law*, p. 21.
36. Ingham, *The Making of Modern Uganda*, p. 119.
37. *Ibid.,* p. 18.
38. Low and Pratt, *Buganda and British Overrule*, p. 260.
39. The Uganda Agreement, 1900, Art. 6, *Laws of Uganda*, Vol. VI, p. 14.
40. *Ibid.,* Art. 9.
41. *Ibid.,* Art. 10.
42. *Ibid.,* Art. 6.
43. The Ankole Agreement, 1901, *Laws of Uganda*, Vol. VI, p. 2; The Toro Agreement, 1900, *Laws of Uganda*, Vol. VI, p. 66. For an interesting account of such earlier treaties, see K. Ingham, "Early Treaties", *Uganda Journal*, Vol. 12 (1948), p. 25.
44. *Laws of Uganda*, Vol. II, p. 1046.
45. *Ibid.,* S. 2.
46. *Ibid.,* S. 3.
47. *Ibid.,* S. 4.
48. *Ibid.,* S. 5.
49. *Ibid.,* S. 6.
50. *Ibid.,* S. 7. It should be noted, however, that in Kigezi no Council was recognized until 1927, and in Lango, towards the close of 1935.
51. *Ibid.,* S. 8.
52. *Ibid.,* S. 10.

53. *Ibid.,* S. 13.
54. *Ibid.,* S. 15.
55. Low and Pratt, *Buganda and British Overrule,* pp. 173–75.
56. *Laws of Uganda,* Vol. II, p. 1058.
57. *Proceedings of the Legco,* 28th Session, 1948/49, p. 118.
58. *Laws of Uganda,* Vol. II, S. 6.
59. *Ibid.,* S. 3.
60. *Ibid.,* S. 4.
61. *Laws of Uganda,* Vol. VI, p. 82.
62. *Ibid.,* S. 15 (1).
63. The Uganda Order-in-Council, 1920, *Laws of Uganda,* Vol. VI, p. 97, S. 6.
64. The Colonial Laws Validity Act, 1865 (28 & 29 vict. c.63) S.I.
65. The Uganda Order-in-Council, 1920, S. 9.
66. *Ibid.,* S. 12.
67. Wallis, *Report of an Inquiry into African Local Government in the Protectorate of Uganda* (hereinafter called the Wallis Report), Pt. II, "Political", p. 14.
68. *Ibid.,* Pt. II, p. 13.
69. *Laws of Uganda* (1955), p. 4, Ordinance No. 1, of 1955.
70. The Buganda Agreement, 1955, *Laws of Uganda* (1955); also Legal Notice No. 138 of 1955.
71. Ingham, *The Making of Modern Uganda,* pp. 191–94.
72. Low and Pratt, *Buganda and British Overrule,* p. 262.
73. Quoted in *ibid.,* Pt. II, p. 168. Sir Donald Cameron was then Governor of Tanganyika.
74. K. Ingham, "Early Proposals for a Federal Uganda", *Uganda Journal,* Vol. 21 (1957), p. 223.
75. Ingham, *The Making of Modern Uganda,* p. 187.
76. For an analysis of indirect rule see Low and Pratt, *Buganda and British Overrule,* Pt. II, "The Politics of Indirect Rule", pp. 164ff.
77. For the application of the principle in Nigeria, see Kalu Ezera, *Constitutional Developments in Nigeria.* A detailed account of this is given later, analysing the forces that shaped Uganda's final constitution before independence.

Chapter 3

1. Ingham, *The Making of Modern Uganda,* p. 172.
2. *Ibid.,* pp. 174–77.
3. *Ibid.,* p. 173.
4. Draft Instructions to the Governor of Uganda, 1920, No. 885, S. 10.
5. *Ibid.,* S. 4

6. *Ibid.,* S. 12
7. *Ibid.*
8. *Ibid.,* S. 25
9. *Ibid.,* S. 26; also found in *Laws of Uganda,* Vol. IV.
10. In his book, *British Policy in Changing Africa.*
11. Draft Instructions to the Governor of Uganda, 1920, No. 885, S. 30.
12. *Proceedings of Legislative Council,* 1946, p. 1.
13. Ingham, *The Making of Modern Uganda,* p. 232; also *The Report of the Constitutional Committee, 1959* (hereinafter called the Wild Report), p. 15.
14. See Low and Pratt, *Buganda and British Overrule,* pp. 272–74; also Apter, *The Political Kingdom in Uganda,* pp. 226–33.
15. *Proceedings of the Legislative Council,* 1946–47, p. 5.
16. *Proceedings of the Legislative Council,* 1949–50, p. 2; also the Wild Report, p. 16.
17. Low, *Political Parties in Uganda,* p. 19.
18. This was contained in the Colonial Secretary's despatch, No. 692 of 20 July 1955.
19. *Proceedings of Legislative Council,* 1956, p. 51.
20. *Ibid.,* p. 52.
21. *Ibid.*
22. The Gold Coast (Constitution) Order-in-Council, 1950, S.I. 1950 No. 2094, S. 62
23. The Jamaican (Constitution) Order-in-Council, 1944, S.R. & O., 1944 No. 1215, S. 5.
24. The Uganda (Amendment) Order-in-Council, 1954, S.I. 1954 No. 1568; the Legislative Council (Powers and Privileges) Ordinance, 1955, No. 11 of 1955.
25. *Proceedings of the Legislative Council,* 1957, Pt. II, p. 36.
26. *The Uganda Argus,* 21 April 1957.
27. No. 692, dated 20 July 1957.
28. *Proceedings of the Legislative Council,* 1957, Pt. I, p. 19.
29. *Ibid.,* p. 21.
30. *Ibid.,* p. 38.
31. *Ibid.,* p. 39.
32. *Ibid.,* Pt. II, p. 43.
33. See Ezeta, *Constitutional Developments in Nigeria.*
34. *Proceedings of the Legislative Council,* 1957, Pt. II, p. 44.
35. *Ibid.,* p. 43.
36. *Ibid.,* p. 44.
37. *Ibid.,* p. 46.
38. *Ibid.,* Pt. I, p. 19.
39. *Ibid.,* p. 82.
40. Colonial Laws Validity Act, 1865, S. 1.

41. *Proceedings of Legislative Council*, 1958, Pt. I, p. 2.
42. *Recommendations of the Namirembe Conference*, 1955; The Buganda Agreement, 1955, Art. 7; *Laws of Uganda* (1955).
43. *The Katikkiro v The Attorney-General* (1957) E.A.L.R.
44. Royal Instructions to the Governor of Uganda, 1958; Legal Notice No. 247/58, Art. 15 (1).
45. British Honduras (Constitution) Order-in-Council, 1953.
46. *Laws of Uganda* (1958), Legal Notice No. 247/58.
47. *Ibid.*, Art. 15.
48. *Ibid.*, Art. 16.
49. *Ibid.*, Art. 17.
50. *Proceedings of Legislative Council*, 1958, Pt. I.
51. *Ibid.*, p. 128.
52. Wild Report, p. 7; also *Proceedings of the Legislative Council*, 1959, Vol. III, gives names of all Members of the Executive and Legislative Councils under the heading "List of Members of the Legislative Council".
53. Royal Instructions to the Governor of Gibraltar, dated 28 February 1950, Ch. 3–14.
54. Royal Instructions to the Governor of Singapore, dated 24 February 1948, as amended on 23 April 1951.
55. Sierra Leone Protectorate Order-in-Council, 1951, S.7.
56. *Proceedings of the Legislative Council*, 1959, Vol. III (II), "List of Members of the Legislative Council".
57. Royal Instructions to the Governor of Uganda, 1958, Art. 18, Legal Notice No. 247/58.
58. *Ibid.*, Art. 19.
59. *Ibid.*, Art. 20.
60. Hon. G. B. Magezi, in *Proceedings of the Legislative Council*, 1960, 40th Session, p. 1526.
61. The Buganda Agreement, 1955, Art. 7 (1), Legal Notice No. 190 of 1955.
62. *Proceedings of the Legislative Council*, 1956, pp. 62, 89–93.
63. *Ibid.*, p. 1; also *The Uganda Argus*, 24 April 1956.
64. Art. 7 (1).
65. *Proceedings of the Legislative Council*, 1956, p. 3.
66. *Proceedings of the Legislative Council*, 1957, Pt. II, p. 23.
67. *Ibid.*, p. 115.
68. *Ibid.*, p. 123.
69. Sessional Paper No. 4 of 1957/58, p. 12.
70. *Proceedings of the Legislative Council*, 1957, Pt. II, p. 20.
71. S.I. 1957, No. 1528, Legal Notice No. 174 of 1957.
72. Ordinance No. 20 of 1957, *Laws of Uganda* (1957), p. 76.
73. *Ibid.*, Pt. II, "Registration of Electors", Ss. 11–15.

74. *Ibid.,* Pt. III, "Elections", Ss. 16–50.
75. *Ibid.,* Pt. IV, "Corrupt Practices and Other Offences", Ss. 51–59.
76. *Ibid.,* Pt. V "Avoidance of Elections and Election Petitions", Ss. 60–71.
77. *Ibid.,* S. 7.
78. *Ibid.,* S. 9.
79. Allen, *Uganda Legislative Council Elections.*
80. The Gold Coast (Legislative Council) Order-in-Council, 1925 to 1939, S. 22.
81. *Ibid.,* Ss. 18–21; also Wight, *The Gold Coast Legislative Council,* pp. 223–24.
82. The Legislative Council (Elections Ordinance), 1957, Ss. 17, 18.
83. *Laws of Uganda* (1960), p. 97, The Legislative Council (Elections Amendment) Ordinance, 1960.
84. *Ibid.,* S.4.
85. "The Principal Ordinance" means the "Ordinance", 1957.
86. The Legislative Council (Elections Amendment Ordinance), 1960, S. 4 (3).
87. *Ibid.,* S. 4 (6).
88. *Proceedings of the Legislative Council,* 1960, Pt. IV, p. 1361; also *The Uganda Argus,* 14 June 1960.
89. The Wild Report, paras. 95, 96.
90. *Proceedings of the Legislative Council,* 1960, Pt. IV, p. 1360.
91. *Ibid.,* p. 1377.
92. *Ibid.,* p. 1376.
93. The Legislative Council (Elections Amendment) Ordinance, 1960, S. 12.
94. *Proceedings of the Legislative Council,* 1960, Pt. IV, p. 1362.
95. *Ibid.,* p. 1391. Hon. A. M. Obote (non-Premia) pressed for the division, as he was the Leader of the Elected Members of the Council.
96. *Proceedings of the Legislative Council,* 1960, Pt. IV, p. 1366.
97. *The Laws of Uganda* (1960); also in *Proceedings of Legislative Council,* 1960, 3rd Meeting of 40th Session, p. 1514; *The Uganda Argus,* 23 September 1960.
98. 3rd Meeting of 40th Session of Legislative Council, 1960, p. 1518.
99. *Ibid.,* p. 1524.
100. *The Uganda Argus,* 23 September 1960.
101. 3rd Meeting of 40th Session of Legislative Council, 1960, p. 1523.

Chapter 4

1. In *British Policy in Changing Africa.*
2. Quoted in Mansur, *The Process of Independence,* p. 27.

3. See supra, pp. 1–21.
4. "The Account on Buganda's Local Government", pp. 10–14, and "Buganda Separatism", p. 111, show this.
5. Low, *Political Parties in Uganda, 1949–62*, p. 15.
6. *Ibid.,* p. 41.
7. See Ingham, *The Making of Modern Uganda*, pp. 123–25, 159–63; Apter, *The Political Kingdom in Uganda*, Ch. 3.
8. There are many available accounts of this conflict; see Ingham, *The Making of Modern Uganda*, pp. 47, 53.
9. Recorded by Tucker in *Eight Years in Uganda and East Africa*, p. 125.
10. Nehru, *The Discovery of India*, p. 412.
11. Low, *Political Parties in Uganda*, p. 20.
12. For a full list of candidates that stood for the 1961 General Elections see "Uganda Legislative Council Elections 1961", pp. 90–97; also *The Uganda Argus* dated 24 February 1963 for the results of Lukiiko Elections in February 1962.
13. Stated in a U.N.C. hand-bill dated 11 January 1961.
14. See Low, *Political Parties in Uganda*, p. 22.
15. Dr. Babumba's Letter to the Conference of Katikkiros and Secretaries-General, dated 22 October 1960.
16. Low, *Political Parties in Uganda*, p. 22.
17. Ingham, *The Making of Modern Uganda*, p. 53.
18. See footnote (†) on page 49.
19. Pelikan, *The Riddle of Roman Catholicism*, p. 89.
20. See "The Democratic Party Manifesto 1960", with the Preface "Forward Ever, Backward Never".
21. *Proceedings of the Legislative Council, 1958*, dated 17 November 1958; also in the Wild Report, Pt. I, pp. 1–2.
22. *Proceedings of the Legislative Council, 1958/59*, Pt. I, p. 95; also *The Uganda Argus* of 5 February 1959.
23. *Ibid.,* p. 125.
24. *Ibid.,* p. 65.
25. Wild Report, paras. 41–42.
26. Despatch to the Governor of Uganda, No. 1461, dated 14 September 1960 p. 1.
27. Wild Report, para. 48.
28. Secretary of State's despatch No. 1461, of 1960, para. 2 (2).
29. Wild Report, para. 60.
30. *Ibid.,* para. 65.
31. Secretary of State's despatch No. 1461, para. 4.
32. Legislative Council (Elections) Ordinance, 1957, S. 9.
33. Wild Report, para. 93.
34. *Ibid.,* para. 95.

35. *Ibid.*, para. 116. For an interesting account of a later argument to lower the age to 18, see infra, p. 170.
36. *Ibid.*, paras. 120, 122.
37. The Secretary of State's despatch No. 1461, paras. 9, 10. For the provisions that became law see supra, "Evolution of the Electoral Process".
38. Wild Report, para. 151.
39. *Ibid.*, para. 153.
40. The Secretary of State's despatch No. 1461, para. 13.
41. *Ibid.*
42. Wild Report, para. 169.
43. This was made known by the Governor in a communication from the Chair to the Legislative Council, on 22 February 1959.
44. Wild Report, para. 174.
45. Despatch No. 1461, para. 19.
46. The Colonial Secretary's despatch No. 1461.

Chapter 5

1. See Moyse-Bartlett, *The King's African Rifles* (Aldershot, 1956), p. 96.
2. Hollingsworth, *The Asians of East Africa*, pp. 40, 45.
3. *Ibid.*, p. 51.
4. *General Report on the Uganda Protectorate for the Year Ending March 1903*, Comd. 1893 (1904), 17.
5. Johnston, *The Uganda Protectorate*, 1, p. 294.
6. See *Report of the Committee, on Immigration from India to the Crown Colonies and Protectorates*, Comd. 5192 (1910), Pt. II, pp. 354–55.
7. Wild Report, paras. 72–73.
8. *Ibid.*, para. 74.
9. *Ibid.*, para. 75.
10. *Ibid.*, para. 77.
11. Also quoted in *ibid.*, p. 20.
12. *Proceedings of the Legislative Council*, 36th session, 1956, p. 1.
13. Wild Report, para. 81.
14. *Proceedings of the Legislative Council*, 1957, Pt. II, p. 23.
15. In his *British Colonial Constitutions*, 1947, p. 28.
16. *Proceedings of the Legislative Council*, 1957, Pt. II, p. 123.
17. *Ibid.*, p. 21.
18. *Ibid.*, p. 115.
19. *Ibid.*
20. *Ibid.*, p. 33.

21. Wild Report, para. 88.
22. For an interesting article on Buganda expansionism, see A. D. Roberts, "The Sub-Imperialism of the Baganda", *Journal of African History*, Vol. 3 (1962), p. 434.
23. For a brief but accurate assessment of this, see Marsh and Kingsworth, *An Introduction to the History of East Africa*, p. 118.
24. Quoted in the pamphlet *Buganda's Independence*, p. 24.
25. See *Journal of African History*, Vol. 3 (1962), p. 434.
26. See Cox's interesting article, "The Growth and Expansion of Buganda", *Uganda Journal*, Vol. 14 (1950).
27. Wilson to Terman, 8 February 99, E.S.A. A4/16, cited by Low and Pratt, *Buganda and British Overrule*, p. 147.
28. See, for example, H. F. Morris, "The Making of Ankole", *Uganda Journal*, Vol. 21 (1957).
29. For fuller accounts on these reforms, see: Apter, *The Political Kingdom in Uganda*, pp. 211–32; Low and Pratt, "The Reforms of Charles Dundas", in *Buganda and British Overrule*, pp. 275–92.
30. Quoted in *The Report of the Sub-Committee of the Lukiiko*, which was set up to examine the recommendations of the Hancock Committee, otherwise called The Kintu Committee. Entebbe, White Fathers Press, 1955.
31. For detailed and official (British) information, see "Withdrawal of Recognition from Kabaka Mutesa II of Buganda", London Comd. 9028; also Low and Pratt, *Buganda and British Overrule*, pp. 317–49; and Ingham, *The Making of Modern Uganda*, pp. 264–78.
32. *Buganda's Independence*, p. 30.
33. Published in *ibid.* The memorandum was submitted in September 1960.
34. *Ibid.,* p. 4.
35. Quoted in *Buganda's Position*, p. 4; also in *Buganda's Independence*, p. 5.
36. This was Art. 13 of the Treaty, quoted in *Buganda's Independence*, p. 6.
37. *Buganda's Position*, p. 7.
38. Quoted from *Buganda's Independence*, pp. 7, 8.
39. *Journal of African History*, Vol. 3 (1962), p. 434.
40. *Buganda's Independence*, p. 11.
41. *Ibid.,* p. 12.
42. *Ibid.,* p. 16.
43. *Ibid.,* p. 15.
44. *Ibid.,* p. 18; also in *Buganda's Position*, p. 16.
45. *Buganda's Independence*, p. 30. This referred to hostile speeches by non-Baganda Members of the Legislative Council.
46. *Ibid.,* p. 28.

47. The reply was in Letter No. EAF/71/6/03, dated 2 December 1960.
48. *Ibid.*, p. 2.
49. Resolution No. 12 of 24 September 1960.
50. Letter No. EAF/71/6/03.
51. *The Uganda Argus*, 2 January 1961.
52. *Proceedings of the Legislative Council*, 40th Session, 1960, p. 1509, Question No. 307 of 1960.
53. *Ibid.*, p. 1549.
54. *Ibid.*, p. 1552.
55. *Ibid.*, p. 1653, Question No. 289 of 1960.
56. *Ibid.*, Question No. 421 of 1960.
57. Kalu Ezera, "The Growth of Tribal Nationalism" in his *Constitutional Developments in Nigeria*, pp. 89–92.
58. *The Government's Revised Constitutional Proposals for Gold Coast Independence*, pp. 5–6.
59. *Ghana Parliamentary Debates*, XVI, 1959, Col. 1682.
60. *The Uganda Argus*, 14 January 1961. PAFMECA means Pan African Freedom Movement for East and Central Africa.
61. *Buganda's Independence*, pp. 7, 8.
62. See Wild Report, para. 179; also, the Memorandum submitted by Ankole Constitutional Committee to the Relationships Commission, dated 20 October 1960.
63. Quoted in the *Report of the Royal Commission on the Australian Constitution* (1929), p. 230, also in Wheare's *Federal Government*, pp. 7, 11.
64. This view is also supported by A. V. Dicey in *The Laws of the Constitution*, Ch. 3, p. 144; also by F. Brown, *Law Quarterly Review*, 1944, p. 305.
65. The Uganda Order-in-Council, 1920, S. 8, *Laws of Uganda*, Vol. VI, p. 97.
66. Wade and Phillips, *Constitutional Law*, Ch. 20, "Foreign Affairs", p. 249.
67. The Uganda Agreement, 1900, *Laws of Uganda*, Vol. VI, p. 14.
68. *Ibid.*, Art. 11.
69. *Ibid.*, Arts. 9, 10.
70. See Ankole and Toro Agreements, *Laws of Uganda*, Vol. VII, pp. 2, 66.
71. These were contained, for example, in the African Authority Ordinance, *Laws of Uganda*, Vol. II, p. 1046, and African Local Governments Ordinance, *Laws of Uganda*, Vol. II, p. 1058.
72. The Buganda (Transitional Provisions) Order-in-Council, 1955, Legal Notice No. 138 of 1955.
73. *Ibid.*, Art. 26 (1).

74. *Ibid.*, Art. 26 (4).
75. *Buganda's Independence*, p. 7.
76. *Proceedings of the Legislative Council*, 1952/53, made at the 32nd Session.
77. Wheare, *Federal Government*, Ch. 3, from p. 37.
78. See the Wallis Report, Pt. II, p. 14.
79. *Report of the Relationships Commission*, para. 103.
80. In *The Federalist*, No. XV, p. 73.
81. *The English Constitution*, chapter on "The Monarchy", pp. 32, 33.
82. See, for example, H. F. Morris, *A History of Ankole* (East African Literature Bureau, 1962); also Beattie, *Bunyoro: An African Kingdom*.
83. *Buganda's Independence*, p. 23.
84. *Buganda's Position*.
85. See *Minutes of the Conference*, Item III—"The Form of Government", dated 29 November 1960.
86. Wild Report, pp. 42–44.
87. *Minutes of the Conference* held at Jinja on 16 August 1961, p. 1.
88. Letter dated 16 November 1960, signed by the Omukama of Bunyoro, who was Chairman of the Conference.
89. *Proceedings of the Legislative Council*, 37th Session, Pt. II, 1957, p. 26.
90. *Ibid.*, p. 29.
91. *Ibid.*, 36th Session, 1956, p. 1.
92. *Ibid.*, 1958/59.
93. Wheare, *Federal Government*, p. 37.
94. *In Representative Government*, pp. 367–68.
95. Wild Report, p. 43.
96. See Mansur, *The Process of Independence*, p. 123.
97. *Ghana Parliamentary Debates*, XII, 1958, Col. 3. See also Rubin and Murray, *The Constitution and Government of Ghana*, pp. 3–5.

Chapter 6

1. *Report of the Uganda Relationships Commission*, 1961 (hereinafter called the Munster Report). The terms of reference were also contained in the Colonial Secretary's despatch No. 1261 of 14 September 1960, addressed to the Governor of Uganda.
2. Peagram, *A Report of the General Election to the Legislative Council of the Uganda Protectorate*, 1961, para. 16.
3. Munster Report, paras. 86–93.
4. *Ibid.*, "British Government Policy", paras. 118–21.
5. *Ibid.*, para. 121.

6. *Ibid.,* "The Choice Before the Country", paras. 79–82.
7. *Ibid.,* para. 99.
8. *Ibid.,* paras. 122–24.
9. Wheare, *Federal Government,* p. 11.
10. Munster Report, para. 123 (iii).
11. *Ibid.,* para. 123 (iv) (c).
12. *Ibid.,* p. 56.
13. *Ibid.,* para. 150 (4).
14. *Ibid.,* para. 150 (2).
15. *Ibid.,* para. 123 (vi).
16. *Ibid.,* p. 45.
17. *Ibid.,* para. 117.
18. *The English Constitution,* p. 70.
19. Munster Report, para. 128.
20. Minutes for the Conference of Katikkiros and Secretaries-General of 18 July 1960.
21. Munster Report, para. 128.
22. *Ibid.,* para. 154.
23. *Ibid.,* para. 151.
24. *Ibid.,* para. 142.
25. *Ibid.,* para. 146.
26. *Ibid.,* para. 147.
27. See *ibid.,* Ch. 8, "The Future Constitution", pp. 55–75.
28. Wild Report, para. 185.
29. Munster Report, para. 156.
30. *Ibid.,* para. 158.
31. See the Nigerian (Constitution) Order-in-Council, 1960, S.I. 1960, No. 1652, Ss. 36–38.
32. *The Government's Revised Constitutional Proposals for Gold Coast Independence,* pp. 5, 6.
33. Munster Report, paras. 161–62.
34. *Ibid.,* para. 163.
35. *Ibid.,* para. 164–67.
36. *Ibid.,* para. 170.
37. *Ibid.,* para. 172.
38. *Ibid.,* para. 176 (b).
39. *Ibid.,* para. 176 (a).
40. *Ibid.,* paras. 182, 183.
41. *Ibid.,* para. 184 (a).
42. *Ibid.,* para. 184 (b).
43. *Ibid.,* para. 188.
44. Wild Report, paras. 43–53.
45. *Ibid.,* para. 52.
46. Munster Report, para. 192.

47. *Ibid.,* para. 191.
48. E.g., Low in *Political Parties in Uganda, 1949–62.*
49. Munster Report, paras. 244–55.
50. *Ibid.,* para. 253.
51. *Ibid.,* para. 255.
52. *Ibid.,* para. 245.
53. *Ibid.,* para. 250.
54. *Ibid.,* para. 255.

Chapter 7

1. Reproduced from the *Report on the Uganda Legislative Council Elections,* 1961, para. 39.
2. *Ibid.,* para. 42.
3. *Ibid.,* para. 48.
4. *Manifesto of the Democratic Party,* 1961, Appendix A, pp. 18–25.
5. *Report on the Uganda Legislative Council Elections,* 1961, p. 96, gives the results of all constituencies, including the number of votes cast for each candidate.
6. *Ibid.,* p. 17.
7. Toro (Provisional) Agreement, 1961, Legal Notice No. 167 of 1961, contained in *Laws of Uganda* (1961), p. 321.
8. The Uganda (Amendment) Order-in-Council, S.I. 1961, No. 62, S. 2.
9. *Proceedings of the Legislative Council,* 1961, Pt. I, pp. 3–5.
10. The Hon. C. K. Patel, C.B.E., Q.C.
11. Embodied in "Additional Instructions" (i.e., to the Governor), Legal Notice No. 30 of 1961, clause 3.
12. As defined by S.I., Colonial Laws Validity Act, 1865.
13. *Proceedings of the Legislative Council,* 1961, Pt. I, p. 4.
14. *Report of the Uganda Constitutional Conference,* 1961.
15. The Uganda (Constitution) Order-in-Council, 1962, S.I. 1962, No. 405, 2nd Schedule, 'The Constitution of Uganda', S. 28.
16. *Ibid.,* S. 20.
17. *Ibid.,* S. 52 (1), (2) (a).
18. *Ibid.,* S. 52 (3).
19. The Independence Constitution, Legal Notice No. 251 of 1962, Ss. 39–40.
20. The Uganda Constitution, 1961, S. 31 (2) (3).
21. *Ibid.,* S. 31 (4).
22. *Ibid.,* S. 30 (1). Cf. Independence Constitution, S. 39, which refers only to Uganda citizens.
23. *Record of the 11th Meeting,* U.C.C. (61), p. 1.

24. *Ibid.*, p. 5.
25. *Ibid.*, p. 7.
26. *Ibid.*, p. 6.
27. The Uganda Constitution, 1961, S. 32 (3).
28. *Record of 11th Meeting*, U.C.C. (61), p. 6. Author's emphasis.
29. The Uganda Constitution, 1961, S. 33 (2).
30. See Kiwanuka's remarks, "Record of 3rd Meeting", U.C.C. (61), p. 1.
31. The Uganda Constitution, 1961, S. 32 (2).
32. *Ibid.*, S. 40 (3).
33. *Ibid.*, S. 44 (2), reproduced in the Independence Constitution, Ss. 41, 42.
34. *Ibid.*, S. 39 (2), reproduced in the Independence Constitution, S. 50.
35. Independence Constitution, S. 49 (1). The detailed procedure for conducting the Assembly's business is contained in the *Standing Orders of the National Assembly.*
36. The Uganda Constitution, 1961, S. 46 (1).
37. *Ibid.*, S. 44 (1).
38. *Ibid.*, S. 46 (2).
39. *Ibid.*, S. 46 (2); S. 46 (1).
40. *Ibid.*, S. 48 (1).
41. *Ibid.*, S. 50.
42. *Ibid.*, S. 51.
43. *Ibid.*, S. 35 (1).
44. *Ibid.*, S. 35 (2). See also the *Report of the Constitutional Conference*, 1961, para. 22.
45. The Uganda Constitution, 1961, S. 34.
46. *Ibid.*, S. 34 (5).
47. *Ibid.*, S. 34 (4). See also *Record of the 3rd Meeting of the Conference*, U.C.C. (61), p. 3.
48. *Report of the Constitutional Conference*, para. 29.
49. The Uganda Constitution, 1961, S. 34 (6).
50. *Ibid.*, S. 53.
51. *Ibid.*, S. 54 (1).
52. *Ibid.*, S. 62 (1).
53. *Ibid.*, S. 60.
54. *Proceedings of the Conference*, U.C.C. (61), pp. 12, 13.
55. *Ibid.*, p. 13.
56. *Ibid.*
57. *Ibid.*, p. 11.
58. The Uganda (Constitution) Order-in-Council, 1962, S.I. 1962, No. 405, Ss. 7 (3), 8.
59. The Uganda Constitution, 1961, S. 11.
60. *Ibid.*, S. 25 (1).

61. *Ibid.,* Ss. 26, 27.
62. *Ibid.,* S. 57.
63. By virtue of S. 52 of *ibid.,* and the Sixth Schedule to the Constitution of Uganda, Pt. I, S. 1—S.I. 1962, No. 405.
64. *Ibid.,* Sixth Schedule, Pt. II, S. 4.
65. *Ibid.,* S. 6.
66. The Uganda Constitution, 1961, S. 54 (2).
67. *Ibid.,* S. 55 (1).
68. See U.C.C. (61), record of the 10th meeting.
69. The Uganda Constitution, 1961, S. 81.
70. *Ibid.,* S. 71.
71. *Ibid.,* S. 83.
72. See *ibid.,* Ss. 84 (1) (a) and S. 82 (1).
73. The Buganda Agreement, 1961, Legal Notice No. 208 of 1961, *Laws of Uganda* (1961), p. 427, contains the full provisions.
74. The Uganda Constitution, 1961, S. 60, (b), (C), (D).
75. The Buganda Agreement, 1961, Art. 14.
76. *Ibid.,* Art. 15.
77. Art. 11 of the Agreement: contained in Pt. I, 7th Schedule to the Agreement.
78. The Uganda Constitution, 1961, Art. 12 (3).
79. *Ibid.,* Art. 12 (1).
80. *Ibid.,* Art. 12 (1) (b).
81. Document U.C.C. (61), p. 17.
82. See *ibid.,* p. 2.
83. *Ibid.,* p. 4.
84. *Ibid.*
85. See the *Report of the Constitutional Conference,* Comd. 1523 of 1961, paras. 111–14; and the Local Administrations Ordinance, 1961. *Laws of Uganda* (1962), p. 143.
86. *Record of 13th Meeting,* p. 1.
87. The Conference Report, para. 109; also, The Uganda Constitution, 1961.
88. The Conference Report, para. 110 (a); also The Uganda Constitution, 1961, S. 77 (5).
89. An instance is the Memorandum by the West Nile delegate, Mr. Okeny, U.C.C. (61).
90. The Uganda Constitution, 1961, S. 75 (1).
91. The Local Administrations Ordinance, *Laws of Uganda* (1962), p. 423, S. 24, Schedule 1 to the Ordinance.
92. *Ibid.,* S. 25, and Schedule 1 to the Ordinance.
93. *Ibid.,* S. 22 (1).
94. *Ibid.,* S. 25.
95. *Ibid.,* S. 32 (2).

96. *Ibid.,* S. 35.
97. For all functions of the chief see *ibid.,* Ss. 39–46.
98. *Ibid.,* S. 48.
99. *Ibid.,* S. 49.
100. The Uganda Constitution, 1961, S. 74.
101. *Ibid.,* S. 76.

Chapter 8

1. See minutes of the Opening of the Conference, U.I.C. (62), pp. 3–4.
2. The Uganda Independence Constitution, Ss. 37, 38.
3. *Ibid.,* Ch. 5, Pt. I.
4. *Ibid.,* S. 40.
5. *Ibid.,* S. 44.
6. *Ibid.,* S. 45.
7. *Ibid.,* S. 73.
8. *Ibid.,* S. 74 (2).
9. *Ibid.,* S. 74 (3).
10. *Ibid.,* S. 78.
11. *Ibid.,* S. 75 (2).
12. See Wade and Phillips, *Constitutional Law,* Ch. 4, on "Parliamentary Supremacy". Also Rubin and Murray, *The Constitution and Government of Ghana,* p. 52.
13. (1803)1, Cranch p. 137.
14. The Uganda Independence Constitution, S. 1.
15. *Ibid.,* S. 74 (1).
16. *Ibid.,* S. 75 (1).
17. Memorandum U.I.C. (62), entitled "The Exclusive Law Making Powers of the Buganda Legislature".
18. *Ibid.*
19. *Ibid.*
20. *Ibid.*
21. *Ibid.,* p. 7.
22. The Uganda Independence Constitution, S. 43.
23. *Ibid.,* S. 77 (2).
24. Ss. 80, 81.
25. *Ibid.,* S. 107 (1).
26. *Ibid.,* S. 124.
27. *Ibid.,* S. 5 (4).
28. *Ibid.,* S. 5 (5).
29. *Ibid.,* S. 5 (4) (5).
30. *Ibid.,* S.5 (1).

31. *Record of 3rd Meeting of the Constitutional Committee*, U.I.C. (CC) (62), p. 4.
32. *Ibid.*, p. 4.
33. Uganda Independence Constitution, S. 61.
34. *Ibid.* See Ss. 62, 63, 65, 66, 67.
35. *Ibid.*, S. 63 (2).
36. Originally from *Life of Robert, Marquis of Salisbury*, Vol. II, pp. 219–20.
37. Uganda Independence Constitution, S. 63 (2).
38. *Ibid.*, S. 26.
39. *Ibid.*
40. *Australian Law Journal*, Vol. 2, p. 26.
41. *Constitutional Problems of Federalism in Nigeria* (Lagos, 1960), p. 4.
42. *State of Madras v Rowe*, 1952, S.C.R.
43. *The Uganda Argus*, 13 December 1962.
44. The Uganda Independence Constitution, S. 23.
45. *The United States v Miller*, 317 U.S. 369.
46. *West Bengal v Banerjee*, 17 *Supreme Court Journal*.
47. The Memorandum, entitled "Emergency Powers", by the Katikkiro of Buganda, dated 19 June 1962.
48. See, for example, the record of the 5th, 6th, 7th meetings of the Constitutional Committee, U.I.C. (C.C.) 62, Items 1, 2.
49. The Independence Constitution, S. 30 (1).
50. For full provisions see *ibid.*, Ss. 30, 31.
51. Briggs, *The Law of Nations*, p. 458.
52. per J. Gray in *U.S. v Wong Kim Ark* (1898), 169 U.S. 668.
53. For detailed provisions relating to acquisition of citizenship see the Independence Constitution, Ss. 6, 7, 8, 9, 10, 13, and The Uganda Citizenship Ordinance, Pt. II.
54. The Independence Constitution, S. 7 (1).
55. The Independence Constitution, S. 7 (2).
56. *Ibid.*, S. 8 (2).
57. *Ibid.*, S. 8 (1) (5).
58. *Ibid.*, S. 8 (6).
59. The Citizenship Ordinance, S. 23 (3), in *Laws of Uganda* (1962).
60. *Ibid.*, S. 4 (1).
61. For detailed provisions on this see the Independence Constitution, S. 12, and the Uganda Citizenship Ordinance, Pt. III.
62. The Independence Constitution, S. 12 (2) (b).
63. *Ibid.*, S. 12 (4).
64. The Uganda Citizenship Ordinance, S. 9.
65. The Independence Constitution, S. 13.
66. The Uganda Citizenship Ordinance, S. 3.
67. The Independence Constitution, S. 29.

68. The Independence Constitution, S. 29 (4) (f).
69. Memorandum No. U.I.C. (62) 7.
70. The Uganda Independence Constitution, Schedule 7, Pt. II (2) (3) (4).
71. Memorandum No. U.I.C. (62) 6.
72. See U.I.C. (62), Record of 5th Meeting, p. 8; also The Independence Constitution, S. 94.
73. The Independence Constitution, S. 87.
74. The Paper on Buganda Police was read by Gratieu, Q. C., to the Constitutional Committee: U.I.C. (62) 14 and *Proceedings of the 11th Meeting*, U.I.C. (C.C.) 62.
75. Munster Report.
76. The Independence Constitution, Ss. 80, 81; Buganda Constitution, S. 39.
77. The Independence Constitution, S. 107.
78. "Notes on Discussions Between the Governor of Uganda and the Rulers of Ankole, Bunyoro and Toro and the Kyabazinga of Busoga", dated 13 June 1962.
79. "Record of Meeting Between the Governor of Uganda and the Toro Delegation", dated 19 June 1962.
80. The Ankole Agreement, Legal Notice No. 229/62, in *Laws of Uganda* (1962).
81. The Independence Constitution, S. 6 (2) (a), also Schedule 8.
82. *Ibid.,* Schedules 2–4, paras. 5–14.
83. Ankole, Schedule 2, paras. 17, 26; Bunyoro, Schedule 3, paras. 16, 25; Toro, Schedule 4, paras. 17, 26.
84. Ankole, Schedule 2, paras. 28, 29; Bunyoro, Schedule 3, paras. 27, 28; Toro, Schedule 4, paras. 28, 29.
85. Schedule 2, para. 30; Schedule 3, para. 29; Schedule 4, para. 30.
86. The Independence Constitution, S. 75 (2).
87. *Ibid.,* S. 75 (3).
88. *Uganda Parliamentary Debates*, First Session 1962–63, 4th Meeting, Pt. I, p. 17; for full text of speeches see pp. 6–82.
89. The Administrations (Western Kingdoms and Busoga) Act, S. 24.
90. *Ibid.,* S. 28.
91. The Independence Constitution, S. 75 and Schedules 2–4.
92. The Administrations (Western Kingdoms and Busoga) Act, Ss. 30–32.
93. *Ibid.,* Ss. 33–38.
94. *Ibid.,* S. 34.
95. The Independence Constitution, S. 108.
96. *Ibid.,* S. 79.
97. The Administrations (Western Kingdoms and Busoga) Act, S. 39.

98. The Independence Constitution, S. 108 (1), S. 109.
99. The Administrations (Western Kingdoms and Busoga) Act, S. 40.
100. *Ibid.,* S. 41.
101. "Limitations on Parliamentary Sovereignty", pp. 246–51.
102. The Independence Constitution, S. 88 (1) (2).
103. *Ibid.,* S. 88 (2).
104. Memorandum, "Federal Status for Kigezi", U.I.C. (62) 16.
105. Memorandum, "Federal Government for Bugisu", U.I.C. (62) 9.

A Select Bibliography and Source List

Books

Allen, C. P. S. *Uganda Legislative Council Elections.* Entebbe: Government Printers, 1958.

Apter, David. *The Political Kingdom in Uganda.* Princeton, N.J.: Princeton University Press, 1961.

Attlee, C. R., et al. *Labour's Aims in War and Peace.* London: Lincolns-Prager, 1940.

Bagehot, Walter. *The English Constitution.* London: Collins, 1963.

Beattie, John. *Bunyoro: An African Kingdom.* New York: Holt, Rinehart and Winston, 1960.

Brierly, J. L. *The Law of Nations,* 6th ed. Oxford: The Clarendon Press, 1963.

Carington, C. E. *The Liquidation of the British Empire.* London: George Harrap, 1961.

Cohen, Andrew. *British Policy in Changing Africa.* London: Routledge and Kegan Paul, 1960.

Davies, H. O. *Nigeria: The Prospects for Democracy.* London: Weidenfeld and Nicolson, 1961.

Dicey, A. V. *The Laws of the Constitution,* 9th ed. New York: Macmillan, 1939.

Elias, T. O. *The Commonwealth: Its Laws and Constitutions—Ghana and Sierra Leone.* London: Stevens and Sons, 1962.

———. *The Nature of African Customary Law.* Manchester: Manchester University Press, 1956.

Ezera, Kalu. *Constitutional Developments in Nigeria.* London: Cambridge University Press, 1960.

Hailey, Malcolm, Lord. *An African Survey*. London: Oxford University Press, 1938.

Hamilton, Alexander. *The Federalist*. New York: E. P. Dutton (Everyman's Library).

Hollingsworth, L. W. *The Asians of East Africa*. London: Macmillan, 1960.

Ingham, Kenneth. *The Making of Modern Uganda*. London: George Allen and Unwin, 1958.

Johnston, H. *The Uganda Protectorate*. London, 1902.

Johnston, John. *The Role of the Military in Underdeveloped Countries*. Princeton, N.J.: Princeton University Press, 1962. (With the following contributors: Coleman and Brice, "The Military in Sub-Sahara Africa"; Guy Parker, "The Role of the Military in Indonesia"; Lucian Pye, "The Army in Burmese Politics.")

Low, Donald A. *Political Parties in Uganda, 1949–62*. London: University of London Institute of Commonwealth Affairs, 1962.

———, and R. C. Pratt. *Buganda and British Overrule*. London: Oxford University Press, 1960.

Lugard, F. J. D. *The Dual Mandate in British Tropical Africa*. London, 1922.

———. *The Rise of Our East African Empire*. Edinburgh and London: Blackwood, 1893.

Machiavelli, Niccolo. *The Prince*. London: J. M. Dent and Sons, Ltd.

Mansur, Fatma. *The Process of Independence*. London: Routledge and Kegan Paul, 1962.

Marsh, Z. A., and G. W. Kingsworth. *An Introduction to the History of East Africa*. London: Cambridge University Press, 1957.

Mill, John Stuart. *Representative Government*. New York: E. P. Dutton (Everyman's Library).

Morison, S. E. *History of the American People*. N.Y.: Oxford University Press, 1965.

Nehru, Jawaharlal. *The Discovery of India*, 6th ed. Calcutta: Signet Press, 1956.

Odumosu, Oluwole. *The Nigerian Constitution*. London: Sweet and Maxwell, 1963.

Oppenheim, L. F. L. *International Law*, 7th ed. Vol. I, *Peace*. London: Longmans Green, 1952.

Pelikan, Jaroslav. *The Riddle of Roman Catholicism*. London: Hodder and Stoughton, 1960.

Roscoe, J. *The Baganda*. London: Macmillan, 1911.

Rubin, Leslie, and Pauli Murray. *The Constitution and Government of Ghana*. London: Sweet and Maxwell, 1961.

Sigmund, Paul E., Jr. *The Ideologies of the Developing Nations*. New York: Frederick Praeger, 1963.

Starke, J. G. *An Introduction to International Law.* London: Butterworth, 1954.

Sukarno, President. *Toward Freedom and the Dignity of Man.* Department of Foreign Affairs, Indonesia.

Tucker, A. *Eight Years in Uganda and East Africa.* London: Edward Arnold, 1911.

Van Doren, Carl. *The Great Rehearsal.* New York: The Viking Press, 1948.

Wade, E. C. S., and G. G. Phillips. *Constitutional Law,* 6th ed. London: Longmans Green, 1961.

Wheare, C. K. *Federal Government.* London: Oxford University Press, 1961.

———. *Modern Constitutions.* London: Oxford University Press, 1966.

Wight, Martin. *British Colonial Constitutions.* Oxford: The Clarendon Press, 1952.

———. *Development of the Legislative Council, 1606–1945.* London: Faber and Faber, 1946.

———. *The Gold Coast Legislative Council.* London: Faber and Faber, 1947.

Woodward, W. H. *Expansion of the British Empire.* London: Macmillan, 1924.

Journals, Reports, and Other Papers

Adimola, A. B. "The Lamogi Rebellion of 1911–12," *Uganda Journal,* Vol. 12 (1948).

Atlantic Charter, The. London: Her Majesty's Stationery Office, 1941.

Buganda's Independence. Kabaka's Government publication, 1960.

Buganda's Position. Kabaka's Government publication, 1960.

Colonial Secretary's Despatch No. 692 of 20 July 1955.

Constitution of the Uganda People's Congress, The. Uganda People's Congress Headquarters, 1960.

Cox, A. H. "The Growth and Expansion of Buganda," *Uganda Journal,* Vol. 14 (1950).

Declaration of Human Rights, The: A Standard of Achievement. United Nations Publication 62-04049, 2nd ed.

Democratic Party Manifesto, The. Democratic Party Headquarters, 1960.

Despatch to the Governor of Uganda No. 1461 of 14 September 1960.

Devonshire White Paper. 1922.

General Report on the Uganda Protectorate for the Year Ending March 1903. London, Command Paper No. 1893.

Government's Revised Constitutional Proposals for Gold Coast Independence, The. Accra, 1956.

Ingham, Kenneth. "British Administration in Lango District, 1907–1935," *Uganda Journal*, Vol. 19 (1955).

———. "Early Proposals for a Federal Uganda," *Uganda Journal*, Vol. 21 (1957).

———. "Early Treaties," *Uganda Journal*, Vol. 12 (1948).

Kintu Committee, The. Entebbe: White Fathers Press, 1955.

Law Quarterly Review, July 1944.

Lukyn-Williams. "Nuwa Mbaguta: Nganzi of Ankole," *Uganda Journal*, Vol. 2 (1934–35).

Minority Report of the Buganda Independence Committee. 1961.

Minutes of the Conferences of Katikkiros and Secretary-Generals held at Fort Portal, Jinja, and Gulu in 1960.

Morris, H. F. "The Making of Ankole," *Uganda Journal*, Vol. 21 (1957).

Peagram, R. C. *Report on the Uganda Legislative Council Elections.* Entebbe: Government Printer, 1961.

———. *Uganda National Assembly Elections.* Entebbe: Government Printer, 1962.

Recommendations of the Namirembe Conference. Entebbe: Government Printer, 1955. Sessional Paper No. 4 of 1957–58.

Report of the Commission of Enquiry into the Management of the Teso District Council. Entebbe: Government Printer, 1958.

Report of the Committee on Immigration from India to the Crown Colonies and Protectorates. (5192 (1910), part 2.

Report of the Constitutional Committee. Entebbe: Government Printer, 1959.

Report of the Constitutional Conference. Command Paper No. 1523 (1961).

Report of the Uganda Independence Conference. 1962.

Report of the Uganda Relationships Commission. Entebbe: Government Printer, 1961.

Roberts, A. D. "The Sub-Imperialism of the Baganda," *Journal of African History*, Vol. 3 (1962).

Srinivasan. "A Decade of Parliamentary Life in Burma," *Indian Journal of Political Science*, Vol. 13, No. 3.

Thomas, H. B. "Capax Imperial: The Story of Semei Kakunguru," *Uganda Journal*, Vol. 19 (1955).

Uganda: The Back-ground to Investment. Kampala: Uganda Ministry of Commerce, 1962.

Wallis, C. A. G. *Report of an Inquiry into African Local Government in the Protectorate of Uganda.* Entebbe: Government Printer, 1953.

———. *British Colonial Judges.* London: Sweet and Maxwell, 1956.

Withdrawal of Recognition from Kabaka Mutesa II of Buganda. London, Command Paper No. 9028.

Court Cases

Nyali Ltd v Attorney-General (1956) 1 QBI.
R v Eyre (1868) LR 3 QB 487.
Hill v Briggs (1841) 3 Moo PCC 465.
Oke Laripekun Laoye v Amac Oyetunde (1944) AC 170.
R v Burah (1878) 3 App Case 889.
R v Crewe (Earl) Ex-parte Sekgome Case (1910) 2 KB 576.
Ndlwana v Hofmeyer (1937) AD 229.
Sobhuza II v Miller and Others (1926) AC 522.
Civil Case No. 50 of 1954 (Uganda); "The Kabaka's Case."
Daudi Ndibarema and Others v Enganzi of Ankole and Others (1960)
    part 1 EALR P 52.
Katosi v Kahizi (1907) 1 ULR 22.
Nasanairi Kibuka v A. E. Bertie Smith (1908) 1 ULR 41.
Duff Development Co v Kelanten Government (1924) AC.
Katikkiro of Buganda v Attorney-General (1957) EALR.
Mighell v Sultan of Johore 1894 IQB 149 C 4.
Marbury v Madison (1803) 1 US 137.
State of Madras v Rowe 1952 SCR.
DPP (Nigeria) v Obi ANLR 1961 part II p. 186.
The United States v Miller 317 US 369.
West Bengal v Banerjee 17 *Supreme Court Journal.*
The United States v Wong Kim Ark (1898) 169 US 668.
Scranton's Trustee v Pearse (1922) 2 Chapter 87 123.
Seaford Court Estates v Asher (1949) 2 KB 481.

United Kingdom Statutes, Orders-in-Council, and Royal Instructions

The Foreign Jurisdiction Act, 1890 (53 & 54 Vict C 37); The Statutes
    Revised, Vol. XI.
Colonial Laws Validity Act, 1865 (28 & 29 Vict C 63).
Interpretation Act, 1889 (52 & 53 Vict C 63).
Statute of Westminster, 1931 (22 Geo V C 4).

Key to abbreviations: AC, Appeal Cases. EALR, East African Law Reports.
KB, Kings Bench (division of High Court of England). LJ, Lord Justice. LN,
Legal Notice. NLR, Nigerian Law Reports. PCC, Privy Council Cases. QB,
Queens Bench (division of High Court of England). SCR, Supreme Court Re-
ports (India). SI, Statutory Instrument. UCC, Uganda Constitutional Confer-
ence. UIC, Uganda Independence Conference. ULR, Uganda Law Reports. US,
United States.

Indian Independence Act, 1947 (10 & 11 Geo VI C 30).

Uganda Independence Act, 1962 *Laws of Uganda* (1962), Vol. III.

Uganda Orders-in-Council, 1902 and 1921, *Laws of Uganda* (1951), Vol. VI.

The Buganda (Agreement) Order-in-Council, 1955 SI 1955 No. 1221.

Uganda (Constitution) Order-in-Council, 1962 SI 1962 No. 405.

Buganda (Transitional Provisions) Order-in-Council, 1955; Legal Notice 138 of 1955.

Uganda (Amendment) Order-in-Council, 1958; Legal Notice 246 of 1958.

Uganda (Public Service Commission) Order-in-Council, 1957; Legal Notice 224 of 1957.

Uganda (Amendment) Order-in-Council, 1954 SI 1954 No. 1568.

Uganda (Electoral Provisions) Order-in-Council, 1957 SI 1957 No. 1528.

Uganda (Amendment) Order-in-Council, 1961 SI 1961 No. 62.

Uganda (Independence) Order-in-Council, 1962 SI 1962 No. 2175.

Uganda (Constitution) Order-in-Council, 1962 SI 1962 No. 625.

Nigerian (Constitution) Order-in-Council, 1951 No. 1172.

Nigerian (Constitution) Order-in-Council, 1957 SI 1957 No. 1652.

Gold Coast Colony and Ashanti (Legislative Council) Order-in-Council, 1946 No. 353.

Gold Coast (Constitution) Order-in-Council, 1950 No. 2094.

Ghana (Constitution) Order-in-Council, 1957 No. 277.

Jamaican (Constitution) Order-in-Council, 1944 No. 1215.

Royal Instructions to the Governor of Uganda, 1920 No. 885.

Royal Instructions to the Governor of Uganda, 1958, *Laws of Uganda*, Legal Notice 247.

Additional Instructions to the Governor of Uganda, *Laws of Uganda* (1961), Legal Notice 30.

Royal Instructions to the Governor of Gibraltar dated February 1950.

Royal Instructions to the Governor of Singapore dated 24 February 1948.

Uganda Legislation and Kingdom Agreements

The Uganda Agreement, 1900, *Laws of Uganda* (1951), Vol. VI (Government Printer, Entebbe, Uganda).

The Toro Agreement, 1900, *Laws of Uganda* (1951), Vol. VI (Government Printer, Entebbe).

The Ankole Agreement, 1901, *Laws of Uganda* (1951), Vol. VI.

The African Authority Ordinance, 1919, *Laws of Uganda* (1951), Vol. II.

The African Local Governments Ordinance, 1949, *Laws of Uganda* (1951), Vol. II.

District Council Administration Ordinance, *Laws of Uganda* (1955), No. 1.

The African Authority (Amendment) Ordinance, *Laws of Uganda* (1955), No. 20.

The Buganda (Transitional) Agreement, 1955, *Laws of Uganda* (1955), No. 141.

The Native Courts Ordinance, *Laws of Uganda* (1951), Vol. II, cap. 76.

The Buganda Courts Ordinance, *Laws of Uganda*, Vol. II, cap. 77.

The African Courts Ordinance, *Laws of Uganda* (1957), No. 1.

Criminal Procedure Code, *Laws of Uganda* (1951), Vol. 1, cap. 24.

The Subordinate Courts Ordinance, *Laws of Uganda* (1951), cap. 4.

The Civil Procedure Code, *Laws of Uganda* (1951), cap. 6.

Legislative Council (Powers and Privileges) Ordinance, *Laws of Uganda* (1955).

The Legislative Council (Elections) Ordinance, 1957, *Laws of Uganda* (1957).

The Legislative Council (Elections) (Amendment) Ordinance, 1960, *Laws of Uganda* (1960).

Elections (Prevention of Intimidation) Ordinance, 1960, *Laws of Uganda* (1960).

The Cotton Ordinance, 1927, *Laws of Uganda* (1951), Vol. IV.

The Co-Operative Societies Ordinance, 1946, *Laws of Uganda* (1951), Vol. V.

The Toro (Provisional) Agreement, 1961, *Laws of Uganda* (1961), Legal Notice 167/1961.

The Buganda Agreement, 1961, *Laws of Uganda* (1961), Legal Notice 208/61.

The Local Administrations Ordinance, *Laws of Uganda* (1962).

The Emergency Powers Act, 1963.

The Citizenship Ordinance, *Laws of Uganda* (1962).

The Ankole Agreement, 1961, *Laws of Uganda* (1962), Legal Notice 229/62.

The Public Service Act, 1963, *Laws of Uganda* (1963).

The Uganda Constitution (First Amendment) Act, 1963, *Laws of Uganda* (1963).

The Administration (Western Kingdoms and Busoga) Act, 1963, *Laws of Uganda* (1963).

Minutes of the Constitutional Conferences and Related Papers

Record of the First Meeting of the Conference U.C.C. (61).

Record of the Fourth Meeting of the Conference U.C.C. (61).

Record of the Eleventh Meeting of the Conference U.C.C. (61).
Record of the Third Meeting of the Conference U.C.C. (61).
Record of the Fourteenth Meeting of the Conference U.C.C. (61).
Record of the Thirteenth Meeting of the Conference U.C.C. (61).
Record of the Fifth, Sixth, Seventh Meetings of the Constitutional Committee U.I.C. (CC) 62.
Record of Third Meeting of the Constitutional Committee U.I.C. (CC) 62.
Record of the Eleventh Meeting of the Constitutional Committee U.I.C. (CC) 62.
Document U.C.C. (61) 20 by B. K. Kiwanuka.
Document U.C.C. (61) 15 by T. Okeny.
Document U.I.C. (CC) (62) 7 "The Exclusive Powers and Law Making Powers of Buganda Legislature".
Memorandum: U.I.C. (62) 7.
Emergency Powers (June 1962) Memorandum by the Katikkiro of Buganda.
Notes on Discussions between the Government of Uganda and the Rulers of Ankole, Bunyoro, Toro and the Kyabazinga of Busoga of 13 June 62.
Record of a Meeting between the Governor of Uganda and the Toro Delegation of 19 June 62.
Memorandum: Federal Status for Kigezi U.I.C. (62) 16.
Memorandum: Federal Government for Bugisu U.I.C. (62) 9.

Parliamentary Debates

Proceedings of the Legislative Council, 1960, Part IV.
Proceedings of the Legislative Council, 1961, Parts I and II.
342 House of Commons Debates, 5 S.
Proceedings of the Legislative Council, 28th Session, 1948–49.
Proceedings of the Legislative Council, 1946–47.
Proceedings of the Legislative Council, 1949.
Proceedings of the Legislative Council, 1956.
Proceedings of the Legislative Council, 1957, Parts I and II.
Proceedings of the Legislative Council, 1958, Part I.
Proceedings of the Legislative Council, 1959, Vol. III (ii).
Proceedings of the Legislative Council, 1960, Part III.
Proceedings of the Legislative Council, 40th Session.
Proceedings of the Legislative Council, 1960, Part IV, 3rd meeting of 40th session.
Ghana Parliamentary Debates, XVI, 1959.
Ghana Parliamentary Debates, XII, 1958.
Proceedings of the National Assembly, 1962, Part IV.

Proceedings of the National Assembly, 1961, Part IV.
Uganda Parliamentary Debates First Session, 1962–63, 4th meeting, Part I.
Uganda Parliamentary Debates, 1962–63, Vol. 17.
Uganda Parliamentary Debates, 1963–64, Vol. 23.

Index